Paradigm Shift

Paradigm Shift
Globalization and the Canadian State

Stephen McBride

Fernwood Publishing • Halifax

Editing: Robert Clarke
Cover art: Richard Slye
Design and production: Brenda Conroy and Beverley Rach
Printed and bound in Canada by: Hignell Printing Limited

A publication of:
Fernwood Publishing
Box 9409, Station A
Halifax, Nova Scotia
B3K 5S3

Fernwood Publishing Company Limited gratefully acknowledges the financial support of the Department of Canadian Heritage, the Nova Scotia Department of Tourism and Culture and the Canada Council for the Arts for our publishing program.

NOVA SCOTIA
Tourism and Culture

Le Conseil des Arts | The Canada Council
du Canada | for the Arts

National Library of Canada Cataloguing in Publication Data

Main entry under title:

McBride, Stephen
Paradigm shift: globalization and the Canadian state

Includes bibliographical references.
ISBN 0-55266-061-3

1. Globalization. 2. Canada-Economic condition-1991-
3. Canada-Commerce. 4. Canada -Politics and government- 1993-
I. Title.

JZ1318.M218 2001   327.71   C2001-901585-2

Contents

Acknowledgements

Several people have been of great assistance in the writing of this book. None are in any way responsible for its contents, but the book would have been much poorer without their help and advice. A number of friends and colleagues read all or portions of an early draft and their comments were very useful when it came to making revisions. To Ted Cohn, Linda Elmose, David Peerla, John Shields and Russell Williams—thanks for responding to my request for feedback in such timely and insightful fashion. David Peerla was also a gold mine of stimulating ideas and helpful references throughout the preparation of the book. Thanks are due also to Libardo Amaya and Russell Williams for their insightful and diligent work as research assistants, and to Sherry Lloyd, who provided valuable secretarial assistance.

Two grants helped the process along: a small SSHRC grant from Simon Fraser University defrayed some research expenses; and a much larger SSHRC MCRI grant on neo-liberal globalism and its challengers, headed by Gordon Laxer, provided the intellectual stimulation of almost twenty colleagues who are focused on similar issues.

Errol Sharpe was, as usual, a most understanding and enthusiastic publisher; and the manuscript benefited greatly from the editing suggestions of Robert Clarke. Richard Slye provided the artwork for the cover and vividly captured the book's themes.

Finally I want to thank my wife, Jan, without whose support and encouragement this book would not have been written.

Stephen McBride

Chronology

1846 Great Britain repeals the Corn Laws, enacted in 1815.

1854 Implementation of the Reciprocity Treaty between Canada and the United States removing all import tariffs on natural products. Abrogated in 1866 by the U.S. congress

1867 The British North America Act creates Canada by combining Ontario, Quebec, Nova Scotia and New Brunswick. It also provides some of the essential elements of the new country's constitution. In 1982, renamed Constitution Act of 1867.

1871 The Treaty of Washington is one of the first moves on the part of Canada towards increased autonomy in making commercial treaties with other countries.

1879 First National Policy unveiled by John A. Macdonald as a broad nation-building policy. It includes tariff protection for Central Canadian manufacturing, massive migration, and the construction of a national transportation system (railroad).

1880 Canada begins to place diplomatic missions abroad. The first mission is the Canadian High Commission, established in London in 1880.

1903 Alaska Boundary Dispute awards a long strip of the northern British Columbia coastline to the U.S. Unreliability of British diplomacy in protecting Canadian interests stimulated demands for greater autonomy in foreign affairs.

1914–18 World War I.

1929 The Great Depression begins—lasts through most of the 1930s.

1939–45 World War II.

1941 Hyde Park Declaration.

1943 Publication of Leonard Marsh's Report on Social Security in Canada.

1944 Meetings in Bretton Woods, New Hampshire, in 1944, which culminate in the creation of the postwar economic order, including the International Monetary Fund (IMF), the World Bank, and the GATT regime.

1945 Introduction of the *White Paper on Employment and Income* as part of the Second National Policy articulated after World War II.

1947 General Agreement on Tariffs and Trade (GATT) signed.

1948 Birth and death of the International Trade Organization (ITO).

1966 Enactment of the Canada Assistance Plan (repealed in 1995).

1967 Introduction of the Medical Care Act.

1968 Publication of the Watkins Report, *Foreign Ownership and the Structure of Canadian Investment.*

1972 Publication of article, "Canada–U.S. Relations: Options for the Future," by Mitchell Sharp, Secretary of State for External Affairs in the Trudeau government, which became widely known as *Canada's Third Option.*

1972 Publication of the Gray Report, *Foreign Investment in Canada.*

1973 Collapse of the postwar economic order established in Bretton Woods.

1973 Initiation of the Tokyo Round of the GATT negotiations (concluded in 1979).

1973 Creation of the Foreign Investment Review Agency (FIRA).

1973 Establishment of Petro-Canada.

1980 Adoption of the National Energy Program by the Trudeau government.

1982 Incorporation of the Charter of Rights and Freedoms to the Constitution Act of 1982, which repatriated the Canadian Constitution from Great Britain.

1984 Enactment of the Canada Health Act.

1984 Election of Brian Mulroney as prime minister of Canada.

1985 Release to the public of the report of the Royal Commission on the Economic Union and Development Prospects for Canada, appointed in 1983 and led by Donald Macdonald.

1986 The Uruguay Round of GATT begins (concluded in 1994).

1987 A package of constitutional amendments proposed by the Mulroney government, the *Meech Lake Accord*, fails to obtain agreement in all provinces.

1989 The Canada–U.S. Free Trade Agreement comes into effect.

1990 Canada becomes member of the Organization of American States (OAS).

1991 Political disintegration of the Soviet Union.

1992 The people of Canada reject the *Charlottetown Accord*, a second attempt by the Mulroney government at comprehensive constitutional change. On October 26, 1992, 55 percent of Canadians say no to the *Accord* in a referendum.

1993 The European Union (EU) is established through the Maastricht Treaty.

1993 Election of Jean Chrétien as prime minister.

1994 The North American Free Trade Agreement (NAFTA) is implemented (signed in 1993).

1995 Establishment of the World Trade Organization (WTO).

1995 Agreement on Internal Trade signed, aimed at eliminating trade barriers among provinces in Canada.

1996 Introduction of the Canada Health and Social Transfer (CHST), replacing earlier forms of funding.

1996 Enactment of the Employment Insurance Act.

1997 Demonstrations against the Asia-Pacific Economic Cooperation Forum (APEC) during its meeting in Vancouver, B.C.

1998 Negotiations on proposed Multilateral Agreement on Investment (MAI) fail.

1999 Demonstrations against the WTO ministerial meeting in Seattle.

2000 Demonstrations against IMF and World Bank meetings in Washington, D.C., in April.

2000 Demonstrations during the IMF/WB Summit in Prague, Czech Republic.

2000 Demonstrations against the World Economic Forum's Asia–Pacific Economic Summit in Melbourne, Australia, in September.

2001 Demonstrations against proposed Free Trade Area of Americas (FTAA), Quebec City, in April.

Introduction

Vancouver 1997 ... demonstrators against APEC pepper-sprayed ... Paris 1998 ... negotiations for a multilateral agreement on investment formally suspended after a mass campaign by non-governmental organizations, and one nation-state, France, announces its withdrawal ... Seattle 1999 ... World Trade Organization meeting stalled; later, delegates meet to the whiff of tear gas and the thud of rubber bullets being fired at demonstrators ... Quebec City 2001 ... wall isolating summit negotiators from popular protest temporarily breached by demonstrators; tear gas, water cannons, rubber bullets and arrests used to restore control....

This book is about how we got to here. "Here" is the globalized world we live in. More precisely, "here" is neo-liberal globalization. "Globalization" refers to the increased levels of interaction and integration around the world. Often, as in this book, the term tends to be used interchangeably with "internationalization," though some authors (for example, Hirst and Thompson 1999), legitimately draw a distinction between the global, which has connotations of "top down," superimposed relationships, and the international, which signifies the prior nature of national units, including the implication that the international economy is constructed from the "bottom up." The term "neo-liberal" refers to the ideology that gives content and shape to the heightened internationalization or globalization characteristic of our times. In some ways neo-liberal is the "paradigm" of the book's title.[1]

Neo-liberalism's prioritization of markets over politics represents a shift from the postwar world, from a time when state co-ordination of the economy and involvement in social policy were accepted as the key to both economic prosperity and social equity. For countries such as Canada, moreover, the state had a long involvement in the process of nation-building. Through its promotion of globalization, neo-liberalism signifies a second shift of paradigm. In the postwar era nation-states might have been involved in close co-operative relations with each other, but they were also accepted as the basic units of economic and political life. No longer. Neo-liberalism denies the possibility or desirability of national economic strategies.

The essential features of neo-liberalism, an updated and embellished version of nineteenth-century classical liberalism, rest in its determination to reduce and alter the role played by the state in human affairs. Instead, neo-liberalism emphasizes market mechanisms and individual rather than collective approaches to solving or handling economic and social problems. Neo-liberalism thus restricts the scope of "politics," preferring most issues to be settled by individuals themselves or by individuals interacting in the marketplace. For neo-liberals, increased globalization based on market principles is unproblematic (Dobuzinskis 2000); it is not only desirable, but also has an air of inevitability about it, because causation is attributed to structural economic and technological pressures.

This view is not uncontested, as the wave of worldwide anti-globalization demonstrations indicates. The book is also about the positions taken by all those demonstrators in Vancouver, Seattle, Prague, Quebec City, and elsewhere—people who believe firmly that neo-liberal globalization is neither desirable nor inevitable and that there are alternatives to current directions. Are they right? Are we living under neo-liberal globalization through choice rather than necessity? Do we still have choices? What might alternatives look like? By what means can they be achieved?

The Conventional Wisdom

The prevailing view on these matters seems to be that there has been and still is little choice. Powerful structural forces—technological and economic developments—over which little control can be exercised have shaped today's world. What is possible, however, is an intelligent adaptation to the new environment.

By this account old institutions and methods will not be useful. The nation-state is all but dead, and we should shed no tears over its remains. As it passes into history, the state's co-ordinating role is being taken over by markets and empowered individuals. For while we may have had little choice over the coming of globalization, this eventuality does not mean the end of democracy, far from it. According to Thomas Courchene, the age of Globalization and the Information Revolution (GIR for short) "will do for human capital what the industrial revolution did for physical capital. Indeed, one can go much further and presume that the ultimate impact of the Internet will be to privilege citizens individually and collectively with a degree of information, influence and power heretofore unimaginable, and one that no government, no matter how powerful, will be able to ignore, let alone to suppress" (Courchene 2000: 6). As Courchene and

Figure 1.1

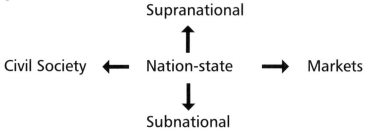

others describe it, it is unlikely that powerful governments will remain. Globalization is said to have stripped the nation-state of many of its powers. The state is seen as losing authority and power upwards to supranational bodies, downwards to subnational governments and sideways to markets and multinational corporations and/or to organizations of civil society. (See Figure 1.1.)

Often the centre of the diagram that depicts this movement is described as "hollowed out." This means that the nation-state, and government, are no longer able to perform the functions traditionally performed at that level. They are losing power in the directions indicated. Other actors, at other levels, are assuming roles formerly played out at the national level. The reason for this diminution of state power and leakage of authority is the state's inability to resist powerful global pressures. Such pressures are said to be structural in origin—the effects of technological innovation, especially in information technology, the consequences of mobile capital, and so on. In a nutshell, the argument is that technology makes borders permeable, and that economic and other actors use this technology to escape the confines of national territories and national controls. Even if it were desirable, there is little likelihood of states being able to control these processes.

The Alternative

This book takes a sceptical view of such arguments. The problem with the conventional version of events is that it ignores the extent to which states have been active participants in their own demise, if demise it be. Indeed, reconfiguration of functions may be a more appropriate description than demise. States have been the authors of the globalization textbook. Rather than being described as having a hollowed-out centre, our diagram should be depicted with an active core. The very term "hollowing out" suggests that globalization is pulling functions and roles away from the state and from the national-state level, which comes to resemble an empty shell. My own interpretation is more suggestive of "domestic push" rather than international "pull."[2]

Acting on the basis of a new economic paradigm and responding to the articulated requirements of capital for freer markets and deregulated profit-making opportunities, states have deliberately shed many of their former functions. But some states, at least, remain crucial actors in the process of constructing globalization. This role does not imply that these states have acted autonomously or independently of the societies of which they are a part. Indeed, the class base to which they have responded has narrowed. But it does mean that we can still look for the explanation for many of the features of globalization at the domestic level, as being embedded in national societies, relying on and susceptible to political processes, rather than beyond the control of states or any other entity.

While today's global economy obviously has its new features, not least the speed and intensity of change, there is also a sense in which globalism is at least as old as capitalism, even if the "globalization" terminology itself is a product of the 1980s. Moreover, in the long run there have been periods, like the one since the early 1970s, when international links have intensified, and other periods in which these links have atrophied or even declined (Chase-Dunn, Kawano and Brewer 2000). A proper scepticism about the globalization hypothesis leads to the conclusion (chapter 1) that more autonomy and capacity reside at the nation-state level than many writers generally concede. One implication, for critics and proponents of globalization alike, is that action at the nation-state level remains an essential part of political strategy.

These findings are particularly relevant for Canada, because there is a sense in which Canada has always been a global nation that has, until quite recently, used the state to manage the terms of its interactions with the global economy. Indeed, this function arguably remains the case, although the management strategy may have radically shifted. Insertion into a global economy has been part of Canada's story from the beginning (chapter 2). Dependence on a single external market has been a continuing part of Canadian history, as has reliance on natural resources as an engine of economic growth. Canada's territory was colonized by European settlers largely for economic reasons. The foundation of the country as a political unit—Confederation—was in considerable measure an economic development project orchestrated by the economic elite of the day. To survive, Canada needed a national policy, and three broad national policies were set in place well before the current strategy, neo-liberalism, arrived on the scene in the mid-1980s. Each of the national policies had a domestic component—an economic and social strategy—and an international component—how to handle Canada's relationship with the international political economy (Albo and Jenson 1997). Each policy required that the country stand apart from and develop an identity somewhat removed from the much larger U.S. republic, while maintaining cordial relations with it.

Two other factors are crucial in an explanation of the embrace of continentalism in Canada (chapter 3). The first is the overwhelming consensus that emerged in the business community in the 1980s in support of continentalism and free trade. The second is the role of free trade as but one component of a broader ideological campaign to change the face of Canada. Engineering a paradigm shift was a crucial element in the pursuit of a globalization strategy.

The domestic impact of this ideological changeover has led, in general, to retrenchment (chapter 4). This retrenchment took form in a variety of discrete measures, including financial stringency, decentralization of federalism through transfer of jurisdictions from the federal state to the provincial (while failing to provide adequate funding for the devolved functions), privatization, and the contracting out of service delivery (see Workman 1996; McBride and Shields 1993, 1997). While the global context and rhetoric surrounding the need to be competitive and efficient in a global economy may have had some influence on the direction of policy, the causation has clearly been domestic. More than one possible explanation exists; indeed, a variety of factors—domestic and international—are no doubt implicated. Still, most discussions of the issue place little (or no) emphasis on domestic factors,[3] even though, as we shall see, it is not necessary to look beyond national borders to explain what happened. The available evidence casts doubt on claims that global developments determine those at the national level.

On the global level, the contents of several international agreements appear to intrude on Canada's capacity to make autonomous decisions (chapter 5). The agreements are those falling under the World Trade Organization (WTO) umbrella, the North American Free Trade Agreement (NAFTA), the proposed, but not ratified, Multilateral Agreement on Investment (MAI), and the still-in-progress Free Trade Area of the Americas (FTAA) initiative. Despite the intrusive nature of the agreements, the Canadian state has been an active supporter of all of them. The architecture of the agreements reflects the neo-liberal concern with constraining the state and freeing investors and markets from state intervention. As such they reinforce neo-liberal measures taken at the domestic level. As part of international law, they have a quasi-judicial and quasi-constitutional aura. Thus their impact is harder to challenge; yet they are as political in construction as any domestic policy.

These international but voluntarily entered constraints or "conditioning frameworks" hold serious implications for the Canadian political system, and its institutions (chapter 6). The broad effects of these constraints will carry over on to the parliamentary institutions, federalism, and the courts. What remains to be considered in the equation, though, is the strength and resilience of the opposition to neo-liberal globalization—its effectiveness and the presentation of alternatives (chapter 7).

States have had choices, and they have exercised that capacity for choice to construct neo-liberal globalization. States are unequal; clearly, some of them, the United States in particular, have been in the forefront of recent developments. Still, this does not mean that other states, such as Canada, have been passive bystanders or victims of the globalization process. Canadian governments have played an active role in shaping the global economy. They have been pressured to do so primarily by business interests, which have pushed hard for the new paradigm. Canadian business has been successful in shaping the environment in which it now operates. Canada's embrace of globalization, then, was not structurally determined; it can be explained quite satisfactorily by reference to domestic political factors, reinforced as they were by international pressures. All of which implies that Canada, like other states, retains a distinct capacity to manage its continuing encounter with globalization.

Notes
1. Technically, paradigm often has a more restricted meaning in that it refers to the constellation of ideas and arguments surrounding policy choices rather than to a full-blown ideology such as neo-liberalism. Hall (1990: 59) defines paradigm as "the broad goals behind policy, the related problems or puzzles that policy-makers have to solve to get there, and, in large measure, the kinds of instruments that can be used to attain these goals." The term is often used when Canada's various national policies are likened to Hall's concept of policy paradigm. Nonetheless popular usage also extends to the broader sense in which the term is employed here.
2. With thanks to Linda Elmose for the suggested terminology.
3. Among the exceptions is Dobbin 1998.

Chapter One

Globalization
A Buzzword Examined

Over thirty years ago an influential account of politics began with the words: "More than ever before men now live in the shadow of the state. What they want to achieve, individually or in groups, now mainly depends on the state's sanction and support.... It is possible not to be interested in what the state does; but it is not possible to be unaffected by it" (Miliband 1968: 1).

In political science, the term "state" has two general meanings. First, it can refer to countries—territorial units recognized by other states as players of equal legal status in the international system. Often, the attribute of equal legal status is called "sovereignty," although the concept is more complex than that term would indicate, and the extent to which states today possess sovereignty is a matter of some controversy (see Krasner 1999). Often—though misleadingly, because few countries comprise a single sociological "nation"—countries are described as "nation-states," a conjunction reflecting the synonymous rise of nationalism and the construction of modern territorial units. The term *nation*-state can be problematic if nation is identified with common ethnicity, an attribute that few if any of today's countries can claim. Eric Hobsbawm (2000: 22–23), suggests that "nation" can just as appropriately pertain to the people occupying the territory of a sovereign state.

Second, "state" can refer to the complex of governing institutions that rule over these sovereign territorial units. Although Miliband provided an original and much debated account of the role of the state, in the sense of a set of governing institutions, the state's centrality to political life in 1968 was uncontroversial. [1]

Today, the state, in both senses of the word, is widely seen as being in retreat in the face of an expanded role for markets. Various thinkers and pundits have proclaimed the decline of the nation-state. Some maintain that the key actors in politics are transnational bodies—whether corporations or international organizations (see Ohmae 1990). And, after two decades of neo-liberal assault on the powers of the state, in the sense of public institutions, the slogan "people now live in the shadow of the market" would seem more appropriate than Miliband's formulation. Markets themselves are depicted as increasingly global rather than national in scope. William Greider's influential book *One World: Ready or Not* represents the growth of global markets as revolutionary:

> The present economic revolution, like revolutions of the past, is fueled by invention and human ingenuity and a universal aspiration to build and accumulate. But it is also driven by a palpable sense of insecurity. No one can be said to control the energies of unfettered capital, not important governments or financiers, not dictators or democrats. And, in the race to the future, no-one dares to fall a step behind, not nations or major corporations.... Even the most powerful players ... are themselves dwarfed by the system and subject to its harsh, overwhelming consequences. (Greider 1997: 12, 26)

The somewhat apocalyptic tone captures the sense of inevitability that pervades many accounts of globalization, popular and academic. Thus, one might suppose that a book like the one you are now reading would echo Greider's words, or those of the Australian foreign minister who remarked: "Whether we like it or not, we are part of an international community which is becoming increasingly global.... Whether people fear globalization or not they cannot escape it" (quoted in Wiseman 1998: 12).

But how true is it that the nation-state is powerless in the face of globalization? How true is it that the state (in the sense of governing institutions) is a passive bystander in the face of global market forces? I would argue that states retain considerable importance, some of it actual, some of it potential, despite claims made about state impotence in the face of globalization. Still, states do show considerable differentiation in their capacities for dealing with global pressures. In the case of Canada, which is far from being a world superpower, our analysis must be mindful of the relative capacity of middle range countries.

Changing Times, Changing Paradigms
The term "globalization" is of relatively recent coinage. Its usage, uncommon before the 1980s, mushroomed in the 1990s (Robertson 1992: 8).[2] Wide ranging definitions have attached themselves to the term, a development that accounts for its ubiquity while perhaps limiting its scientific utility. It is in some danger of becoming all things to all people, of being used to explain everything, and thus perhaps at risk of explaining nothing.

Moreover, like a preceding and related concept, "modernization," it is ideologically suspect in that "it appears to justify the spread of Western culture and of capitalist society by suggesting that there are forces operating beyond human control that are transforming the world" (Waters 1995: 3).

Most definitions of globalization include economic, political and cultural aspects (see Waters 1995 for detailed discussions). Our focus here is on the economic and political dimensions. Economically, globalization is marked by major increases in international trade and investment, the evolution of global production by transnational corporations, and unregulated flows of capital. Politically, globalization theorists point to the erosion of nation-states as the key unit in which political decisions are made; the leakage of sovereignty to supranational organizations on the one hand and to subnational units on the other; and, sometimes, to the emergence of neo-liberalism as a global ideology. Culturally, globalization is held to bring a rather chaotic mix of homogenization (the McDonaldization of the world) and differentiation (the rise of ethno-nationalism on one side and identity politics on the other).

If the term is generally conceded to be relatively new, more debate exists about the longevity of the process of globalization itself. Clearly, voyages of discovery and transborder trade, communications, and migration, not to mention invasions and colonization, have a long history (Wiseman 1998: 14–15). A corollary of this, though perhaps not a particularly helpful one, is that globalization is as old as history itself (Waters 1995: 4). More commonly, analysts link globalization to the rise of mercantile and, subsequently, industrial capitalism and its gradual, though hardly peaceful spread from Western Europe to the rest of the world. Others emphasize the revolution in the technology of information and communications over the past three decades and the compression of time and space that has resulted (Harvey 1989). As for myself, I would argue that Canada has always been a global nation. Today's globalization may exhibit a number of novel features—the speed and intensity of economic interactions and information flows, the rise of a single hegemonic ideology— but the facts of insertion into an international economy and dependence on foreign markets have been ever-present in Canadian history.

The case for globalization's novelty typically includes reference to empirical data on trade, investment and financial flows. One of the key indicators is growth in international trade. The total volume of world trade increased from an estimated $126 billion in 1950 to about $4 trillion in 1980 and $7 trillion in the mid-1990s (Pearson and Payaslian 1999: 161). The growth in the value of traded goods was more than double the increase in global output (Axford 1995: 104).

Discussions of trade generally focus on the doubling of merchandise exports as a percentage of Gross Domestic Product (GDP) since 1950. In recent years that growth has slowed considerably (Bairoch 1996: 176–77). However, the increase in the volume of international financial transactions dwarfs the value of foreign trade. In the early 1990s, for example, the daily volume of trading in foreign exchange markets approached $1 trillion, about forty times more than the daily value of international trade (Helleiner 1996: 193). There is little doubt that global integration has proceeded furthest in the area of short-term, liquid financial flows. It is here that the image of a footloose international capital has greatest resonance (Epstein 1996). But even in the more stable area of foreign direct investment flows, growth in investment outpaces growth in trade by a wide margin (Bairoch 1996: 183). Thus, in the economic sphere the indicators of globalization are ranked: short-term financial flows show the greatest degree of integration, followed by direct investment and then trade. All of these indicators are growing much faster than economic output as a whole.

Political globalization becomes an understood consequence of this greater economic integration. Essentially, advocates of this view judge the economic system to have outgrown its political counterpart, the territorially based nation-state, and argue that the state can do little to control economic outcomes (Teeple 1995, 2000). As a result, states, in both senses of the term, have suffered a diminution of their capacities. For Roger Burbach and William I. Robinson (1999: 30), "The whole set of nation-state institutions is becoming superseded by transnational institutions." States supposedly lose sovereignty, policy-making capacity, and their status as a focal point of identity (Axford 1995: 138–51). Given Canada's reliance on a degree of state intervention to manage its insertion in the global economy and to create a "political nationality" (Smiley 1967) in the northern half of North America, this erosion of state capacity becomes a serious matter.

Gary Teeple (2000: 131) argues that states have responded to globalization by adopting neo-liberal policies, but the triumph of neo-liberalism should not be understood as a domestic ideological victory. Rather, it is an internationally induced structural necessity: "If the national economy is to remain capitalist, the agenda must be accepted by the world's governments. Yet, at the same time, such acceptance will harmonize the national with the international; it will spell the end of the national economy and of the nation-state as we have known it."[3] Others, agnostic as to causes, argue that regardless of the origins of the changes, the result has been the implementation by national governments of a series of deregulatory actions that have liberated capital from national constraints; this, in turn, makes any reassertion of national power problematic (Scharpf 1987: 244–46).

In a nuanced account of the implications of globalization for the state, Jan Aart Scholte (1997: 440–49) notes a lack of uniformity. States have responded to globalization it in different ways. Nonetheless, a number of common themes stand out, though their impact will be different in different cases. In contrast to those who posit the end of the nation-state, Scholte argues that the state will survive, but it has been or will be transformed. States have lost sovereignty as a result of the growth of transborder capitalism, and they have acquired new constituents in the shape of transnational entities, with which they must now interact. They are less likely to engage in interstate warfare because of greater economic interdependence and the growth of multilateral pressures emanating from transnational capital. And, not least, the achievement of democracy has been rendered more difficult. This is because of the lack of accountability implied by the overlapping decision-making systems that characterize what some have termed the "new medievalism" (Bull 1977). Even those who are otherwise sceptical of some of the claims made on behalf of globalization erect a weak framework for the continued salience of the nation-state.[4]

The Debate: Grounds for Scepticism?

Laurent Dobuzinskis (2000) characterizes a broader discourse about globalization as consisting of "three worlds." The first world, composed of liberal thinkers and their allies in the business world, finds the process unproblematic insofar as it represents the spontaneous and inevitable evolution of markets to a global level. The second and by far largest grouping of opinion includes the work of most economists, centrist politicians of all parties, most bureaucrats and business people; it considers globalization as a momentous development that is largely inevitable. However, since the course of globalization is unpredictable, this grouping recognizes the necessity of making difficult adaptations and adjustments. They see that the state has a role to play, particularly in fostering adaptability and flexibility in order to enable its citizens to compete effectively in the global marketplace (Cerny 2000).

The third world includes the sceptics who are opposed to globalization. A few of them have right-wing nationalist roots, but most of them are leftist anti-globalists who emphasize the destructive social impact of globalization and/or of the neo-liberal policies employed by its adherents.[5]

Scepticism about the demise of the national springs, for one thing, from the exaggeration of globalization as a new phenomenon. To the extent that globalization is instead a constant, then the decline of the national can be attributed to other causes. Sceptics also argue that the structural pressures connected to globalization are overemphasized and that therefore the space for political mediation is more expansive. They indicate that the outcomes of domestic politics at the nation-state level may be more responsible for globalization than vice versa. As well, the resulting degree of both political convergence and incapacity is more limited than is generally supposed. The continued differentiation of national policies reveals that choices do continue to exist and can be made at the nation-state level. Again, this line of thought would imply that the determining impact of globalization has been overstated. Finally, the international economic agreements, such as the WTO and NAFTA, which clearly do constrain national choices are equally clearly the result of political agreements between states. To the extent that these arguments are plausible, a strong case can be made that significant autonomy and capacity continue to reside at the nation-state level. It may be that more autonomy exists than is actually exercised by national elites. If so, the responsibility for direction would seem to fall on domestic politics underscored by class preferences rather than on global structures.

Major debates exist on all these issues. Paul Hirst and Grahame Thompson (1996: ch.2–4), for instance, demonstrate that the degree of international economic integration is not unprecedented. Some indicators, such as labour migration, show less integration than witnessed in the period immediately prior to the First World War. From this they infer that the internationalization of economic activity, and any related damage to national autonomy, may be uneven and cyclical rather than linear as argued in many recent depictions of globalization (see also Chase-Dunn, Kawano and Brewer 2000). Hirst and Thompson also find that the dramatic increase in foreign direct investment is heavily concentrated in the advanced industrial countries plus a small number of newly industrializing countries (NICS). Foreign direct investment is thus far from being truly global and, in addition, may not be producing some of the consequences attributed to it.

A case in point is the oft-cited spectre of competition from low-waged labour. This competition may well be exaggerated, because overseas investment is for the most part in comparable countries with comparable standards of living and wage structures. Hence the drive to lower wages in some of the advanced industrial countries may have less to do with structural pressures than with the course of internal class politics. Open to similar scrutiny is the proposition that multinational corporations are becoming truly transnational in the sense of having no national base.

International businesses remain largely multinational in terms of operations, but they are otherwise "nationally embedded." As a result it is "not beyond the powers of national governments to regulate these companies." The deficiency in the regulation of these entities is most likely to be political rather than structural (Hirst and Thompson 1996: 98). Other evidence suggests that multinationals show durable national differences: "At a time when many observers emphasize the importance of cross-border strategic alliances, regional business networks, and stock offerings on foreign exchanges—all suggestive of a blurring of corporate nationalities—our findings underline, for example, the durability of German financial control systems, the historical drive behind Japanese technology development through tight corporate networks, and the very different time horizons that lie behind American, German, and Japanese corporate planning" (Pauly and Reich 1997: 59). As a result, "The globalization template upon which much current theoretical and policy debate rests remains quite weak" (Pauly and Reich 1997: 60).

Robert Wade (1996) offers a detailed discussion of evidence that qualifies the globalization thesis in regards to trade, foreign direct investment, finance capital, multinational corporations and technology. He argues:

> The world economy is more inter-national than global. In the bigger national economies, more than 80 per cent of production is for domestic consumption and more than 80 per cent of investment by domestic investors. Companies are rooted in national home bases with national regulatory regimes. Populations are much less mobile across borders than are goods, finance or ideas. These points suggest more scope for government actions to boost the productivity of firms operating within their territory than is commonly thought. (Wade 1996: 61)

Even in finance, the most internationally integrated economic activity, the picture is uneven. Only a few financial products, principally currency, government bonds and futures, are sold in truly global markets. Most of the rules surrounding finances, including taxation, regulation, legislation, accounting conventions and the like, remain national. Evidence exists that domestic investment in the advanced industrial countries remains highly correlated with domestic savings. This finding suggests that globalization has had only a limited impact. Finally, major differences obtain between countries in real interest rates, and opinions differ about whether these differences are declining or remaining constant. This discrepancy means that the equalization of capital costs that is expected in a global market has so far failed to materialize (Wade 1996: 73–76). These findings have very different implications for the possibility of national regulation, or co-operative regulation by nations, than much of the globalization literature suggests.

Other analysts point to the role of nation-states themselves in bringing about the neo-liberal phase of globalization. In Janine Brodie's evocative phrase, governments have been "acting as the midwives of globalization" (Brodie 1996: 386; see also Panitch 2000). Eric Helleiner (1996: 193) argues that the development of international financial integration has been "heavily dependent on state support and encouragement," particularly decisions to abolish state controls on capital. The corollary is that this integration represents a political choice that, under appropriate circumstances, could be reversed. Domestic politics have been depicted as the cockpit in which choices are made about the kind of foreign capital that needs to be attracted. This position does not imply that the choices are easy. All countries exercise choices within certain constraints: "Given the high degree of short-term capital mobility that currently exists … all countries are constrained to try to maintain the confidence of short-term investors, or they must interfere with short-term capital mobility if they are to pursue independent policies" (Epstein 1996: 212).

Even staunch advocates of globalization have occasionally alluded to its being politically created and, hence, that it is potentially capable of being politically reversed. In 1995 *The Economist* (7 Oct.) pointed out, "Those who demand that the trend of global integration be halted and reversed are frightening precisely because, given the will, governments could do it." Five years later, the magazine remained concerned about this issue. It warned:

> International economic integration is not an ineluctable process, as many of its most enthusiastic advocates appear to believe. It is only one, the best, of many possible futures for the world economy; others may be chosen, and are even coming to seem more likely. Governments, and through them their electorates, will have a far bigger say in deciding this future than most people appear to think. The protestors are right that governments and companies—if only they can be moved by force of argument, or just by force— have it within their power to slow and even reverse the economic trends of the past 20 years. (*The Economist* 23 Sept. 2000)

Analysts often see globalization as producing convergence in state policies, taking this convergence as evidence of powerful structural pressures to conform. Suzanne Berger (1996: 1) summarizes this view: remaining national variations are attributable to historical legacies, politics, or special interests that hinder the unfolding of "competition, imitation, diffusion of best practice, trade and capital mobility," which together "naturally operate to produce convergence across nations in the structures of production and in the relations among economy, society and the state." Such a view has been attributed to the influence of neo-classical theory (Boyer 1996: 58). From this point of view, policy deviations from the neo-liberal model are irrational, because the best performance is to be obtained by following that approach.

The grounds for expecting neo-liberal convergence lie in what happened between 1975 and 1985. During that period macroeconomic policy was transformed by advocates of a refurbished version of neo-classical economics, known variously as neo-liberalism or neo-conservatism.[6] This force fought and won a battle for ideological hegemony against their Keynesian opponents—a battle pitched in leading capitalist countries such as the United States and Britain (see Hoover and Plant 1989) and emulated elsewhere.[7] The same set of ideas came to inform the actions of international organizations (Chossudovsky 1997). These developments set the scene for neo-liberal convergence or what might be termed the "There Is No Alternative" hypothesis.[8] A common pattern of responses would suggest that little alternative exists.

Even the Keynesian era included examples of policy convergence between states. Since Keynesianism is built upon *national* economic management, whereas neo-liberalism seeks to dismantle such policy regimes, one might reasonably expect convergence to have increased, especially in view of increased participation in regional blocs such as the European Union and NAFTA. But the record is decidedly mixed. In the European Union (EU), the most integrated of the regional blocs, a study of France and Germany revealed a certain convergence at the macroeconomic policy level, with France moving closer to the German model, especially in the monetary policy area. But there was no equivalent convergence at the microeconomic management level (Boltho 1996). Similarly, Geoffrey Garrett (1998) argues that for the period up to 1990, countries such as Austria, Denmark, Finland, Norway and Sweden were governed under social-democratic corporatist arrangements. With left-labour political power and highly institutionalized labour markets, they pursued distinctive fiscal policies even as the process of globalization grew apace. There were resulting differences in economic performances between these countries and other advanced industrial countries that practised market liberalism, such as Canada, France, the United Kingdom and the United States. Although economic performance in the 1990s slipped in the social-democratic corporatist countries, Garrett nevertheless argues that this decline had little to do with globalization per se, but more to do with policy mistakes and the specific geographical and economic impact of the collapse of the Soviet Union. In any event he finds sufficient evidence of the exercise of policy autonomy and different economic outcomes, such as lower incidences of poverty, to conclude that the homogenizing effects of globalization are exaggerated (see Garrett 1998, ch. 6).[9]

In North America neither the Free Trade Agreement (FTA) nor its NAFTA successor approaches the degree of economic integration of the EU. Nonetheless, there has been considerable speculation that Canadian public policy would converge with that of the stronger power in the agreements, the United States.

Reviewing empirical studies of individual policy areas, Keith Banting, George Hoberg and Richard Simeon (1997b) note considerable variation. Macroeconomic and industrial policy show convergence, though the macroeconomic area also reveals instances of Canada pursuing an autonomous policy. In the social policy area the chief finding is one of persistent differences—a result that "offers some reassurance to those Canadians who are fearful of harmonization pressures as a consequence of free trade" (Simeon, Hoberg and Banting 1997: 393). More generally, these analysts conclude, "Globalization does increase the costs of distinctive policy choices in some crucial areas, but it does not eliminate them. Trade-offs may be more painful than they once were, but they are still there to be made, and domestic social and political factors continue to influence policy responses" (399). Even where convergence is identified, it need not flow from globalization (Bennett 1991; Banting, Hoberg and Simeon 1997a: 16–17). Other possible causes of convergence include parallel domestic pressures and emulation.

Our assessment of the grounds for scepticism about exaggerated claims made on behalf of globalization, then, produces relatively optimistic conclusions from the perspective of the continued national capacity to moderate the pressures. However, it is clear that strong international political pressures are directed not only to producing particular policy responses, especially neo-liberal ones, at the national level, and also to limiting the future capacity of nation-states to deviate from such a response. In the case of international trade agreements between economically advanced countries the conditions are clearly self-imposed, at least as far as the domestic elites governing these countries are concerned. The agreements entrench a minimalist view of the state and "modify the conditions under which economic and social decision-making is conducted domestically"(Grinspun and Kreklewich 1994: 34). Essentially, for their own economies and polities, domestic elites engineer an external constraint similar to that imposed, via international institutions, on the developing countries.[10] The staitjacket within which most nation-states operate is constructed politically rather than structurally. By extension, reports from international organizations, such as the Organization of Economic Co-operation and Development (OECD), can be used to validate policy choices whose origins lie in the domestic preferences of some actors.[11]

A Post-Sceptical Synthesis

Many of the sceptical arguments are compelling. A good case can be made that globalization is neither new nor primarily determined structurally. Further, its origins lie in domestic choices, and continued policy diversity shows that nations can still make choices in the face of globalization. However, sceptics do have a tendency to counterpose the concepts of globalization and state autonomy. It may be more useful to consider states as integral actors in the globalization process, to recognize that states clearly favour some sectors of their own societies at the expense of others. We need, then, to analyze the domestic and international forces that have successfully induced states to identify their interests by way of fostering globalization.[12]

In a seminal critique of the notion that states are powerless in the face of globalization, Linda Weiss (1997) argues that those making the case typically overstate the powers of the state in a pre-global era, and that this device exaggerates the state's impotence now (see also Weiss 1998). Further, the analysts, she says, also overstate the uniformity, or convergence, of state responses. If a diversity of state responses exists, that would imply a continued capacity to act with some degree of autonomy (see also Palan and Abbott with Deans 1999). Finally, Weiss argues that the incapacity of the state is a politically constructed concept:

> Political leaders—especially in the English-speaking world dominated by neo-liberal economic philosophy—have themselves played a large part in contributing to this view of government helplessness in the face of global trends. In canvassing support for policies lacking popular appeal, many OECD governments have sought to "sell" their policies of retrenchment to the electorate as being somehow "forced" on them by "global economic trends

over which they have no control." (Weiss 1997: 16; see also Evans 1997; McQuaig 1998)

Weiss goes on to argue that state functions may be adapting to new conditions, but this is not the same as declining. Strong states, rather than being victims of globalization, are facilitators of it, and some states are acting as catalysts and consolidating regional blocs in which common trade and investment rules apply. Her analysis points to the need to analyze domestic power relations within particular states if we are to understand the state enthusiasm for pro-globalization, or neo-liberal, policies.

Where should Canada be located in such a typology? If the United States has been a catalyst in constructing a regional bloc, NAFTA, in its own neo-liberal image, Canada should be cast in one of the other roles.[13] Despite the temptation in some circles to see Canada as a victim, as befits a country whose development has been marked by "dependency," the label "facilitator" probably better describes the role of the Canadian state. Canada not only was the initiator of the original free-trade agreement with the United States but also remains deeply wedded to market liberalization at home and abroad. The Canadian state has been extraordinarily enthusiastic about globalization.

The reasons for this rest above all else in the internal politics of the country and in the social forces whose interests are served by the particular policy stance. This explanation is all the more important because some versions of the "states matter" perspective have been criticized for failing to take domestic factors, such as class, into account (see Moran 1998). From the class-analysis perspective, states certainly have mattered. However, many state policy initiatives over the past two decades have been understood as stemming from political choices, not global financial constraints. The focus on deficit reduction and deflationary policies such as high real interest rates may thus have been engineered partly to win the confidence of international investors and prevent capital flight. But it was also engineered as a domestic distributional contest between classes. In such a conflict ideological representations of the severity of budget deficits played a key role: "We must view the deficit discourse as a mechanism of social and political hegemony construction and maintenance ... linked to the particular interests of globalizing elites." (Sinclair 2000: 185–86; see also Workman 1996; McQuaig 1995; Klein 1996). Reducing the state's size, especially its role as a provider of social support, together with pursuit of deflation and acceptance of higher unemployment, served to recast labour/capital relations on terms more favourable to capital.

This push was reinforced by a globalization that added plausibility to any threat by capital to move elsewhere. But globalization was "not just a structural imperative but a class strategy" (Meiksins Wood 1998:25). By this logic, the argument that global market forces compelled the shift to neo-liberal domestic policies was and is one of convenience (Moran 1998:66–67). For Jonathan Moran, empirical evidence from Britain, Australia and Sweden indicates that the traditional strategies of confrontation with labour (Britain) or its incorporation (Australia) were crucial to managing the shift to globalizing strategies by those states. In Sweden, Moran argues, capital used internationalization as "an ideological battering ram whose main intention was domestic, to weaken the state-working class alliance that lay at the core of social democracy" (Moran 1998:70). Others, too (for example, Cowling and Sugden 1987), have noted that the growth of the transnational corporation is partly a response to and an attempt to escape the constraints of political democracy and the power of labour.

Our initial foray into the globalization debate, then, yields the conclusion that globalization's impact on the capacities of the state may be exaggerated. This is true even in the case of a country such as Canada, which is far from superpower status. In examining the connection between globalization and the Canadian state, therefore, we might find a more worthwhile approach in positing that while globalization pressures certainly do exist, Canada's increased integration into the global economy, and the domestic policy changes associated with that integration, are matters of choice rather than necessity. States, including those of semi-peripheral countries like Canada, have been deeply implicated in promoting globalization and engineering the required domestic adjustments. Given this contingency, it would be rewarding to focus on the domestic determinants of that political choice. That investigation in turn requires a discussion not only of Canada's historical pattern of integration within the international system, but also of the characteristics of Canadian capitalism.[14]

Notes

1. To some extent the state's centrality was so much a part of the landscape that political scientists often neglected its role in favour of a focus on political behaviour and political processes. To remedy this omission, various schools of political analysis arose, from different theoretical perspectives, premised on "bringing the state back in" to political analysis (see, for example, Evans, Rueschemeyer and Skocpol 1985).

2. A computer search for the term, kindly made available by David Peerla, provided examples from 1976.

3. This explanation has been challenged by those who attribute the erosion of national state capacity primarily to domestic political factors, with structural influences emanating from the international economy playing a secondary

role (Hirst and Thompson 1996; McBride and Shields 1997).

4. See Hirst and Thompson 1996: ch. 8 and the critique of their concept of the state under globalization by Weiss 1997: 17.

5. A similar account can be found in Wiseman 1998: 18–23.

6. Neo-liberalism and neo-conservativivism have been used almost interchangeably to refer to the revival of classical market liberalism and the policies of leaders such as Margaret Thatcher and Ronald Reagan. Some writers reserve the term neo-conservatism for the combination of neo-liberal economic policies and social conservatism they take as hallmarks of the Reagan years. Based on that distinction, I use the term neo-liberalism here.

7. For the Canadian case, see McBride 1992; for Mexico, see Otero 1996.

8. Thatcher used this term, and concept, to justify her turn to neo-liberalism.

9. Gobeyn (1995) notes the absence of corporatist institutions at the European level, a phenomenon he attributes to market conditions having reclaimed corporatism's functional role of securing wage restraint and labour discipline. In these circumstances, business finds it unnecessary to deal with trade unions in the way implied by corporatist institutions.

10. Because of growing levels of external debt since the early 1980s, many developing countries have found themselves in the position of having to renegotiate debt payments and, as a condition of receiving relief, of being bound to apply neo-liberal policies insisted upon by the International Monetary Fund (IMF) and World Bank. Indeed, the IMF's menu of "budgetary austerity, devaluation, trade liberalisation and privatisation is applied simultaneously in more than 100 indebted countries" (Chossudovsky 1997: 35).

11. Clarkson (1993) presents a perceptive account of the constitutionalizing impact of international trading agreements. In his view, international law, expressed in treaties and agreements to which the state has bound itself, forms part of the constitutional system. The main constitutional effect of the Free Trade Agreement lay in the limitations it placed upon government, specifically the Canadian government. In many respects it was not binding upon the United States. However, while the FTA is part of Canada's constitution it does not follow, given asymmetrical power relations and different circumstances, that it is part of the American constitutional system. In an analysis of NAFTA, Robinson (1993: 20–24) points out that the agreement extends the deregulatory approach to international trade and economics that are entrenched in the General Agreement on Tariffs and Trade (GATT) and the FTA. Thus, NAFTA's principal focus "is constraining governments' capacity to regulate the behaviour of foreign and domestic corporations in their roles as importers, exporters, and investors" (20). Much of the opposition to the OECD's sponsored Multilateral Agreement on Investment focused on its quasi-constitutional restrictions on the capacity of democratically elected governments to act.

12. As Panitch (2000: 5) notes, having played an "active and crucial role in making globalization happen," states are increasingly "encumbered with the responsibility of sustaining it" in the wake of market volatility and various crises.

13. Here, Weiss does not imply that the United States is a strong state in terms of

its institutional capacity. Indeed, most analysts would regard it as a weak domestic state. It is in the other meaning of "state," that of country, that the United States qualifies as strong. Weiss (1997: 25) notes: "It is often the domestically weaker states which take the lead in seeking out this external path [of using international agreements], aspiring to constrain others to adopt their own more 'hands off' approach to trade and industry."

14. Reflecting on developments within political economy in the 1980s and 1990s, Panitch (2000: 8) argues: "The abandonment of attempts to develop Marxist theories of the capitalist state in favour of notions of state autonomy was a disastrous diversion." In some measure my work here returns to the themes of class and state that characterized earlier political economy.

Chapter Two

Canada
An (Always) Global Nation

The need and the efforts to deal with the problems posed by its insertion into the global economy are nothing new for the Canadian state. Indeed, there is a sense in which the political history of Canada consists of little else. The territory that became Canada was colonized by European powers in pursuit of natural resources for shipment to home markets, and its economic development became dependent on a succession of resource staple products—fur, fish, timber, wheat, minerals—and was unusually subject to the ebb and flow of demand for these products abroad.

An indigenous tradition in political economy, described in Harold Innis's staples theory, developed in response to the Canadian conditions. Its central thesis was that Canada was an "open economy" dependent on international resource markets. Staples theory thus "emphasized the external determination of much of what happened in Canada. Canada should not be studied, it was thought, as a self-contained economy using Ricardian assumptions of international trade, namely that capital and labour were relatively immobile. Staple-exporting sectors were analyzed in their global contexts. Canada was an 'open economy'" (Laxer 1991: xiv-xv).

The degree to which Canada has always been a globally integrated economy and the degree to which Canadian political economists have always understood this make the current focus on the "novelty" of globalization puzzling. Canada was one of the first globalized nations, and Canadian political economists were among the first to seek to understand the impact of global relations on domestic economic and political development (often with a view to reducing the global impact rather than embracing it).

Even in the pre-Confederation period the Canadian colonies were dependent on resource exploitation and trade to a much higher degree than their southern neighbours (Pomfret 1981: 19). It was resource- and export-dependency and lack of economic self-sufficiency that staples theory sought to explain. This trade has, though, been narrowly focused on a limited number of markets. Once Canada was dependent on a single colonial power, Britain, for trade and investment; today it is overwhelmingly dependent on the United States. Little has changed, other than the location of the primary market. In short, for Canada there is little that is new about market dependency; and the intrusion of international factors and concerns into the domestic political economy was the central concern of Canadian political economy long before the concept of globalization was coined.

The decision to found Canada, to move towards Confederation, had its roots in trade. Britain had repealed the Corn Laws in 1846 and, with that step ended the preference for Canadian producers. This shift necessitated a search for alternatives in the colonies of British North America. Economic factors were a major motivation in the search for a strategy that eventually led to the foundation of the Canadian nation-state. The initial "solution" for Canada's new trading problem was negotiation of a Reciprocity Treaty with the United States. The treaty covered only natural products, and its abrogation by the United States in 1866 was declared, in U.S. press reports of the day, to be a precursor to annexation (see Ryerson 1973: 338–39). Instead, the move reinforced pressures for economic and political union in British North America. As a result, the new Dominion of Canada devised various "national policies" to ensure its survival.

The need for national strategies, or policies, derived from Canada's marginal semi-peripheral position within the international political economy. In this sense, the term "semi-periphery" conveys the image of a country whose reality includes relative affluence (and hence is hardly "peripheral") but which has an industrial structure that is in some ways not fully developed, leading to unequal relations with major powers (hence not "core"). It was a large, sparsely populated entity, dependent on foreign capital to exploit its abundant resources and, right from the beginning, heavily dependent on a limited number of overseas markets. As early as 1870, for example, 89.5 percent of Canada's exports and 88.5 percent of its imports involved Britain and the United States (Glazebrook 1966, vol. 1: 101). Over time the U.S. market displaced the British (see Table 2.1).

Confederation and the National Policy

As with any major project, a number of factors combined to produce the 1867 constitutional deal that led to the creation of a new country. Relations between the French and English populations of the Province of the United Canadas were deadlocked. A new set of political structures offered a way out. A perception of external threat existed as a result of events and conditions in the United States—the Civil War was ending and,

Table 2.1
Canadian Exports, Selected Years (in $ millions)

	United States	United Kingdom	U.K. as a % of U.S.
1886	34	37	109
1896	38	63	166
1906	84	127	151
1916	201	452	225
1926	452	459	102
1936	333	395	119
1946	884	594	67
1956	2,803	811	29
1966	6,046	1,123	19
1975	21,074	1,795	9

Source: Data Extrapolated from Statistics Canada, *Historical Statistics of Canada*, Series G389-400, 401–407, (Ottawa, 1983).

in fighting it, the Americans had established a powerful military machine; and Irish republicans (Fenians) in the United States were engaged in occasional border raids. From both the British and Canadian viewpoints a united Canada would be more defensible and better able to bear a greater share of the costs of defence. The colonial elites undoubtedly held a desire for more responsible government and greater autonomy from London, while maintaining the British connection.

On the part of the economic and political elites of the day, there was a sense of great potential being hindered by an inability to launch an economic development strategy. The strategy in question included railway-building to unite the country (and prevent the West from being annexed by the United States), settling the Prairies for agricultural production, exploiting the North for its timber and minerals, and stimulating the manufacturing sector in Central Canada. Alfred Dubuc (1966: 114) argued:

> In economic terms Confederation was essentially an instrument of public finance whose object it was to make available to those responsible for effecting investment, the resources necessary for the unified economic development of the British colonies in North America. It was based on a fundamental project of economic growth: the opening up of new regions to agriculture and forestry; the development of national industry protected by tariffs from foreign competition; the development of an abundant work

force through a vigorous immigration policy; and the intense cultivation of commercial relations with the British Empire.

Here, Dubuc is running together the actual Confederation agreement with the National Policy, which followed in 1879. The trajectory was, perhaps, not as smooth as suggested because of the flirtation, in the 1870s, with renewed reciprocity with the United States. Failure to reach agreement with the Americans doomed this initiative (see White 1989: 59–60). Still, there is every reason to concur with Dubuc's assessment of Confederation: that "it had as its goal the creation of adequate institutions for the pursuit of a centralized policy of long-term economic development" (Dubuc 1966: 117).

Canadian economic development was subsequently shaped by a number of "national policies" that succeeded one another, with overlaps, as the guiding principles for detailed public policy (see, for example, Bradford 1998; Brodie 1990; Eden and Molot 1993; Fowke 1967; Leslie 1987). The term "national policy" has been variously defined as "conscious nation-building policies of successive federal governments" (Eden and Molot 1993: 232) and "overarching federal development strategies for achieving economic growth and social cohesion within the Canadian political community" (Bradford 1998: 3). The concept clearly has affinities with the notion of policy paradigm: "the broad goals behind policy, the related problems or puzzles that policy-makers have to solve to get there, and, in large measure, the kinds of instruments that can be used to attain these goals" (Hall 1990: 59).

The first National Policy, implicit in the Confederation agreement and taking definite shape with John A. Macdonald's subsequent initiative in 1879, consisted of creating the transportation link for a national, east-west economy through railway-building (projects that also served as a stimulus to the manufacturing industries of Central Canada). High tariff barriers on imports served as a further aid to manufacturing and industrialization. Finally, the government pursued an active immigration policy to settle the West and provide some of the labour-power necessary in the new manufacturing industries.

Neo-classical economists such as John Dales (1966) predictably considered the extent of government involvement through the National Policy as being costly and unproductive. Others, like Tom Naylor (1972, 1975), viewed it as less of a national policy and more of a self-interested strategy by a predominantly commercial elite intent on risk-avoidance and content to allow manufacturing in Canada to take place under the aegis of foreign, primarily U.S. investors, who established branch plants to

Table 2.2
Estimated Percentage of Total Foreign Capital Invested in Canada
(Selected Years)

	United States	United Kingdom	Other Countries
1900	14	85	1
1905	19	79	2
1910	19	77	3
1915	27	69	4
1920	44	53	3
1925	56	41	3
1930	61	36	3
1933	61	36	3
1939	60	36	4
1945	70	25	5
1950	76	20	4
1955	76	18	6
1960	75	15	10
1965	79	12	9
1970	79	9	12
1974	77	9	14

Source: M.C. Urquhart and K.A.H. Buckley, eds., *Historical Statistics of Canada*, 2nd ed. (Ottawa: Statistics Canada, 1983) tables G188-202.

surmount the tariff wall (see Table 2.2).

But it is more likely that the degree of foreign direct investment was an unintended rather than intended consequence of the high tariff policy. More accurately, perhaps, the elites did not anticipate the long-term consequences of high levels of foreign direct investment: "Foreign economic domination was never perceived as a real threat during that period. American investment was stimulated, but not in amounts that would raise fears. Macdonald ... does not bear the responsibility for the failures of twentieth-century Canadian leaders to readjust to changed economic circumstances" (Scheinberg 1973, quoted in Clement 1975: 66).

The high level of U.S. foreign ownership in Canada has had less to do, then, with a conspiracy on the part of merchant capital than it has with Canada's location next door to the major twentieth-century capitalist power at the very time it was attempting to industrialize and expand its international presence (McBride and Shields 1997: 121). The process of creating a transcontinental economy out of British North America, in large measure centred around the building of a national railway, was also integral to the development of a national community. The National Policy, "aimed at extensive growth and economic diversification, was a defensive reaction to the threat of U.S. expansionism balanced by the desire to emulate U.S. industrialization and westward expansion" (Eden and Molot 1993: 235). The construction of a political community or nationality (Smiley 1967) was essential for this economic strategy, and the Canadian state's economic policies played a central role in this process (see Laxer 1992: 202–03; and Resnick 1990: 207–20).

The framework of the National Policy of 1879 was reaffirmed by the results of the 1911 federal election. Rejection of reciprocity with the United States was a clear victory for the conservative nationalist approach (see Granatstein and Hillmer 1991: 46–56). Even though free trade was rejected as a policy, and anti-American rhetoric periodically surfaced until the Cold War cast a cloud of disloyalty over such sentiments, trade, communication and culture grew in a north-south direction as the United Kingdom declined and the base of the staples trade shifted. Other problems included persistent regional inequalities—and perceptions in both West and East that these inequalities were the product of national policies favouring Central Canadian interests (see Bercuson 1977).

The Second National Policy

A second national policy (Neill 1991: 173) was fully articulated following World War II. A Keynesian demand-management strategy complemented by the construction of a social welfare state was the main feature (Brodie and Jenson 1988: 293; Smiley 1975: 47–48). The approach went along with an active pursuit of a liberalized international trading system (see Eden and Molot 1993: 235–40). According to Robin Neill (1991: 183), where Keynes had assumed a closed, mature economic system, "By introducing considerations relating to development and trade into Keynesian general equilibrium analysis Canadians ... made major contributions to the development of economics." Canadian Keynesians, such as W.A. Mackintosh, were responding to factors that today would be associated with globalization. Intimately aware of the realities of staples dependency, the early Keynesians knew that the application of their approach would be difficult in Canada because "the Canadian economy was open, regionally diversified, relatively dependent on primary product exports, and governed by a federated state" (Neill 1991: 173).

Wolfe (1985: 48) argued:

> The adoption of Keynesian ideas in Canada was based on several prior assumptions. The most important of these was the assumption that Canada had always been, and would remain, an open

trading economy specializing in the export of resource staples. Consequently, Canada could only hope to apply the Keynesian policies in a liberalized post-war trading environment that would stimulate the export of its resource products. Thus in adopting Keynes to the Canadian context, government leaders and their economic policy advisors fashioned a uniquely Canadian synthesis of the more general Keynesian theory with the traditional staples approach to Canadian economic development.

The postwar *White Paper on Employment and Income* (April 12, 1945) focused on increasing exports as the key to prosperity. It argued that the Bretton Woods system and the proposed international trade organization offered the best prospects for economic growth in Canada. Thus Canadian Keynesianism was to a certain extent subsumed by an "export-led growth theory," by which a liberalized international economy would be a major contributor to full employment.

In the postwar world most western countries adopted some version of Keynesianism, or a functional equivalent. Long-term factors such as industrialization and urbanization partly account for this cohesion. Other factors included the recent experience of the Great Depression, the challenge of an ideological competitor in the shape of the Soviet Union (still basking in wartime prestige, particularly in working-class circles), the intellectual influences of Keynes's economic theories and the Beveridge Report on postwar reconstruction and social policy in Britain,[1] together with pressure from below for full employment, labour rights and economic security. The war itself had also legitimated the notion of an active state.

Many scholars have interpreted the postwar Keynesian era[2] as a tacit class compromise between capital and labour. Certainly both these social actors received benefits from the social contract constructed in Canada after the Second World War. Capital had to tolerate a more active and interventionist state; but the intervention was largely at the level of initiatives on fiscal and monetary policies designed to maintain aggregate demand at something like the level necessary to sustain high and stable levels of employment and income. As a result, economic growth and profit-making opportunities were good. Keynesianism did not imply higher levels of public ownership or state control of investment or other investment decisions. Labour won collective bargaining rights, even though legally circumscribed, and commitments that the state would construct a welfare state and, in its economic policies, aim for high employment levels.

Researchers have expressed doubts about the strength of the commitment to full employment in Canada—and, indeed, the actual commitment was only to the phrase "high and stable levels of employment" (Canada, Department of Reconstruction, 1945). For much of the postwar period unemployment, though low, exceeded levels in other Western countries (see McBride 1992: ch.2). Some commentators have drawn attention to the passivity of fiscal policy in this period. Budgets, for example, tended to be passive rather than countercyclical. Policy goals were not limited to those favoured by the Keynesians, and the priority of various goals was contested rather than the subject of a consensus. Full employment was not necessarily the primary goal of government:

> The economy experienced a few brief periods of "full" employ-ment, but there were far more jumps than declines in the level of unemployment. In thirteen years in the post-war period [1945–75], government economic policy was unsuccessful in preventing a substantial rise in the level of unemployment. In six other years, government policy did not encourage a fall in the level of unemployment. In the remaining years, a low level of unemploy-ment was the result of healthy economic conditions. (Campbell 1987: 191)

Nonetheless, the commitment to high levels of employment was always part of the discourse. Much of the repertoire of government policy was rationalized as contributing to its achievement.

The Canadian version of the Keynesian welfare state emerged gradu-ally. The Second World War provided a stimulus and saw the creation of some programs, but the process as a whole continued for years, culminating with the reform and expansion of the unemployment insurance system in 1971.

Canada's version of the U.K. Beveridge Report, Leonard Marsh's Report on *Social Security in Canada*, appeared in March 1943. Few of its recommended policies—full employment, supplementary programs for occupational training, comprehensive systems for social and medical insurance (covering unemployment, sickness, maternity, disability, old age and health), family or children's allowances and general welfare assistance saw the light of day in the short term (Guest 1987: 212–13). Nevertheless, the federal government did incrementally introduce a wide range of social programs. Canada was not in the vanguard internationally, but a gradual piecemeal extension of programs did occur, producing a more compre-hensive social network than found in the United States.

Many of the programs involved federal and provincial co-operation.

Indeed, the heyday of the Keynesian welfare state in Canada was also the heyday of "co-operative federalism." Shared-cost arrangements emanated from the fact that much of the social policy area was under provincial jurisdiction whilst the predominant power of taxation was in the hands of the federal authorities. Since, over the postwar years, the federal level was inclined to pursue an agenda of building national standards in social policy, the scene was set for bargaining between the two orders of government about the generosity and shape of that policy. Some of the programs, such as family allowances, were universal and funded from general revenues. Others, such as the Canada Pension Plan and unemployment insurance, were based partly on insurance principles. In addition to providing income-support programs, the federal government made dollars available to the health, education and social assistance systems. Frequently, as with the Medical Care Act or Canada Assistance Plan, Ottawa would attach conditions to its funding. Provincial health systems, for example, had to meet the criteria of universality, comprehensiveness, portability, accessibility and public administration to qualify for federal financial contributions.

As time passed, and as certain types of unemployment—regional and seasonal among them—seemed resistant to Keynesian measures, the paradigm itself came under challenge. The challenges picked up strength in the 1970s when Keynesianism appeared to be unable to account at the theoretical level for the simultaneously high levels of inflation and unemployment. More to the point, the approach seemed to have no policy solution for these problems.

The Post-Keynesian Experiment with State Intervention

Postwar Keynesianism began to unravel in the 1970s.[3] In retrospect, when the long postwar boom was over and succeeded by decades of crisis and uncertainty, observers "began to realize that the world, particularly the world of developed capitalism, had passed through an altogether exceptional phase of its history; perhaps a unique one. They looked for names to describe it: the 'thirty glorious years' of the French ... the quarter-century Golden Age of the Anglo-Americans.... The gold glowed more brightly against the dull or dark background of the subsequent decades of crisis" (Hobsbawm 1995: 257–58).

As the "golden age" unravelled, social expenditures came increasingly under attack as unaffordable. Two successor strategies emerged. One, sometimes partially endorsed by the Liberal Party, was a nationalist-inspired industrial strategy that would actively use the state to stimulate the economy and promote domestically controlled capital accumulation. The Progressive Conservatives, by contrast, gradually came to view the state as a major cause of the crisis and based their cure in free-market solutions (Brodie and Jenson 1988: 294). The Chrétien Liberal government of the 1990s also adopted that perspective.

The set of policies taken up by the Liberal governments of Pierre Trudeau represented an embryonic state-directed industrial strategy, with a highly interventionist role reserved for the federal government. The federal state, as in the first National Policy, would be utilized in an attempt to restructure the national economy (Leslie 1987: 8). The core of the industrial strategy eventually came to be the National Energy Policy (NEP), adopted in 1980, which attempted to base economic strategy upon "a resource-driven restructuring of the industrial sector" (Brodie and Jenson 1988: 314). This was part of the Liberal government's ongoing nationalist policy, as evidenced by its earlier creation of the state oil company Petro-Canada (see Fossum 1997) and the Foreign Investment Review Agency (FIRA).

The Trudeau energy policy "was interventionist, centralist, and na-tionalistic" (Pratt 1982: 27). It aimed to achieve 50 percent Canadian ownership of the industry and energy self-sufficiency as well as insulate Canada from international oil crises (Lalonde 1982: 107). Energy security would also provide a strategic advantage to Canadian-based capital. Not only was it the first attempt by a Canadian government since World War II to reclaim for Canadian ownership a key foreign-controlled sector of the economy, but it also aimed at strengthening the fiscal hand of the central state. Further, the policy was geared towards giving "the national state far greater control over one of the real commanding heights of the Canadian economy." This approach had nothing to do with socialism. The NEP utilized the federal state to promote indigenous capital over foreign business interests; the state was employed primarily to advance the interests of private capital accumulation (Pratt 1982: 28, 40–41).

This new, third national policy failed for two reasons. First, it was dependent upon the fortunes of the international commodities market. To sustain the strategy and support the energy megaprojects, oil prices had to keep rising; but they dropped. Second, the initiative ran into major ideological opposition from U.S. and Canadian business. The pressures emanating from these sources were accentuated by structural factors. Increased Canada-U.S. trade had made the economy vulnerable to U.S. policy and threats of retaliation (Brodie and Jenson 1988: 318). U.S.-based capital successfully encouraged its state to pressure Canada to abandon its new national policy. Indeed, Canadian business generally, both indigenous and foreign-owned, became increasingly nervous about the degree of state interventionism inherent in the Liberal strategy and evident in such initiatives as the earlier Anti-Inflation Program as well as the NEP. The concerns prompted business to increase its representative capacity—hence the formation of the Business Council on National Issues (BCNI) in 1975 (Langille 1987).

The collapse of the Trudeau Liberals' new national policy opened the door to the Conservative Party's neo-liberal economic agenda based on free-market principles. In the energy field this meant abandoning a national policy (energy, or otherwise) in favour of the continentalist approach, which was eventually embodied in the North American Free Trade Agreement. The provisions of that agreement continentalized the disposition of Canadian energy.

The evolution from one national policy to another took place under conditions in which Canada's international trade exposure remained significant (see Table 2.3). Over the course of the twentieth century, a remarkable stability existed in the proportion of the Canadian economy that was trade-oriented. Indeed, if Canada's trade is calculated as a percentage of GDP, Canada was no more trade-dependent in the 1980s and early 1990s than it was in 1926, although the percentages were increasing. By 1994, trade dependency was clearly higher than in the 1920s (see Table 2.3).

Table 2.3
Canadian Global Trade Exposure

	GDP (millions)	(Exports at market prices) (millions)	% of GDP	Imports (millions)	% of GDP
1926	5,354	1,601	30	1,233	23
1931	4,975	903	18	782	16
1936	4,879	1,338	27	845	17
1941	8,532	2,396	28	1,659	19
1946	12,167	3,189	26	2,487	20
1951	22,280	4,908	22	5,045	23
1956	32,902	6,141	19	7,007	21
1961	40,886	7,296	18	7,450	18
1966	64,388	12,564	20	12,584	20
1971	97,290	21,173	22	19,531	20
1976	197,924	44,252	22	45,279	23
1981	355,994	96,880	27	93,001	26
1986	505,866	138,119	27	133,369	26
1991	676,477	164,849	24	172,805	26
1994	750,053	249,371	33	243,756	32

Source: Statistics Canada, Canadian Economic Observer: Historical Statistical Supplement 1994/95, Catalogue no 11-210, Table 1 (Ottawa).

During the peak years of postwar prosperity, from the mid-1950s to the mid-1970s, trade dependence was relatively low by Canadian standards. The relatively low dependency on trade during the Keynesian era may indicate that postwar economic development, based on "national" Keynesianism, was working as intended. Significantly, however, exports as a percentage of GDP increased sharply before the enactment of the Free Trade Agreement.

Foreign Relations: Three Interpretations

Canada's three national policies all sought to facilitate economic development in the context of a relatively trade-dependent economy integrated into world markets. That is, these policies "spoke" to international questions, such as trade and foreign investment, as well as domestic issues. Canada's foreign policy has, of course, covered a wide range of issues. However, it has normally shown a healthy regard for economic matters, as befits a major trading country.

The early foreign policy of a self-governing Canada was focused on commercial matters. H.G. Skilling (1945) notes that the first Canadian overseas representatives, as early as 1868, were emigration agents, and they were closely followed by trade commissioners. A Trade Commissioner Service was established in 1892, long before the establishment of diplomatic missions per se (Howlett, Netherton and Ramesh 1999: 123). Even when Canadian high commissions abroad began to be set in place, beginning with London in 1880, they were necessarily "considered a phase in the development of autonomy on commercial negotiations" (Skilling 1945: 90). George Glazebrook (1966, vol. 1: 204) noted "It was through the frequent negotiations with foreign governments, chiefly on tariff questions, fisheries and the use of inland waters, that Canadians played their most active and most direct part in diplomacy."

Autonomy in foreign affairs thus first manifested itself in the economic sphere. The "high politics" were largely left to Britain, certainly until the early 1920s. Prior to World War I the context of Canadian foreign policy (see Glazebrook 1966, vol. 1) had been one of loyal, and usually uncritical, ally of the United Kingdom, which was still the predominant world power. Because of an increasing concern about the role of Germany the British had an interest in maintaining friendly relations with the United States. Many Canadians believed that in pursuit of that relationship Britain was willing to sacrifice Canadian interests. The Treaty of Washington and the Alaska Boundary Dispute loomed large in such perceptions. Consequently, Canada increasingly demanded and got an independent foreign policy vis-à-vis Canadian-U.S. relations and with respect to foreign economic and commercial policy.

After the First World War came a period of close co-operation with Britain and the other autonomous dominions. But thereafter, for the rest of the interwar period, Canada adopted an autonomous, albeit isolationist, stance characterized by a refusal to engage in collective decision-making and an avoidance of all commitments that might lead to involvement in another European war (Rosenbaum 1969). Economically, meanwhile, Canada and the United States waged what J.B. Brebner (1947) called "an almost continuous tariff war," which continued until 1935, when under the impact of economic crisis the two countries took first steps towards closer continental co-operation.

World War II led to ever-increasing Canadian co-operation and consultation with the United States. Joint policy declarations, notably the Hyde Park Declaration in 1941, left no doubt that a complete integration of North American resources and facilities was the common aim. To a large extent North America became the arsenal of the Allied forces. Even while the war was being prosecuted, however, "normal" power politics continued to operate. Within Canada, as Ernest Forbes (1986:5) shows, the Maritime provinces were bypassed in decisions on industrial location, even when a logical military or economic rationale existed:

> While the demands of Canada's allies were concerned with immediate efficiency in wartime, C.D. Howe and his controllers[4] often appeared to be following an agenda for industrialization based on their perception of Canada's needs after the war. Their vision of a centralized manufacturing complex closely integrated with the United States apparently did not include the Maritimes in any significant role.

Projects such as lend-lease enabled Britain and other Allied countries to purchase arms and supplies. However, at U.S. insistence, one aspect of the lend-lease agreements was the inclusion of commitments, such as the elimination of imperial preference by Britain, to produce a "non-discriminatory commercial policy" in the postwar world (James 1949: 37).

In the generally prosperous postwar years, the international economic regime was relatively tolerant of national diversity in economic and social policy regimes. State interventionism, which had been part of Canadian national policies since the country's inception, was the norm in the Western world. These were, after all, the Cold War years, and social cohesion was an important factor in waging the war. In line with other Western countries, Canada added a social dimension to the underlying economic strategy. The battle between alternative systems was in part ideological; but conferring real benefits on subordinate classes also served to reinforce the ideological hegemony of liberal capitalism. In the foreign policy arena Canada was clearly and enthusiastically a member of the Western alliance. Canada supported the NATO alliance, contributed troops to the Korean War, joined NORAD (a bilateral air defence agreement with the United States) and stationed armed forces in Europe.

Descriptions of Canadian foreign policy in this period usually focused on three images: Canada as a "middle power" (or "honest broker"), a "principal power," and a satellite of the United States (see Cooper 1997). The different images capture some of the ambiguities in Canadian foreign policy. Canada made significant efforts to construct a role as a "middle power." Some analysts considered that over time Canada achieved this goal and actually made the transition to being, if not a great power, then at least a "principal" power. But it is not easy to be a loyal ally to one power and simultaneously an "honest broker" between it and others. Others detected a growing subservience to the United States that rendered all of the categories pure imagery. They saw the roots of Canadian subservience as lying in the close integration of the Canadian and U.S. economies (see Tables 2.1 and 2.2).

Political factors, of course, also played a role. After the election of the Mulroney government in 1984, Canada pursued a policy of loyal and uncritical alliance with the Americans. The policy was pursued overtly and, to critics, on occasion obsequiously, an approach that stood in partial contrast to the policy, and more emphatically in contrast to the political optics, of the Trudeau era. Under Trudeau, Canadian efforts to maintain a sense of distance from the United States had at least limited substance, expressed through initiatives like the Foreign Investment Review Agency, the Third Option, and the National Energy Program. Perhaps, as Stephen Clarkson and Christina McCall (1994: 111) put it, these efforts "were too cursory and too cynically cosmetic to satisfy most ardent nationalists. But they alienated big businessmen further from a government that seemed to them decidedly out of touch with the private sector's desire to accelerate, not reverse, Canada's integration into the U.S. economy." The shift from Trudeau to Mulroney has been represented as a redefinition of Canada's middle-power role—from an approach partially exercised in a "counter-consensus" direction to one that was "limitationist," reflecting "an orientation more in keeping with existing power and privilege in Canadian society and in the global order" (Neufeld 1995: 22).

The 1980s saw a re-emergence of economic priorities in Canada's foreign policy, symbolized by the addition of international trade to the external affairs ministry and its renaming as the Department of Foreign Affairs and International Trade (DFAIT) (see Doern, Pal and Tomlin 1996b: ch. 10). Increasingly, Canada's interests were defined in bilateral rather than multilateral terms.

The term "middle power" has been applied to Canada in two related senses: first, as "occupying the 'middle' point in a range ... usually measured by reference to such quantifiable attributes as area, population, size, complexity and strength of economy, military capability, and other comparable factors" (Cooper, Higgott and Nossal 1993: 17);[5] second, on the basis of function and behaviour in the international system. Canada, with countries such as Denmark, the Netherlands, Norway and Sweden, actively supports the international community through the provision of more nationals to the international civil service, more military personnel to peace operations, and more funds to overseas development assistance through multilateral agencies than other countries. Overall, these states "have both the capacity and the will to play an important role on the international scene" (Pratt 1990: 14).

Considered as a middle power, Canada's greatest influence has been exercised multilaterally through its membership in various international institutions and organizations. Its foreign policy has been functionalist, in that it has deliberately focused on those issues in which it has had the greatest potential to exert influence in the international system. Multilateralism and functionalism, therefore, often go together. As a middle power, Canada's interests and foreign policy objectives are said to have been based largely on its need for co-operation in the international system (Holmes 1976: 13).

In economic terms, the middle-power approach assumes that rules and norms have a significant impact on interstate relations and that, as a functioning middle power, Canada has the potential to play an important role in multilateral and bilateral arrangements. From this point of view, strong multilateral regimes become a means of enhancing economic welfare and peace in an interdependent global system and of reducing U.S. domination of the economy. These goals are usually articulated by federal representatives extolling the benefits of Canada's membership in these regimes: "Indeed, Canadian foreign policy officials stress that Canada has a strong interest in multilateralism and economic liberalization because this enhances economic welfare and Canadian influence in international affairs" (Cutler and Zacher 1992a: 3).

Michael Hart (1985) and Frank Stone (1992), for example, cite the development of international economic regimes such as the GATT and the FTA as important mechanisms for managing systemic changes related to globalization. Stone (1992: 1) suggests that the GATT constituted "a great advance in international cooperation over the anarchical conditions that characterized world trade relationships during the inter-war period, and indeed, represents one of the most successful efforts in international cooperation of the post-war period." Tom Keating (1993: 13) also stresses the importance of multilateralism and suggests that Canadian policy-makers have repeatedly relied on both economic and security regimes in an attempt to fulfil a wide range of foreign policy objectives. For Canada to wield influence and authority, the most effective medium is a co-operative and rules-based system whereby Canada's strength is derived, it is said, not from traditional sources such as military capabilities or economic status, but instead from its ability to generate ideas.

For others, Canada's traditional commitment to multilateralism and the establishment of regime-based norms has been less than impressive. Certainly Canada has pursued bilateral as well as multilateral agreements. Thus: "The Canadian commitment to multilateralism and liberalization is an exaggerated one, and in some cases, an inaccurate portrayal of Canadian foreign economic policy" (Cutler and Zacher 1992a: 4; see also Cooper 1997: ch. 2; Keenes 1995).

Thus one analysis of Canada's postwar international trade policy argued that the Canadian commitment to international economic regimes was never absolute (Finlayson and Bertasi 1992). Similarly, Christopher Thomas (1992) examined the establishment of a bilateral trade regime with the United States in terms of Canada's growing disillusionment with the GATT and the need to reinforce the economic relationship with its largest trading partner. Such initiatives build upon a long history of "creeping continentalism," from the wartime Hyde Park Declaration through the Defence Production Sharing Agreement of 1958 to the 1965 Auto Pact (Black and Sjolander 1996: 14). Theodore Cohn (1992), in a study examining Canadian agricultural policy, suggests that pressure from domestic sectoral interests has a greater impact on governments than do international regimes. Specifically, Cohn perceives agriculture as its own opposing internal "regime," which creates a great deal of tension between international norms and rules and those established at the domestic level.

Outside the economic sphere the functionalist view of Canadian foreign policy is closely tied to the concept of "niche diplomacy," whereby nations concentrate resources in the specific areas that offer the best returns (Potter 1997; Cooper, Higgott and Nossal 1993). By such means Canada's strength as a mediatory middle power emphasizing the importance of co-operation, as well as technical and informational expertise, might be maximized.

The Canada 21 Council (1994: 12) concluded that Canada, which draws on a wide range of instruments and resources, must rely on its social, human and intellectual capital to carve out an influential role for itself in the international arena. Andrew Cooper, Richard Higgott and Kim Richard Nossal (1993: 13) consider that waning U.S. hegemony had given way to alternative forms of leadership whereby "games of skill" increasingly replaced "tests of will." Emphasis on technical and entrepreneurial leadership refers to what Foreign Affairs Minister Lloyd Axworthy termed "soft power," a concept that he argues must be cultivated and wielded by Canada if it were to emerge as an important and influential actor in the twenty-first century (Axworthy 1997: 192). Such efforts, as one would expect, have intensified since the end of the Cold War and end of the "Soviet threat." Reduced Cold War tensions should have expanded the terrain in which "middle powers" could operate. But for Canada the end of the Cold War seemed to increase the contradictory nature of its foreign policy.

In its participation in U.S.-organized military ventures such as the Gulf War and Kosovo (Allen 1999; P. Phillips 1999) in the 1990s, Canada operated very much as an agent of U.S. foreign policy. Still, by participating in peace-building and campaigning to outlaw anti-personnel land mines, promoting the concept of human security, and advocating a U.N.-sponsored international criminal court, Canadian foreign policy demonstrated its aspirations to a middle-power role. In the words of the former director-general of the Planning Secretariat at the Department of Foreign Affairs: "While we have been proud of our respected role as middle power in the past, today, objectively, we are aiming at a global reach. Therefore we think that 'global' middle power would fit the bill" (quoted in David and Roussel 1998: 131). In this view, the growth of multilateralism and international institutions since 1990 has considerably broadened the scope of action for middle powers. Such factors as the reform and enlargement of NATO, membership in the Organization of American States (OAS) and the increased incidence of peacekeeping represent new opportunities for countries such as Canada to assert their views. Issues traditionally promoted by middle powers, such as human rights, environmental protection and human security have assumed a higher profile, which suggests to middle-power theorists that these countries will increase their international role.

This sense of the growing importance of middle powers spawned another interpretation: that Canada made the transition to being a "foremost" (Eayrs 1975), "major" (Lyon and Tomlin 1979; Gotlieb 1987) or "principal" power (Dewitt and Kirton 1983). John Kirton has argued that despite the apparent rise during the 1990s of the United States as the only superpower, the Asian financial crisis of 1997–99 affirmed Canada's position as a principal power. According to Kirton (1999: 607), "In the diplomacy behind the Hong Kong reform package, Canada acted as an equal member of the G-7 concert in which different members lead on specific issues and mutually adjust to create a new and effective consensus." Thus Canada's diplomacy during the financial crisis calls into question traditional interpretations of Canadian foreign policy. The crisis, Kirton argues, demonstrates that Canada remains a global player, rather than one forced by diminishing relative capabilities in the 1990s to turn to a more restricted, niche-based, regional focus (624). However, other commentators make strong arguments to the contrary. For example, Michael Webb (1992) holds that small and medium-sized countries are ineffective in multilateral settings, which is why Canada turned to a bilateral agreement with the United States—not from strength but rather from weakness. Others consider that the closing of the Cold War ended the conditions in which middle powers found space in which to act (David and Roussel 1998).

In contrast to arguments suggesting middle- or principal-power status, an alternative interpretation portrays Canada as a dependent, satellite state. By the late 1960s the middle-power image of Canada was already being "greeted with scepticism by some and complete rejection by others" (Nossal 1997: 60). In this view Canada's capacity for independent and autonomous action in international affairs had been eliminated by its successive membership in the British and U.S. empires. Canada went from colony to nation to colony, so "what for some marked the emergence of a middle power in world politics was, for others, merely a transfer of dependent orbit, with Canada consigned to the periphery—or at best the 'semiperiphery' of the world economy" (Nossal 1997: 60–61; see also Hawes 1984; Clarkson 1968; Lumsden 1970).

David Dewitt and Kirton (1983: 28), who have advanced the idea of Canada as a principal power, labelled this perspective as the "peripheral-dependence" perspective because it stresses Canada's cultural, political and economic dependence on a more powerful international actor. It also highlights the reliance of the Canada on the U.S. market for international trade, and the predominance of U.S. investment in Canada.

Growing nationalism in the late 1960s and 1970s led to a number of measures that suggested, even to supporters of the satellite interpretation, that this situation might be reversed. For example, the so-called Third Option represented a desire to "lessen the vulnerability of the Canadian economy to external factors, in particular the impact of the United States"

(Sharp 1972). This approach was stimulated as much by domestic U.S. politics as by Canadian preferences. Under President Richard Nixon the United States signalled that self-interest, narrowly defined, would be the determining factor in its economic policy. Henceforth any "special relationship" for Canada would be hard to achieve. Despite the Third Option's lack of success, nationalist hopes were aroused periodically, as with the nationalist measures taken by the Trudeau government of 1980–84.

Indeed, it could be argued that by the 1970s Canada was close to achieving, or had achieved, middle-power status as measured by autonomy from the United States, but that later events returned the country to a satellite-like status. Clarkson (1991) considers that although the Canadian state had reached a point in history where it was at its most advanced stage of development, the federal government's decision on the Free Trade Agreement with the United States abdicated most of Canada's economic and cultural sovereignty. Efforts at greater autonomy, such as the attempt at a third national policy and the Third Option trade initiative, proved to have lasted only as long as the global balance of power was conducive to the more autonomous role. The arrival of President Reagan signalled a much more aggressive U.S. stance, and the arrival of Prime Minister Mulroney signalled the end of any Canadian attempt to retain autonomy in the face of the new U.S. stance.

Once this shift happened, the most important international agreements understandably were the bilateral ones with the United States. Canada's involvement in multilateral economic regimes was primarily designed to support U.S. preferences and policies—"Multilateralism was always first and foremost a product of American hegemony" (Black and Sjolander 1996: 27). In sum, Canada's multilateral involvement "provides direct reinforcement for United States foreign policy doctrines and limits [Canada's] dissent from U.S. positions to marginal aspects. Bilaterally [Canada] assigns the highest importance to themes of harmony and commonality in the 'special relationship' ... and encourages a flow of transaction from the United States into Canada" (Dewitt and Kirton 1983: 28).

The foreign and domestic policy response of the Mulroney government gave fresh impetus to the view that Canada was part of the American imperialist orbit (Nossal 1997: 62). The policy record of the Mulroney years—the Canada-U.S. Free Trade Agreement, the pursuit of deregulation, the elimination of some of the key elements of the welfare state and the embrace of a more hawkish foreign policy—provided clear signs that Mulroney had "closed down the Canadian dream" of autonomy and independence (Martin 1993: 272–73).

Notes
1. The wartime Beveridge Report "set out a comprehensive long-term programme for the provision of security against need in all its forms, personified
   as the five threatening giants, want, disease, ignorance, squalor and idleness, and
   covering the entire population" (Deakin 1987: 41). It became enormously
   popular and played a major role in the reconstruction agenda in Britain and,
   by emulation, elsewhere.
2. For a fuller account see McBride and Shields 1997: ch.2.
3. For an in-depth evaluation of the "golden age" internationally, see Webber and
   Rigby 1996.
4. Government-appointed controllers of major industries whose task was to
   develop and implement plans for industrial expansion.
5. As noted earlier, the middle-power concept corresponds to some extent with
   the political economy depiction of Canada as a "semi-periphery"—affluent
   but in a relationship of structured inequality with larger powers.

Chapter Three

Canadian Capital and Globalization

The ratification of the Free Trade Agreement seemed to resolve, at least temporarily, a long-standing tension between continentalist and economic nationalist tendencies in Canadian history (see Merrett 1996: ch. 2). The FTA, and subsequently NAFTA, heralded much closer continental economic integration. Opponents argued that loss of political autonomy and national and cultural identity would follow (see Ayres 1998: ch. 2). In essence, the move to continental integration was a product of the growing maturity and strength of Canadian capital. The state complied with business pressures and negotiated agreements, ostensibly about trade, that had far-reaching consequences beyond any reasonable definition of that term.

Canadian Capital: Dependent or Triumphant?

The oldest strand in Canadian political economy, staples theory, pictured Canada as locked into dependent relations, first with France, then Britain, later with the United States. Dependency on the world's hegemon was not without its compensations. Even critics of the close relations noted that the United States' "greater dynamism has tended both to facilitate Canadian growth and to constrain it" (Watkins 1989: 28). Canada's trajectory was the consequence of its having been "developed to exploit a series of raw materials for more industrially advanced metropolitan nations. Canada's reliance on resource exports led to a failure to capture the benefits of the 'linkages' associated with the inputs into production and processing of raw materials" (Clement and Williams 1989a: 7). In this view, economic activity in the periphery or margins of the international political economy was derivative of developments at the centre. Hence, economic activity at the margin was distorted (see Clement 1989: 38).

Later dependency theory depicted an unequal relationship in which the United States used its superior power to extract economic advantages in its dealings with Canada (Brym 1989a). As in the staples theory analysis, this relationship might be portrayed in "agentless" terms, as the product of a technological gap (Britton and Gilmour 1978) resulting from staples production. In the harsh climate and environment of Canada, this gap proved difficult to close.[1] More commonly, from the 1970s the relationship might be couched in class terms, with much discussion focused on the characteristics of Canada's capitalist class.[2]

Class analyses often overlap with studies that focus on a ruling elite or elites. Many political economists and political sociologists have conducted investigations of the composition and character of Canada's capitalists (Porter 1965; Myers 1972; Park and Park 1962; Clement 1975; Newman 1975; Carroll 1986; Veltmeyer 1987). Sometimes these studies were written from a class perspective; sometimes from the standpoint of elite theory. The great wealth of the corporate elite and the density of personal and economic connections between them—for example, through interlocking directorships on corporate boards—make it clear that the distribution of economic power is highly concentrated in a relatively few hands. Discussion of class-based inequalities of condition and power within the economy leads logically to a consideration of possible links between the economic and the political. Because relations of political power find expression in the state—meaning, in this case, not "country" but rather the political system that governs a particular country—theorizing the role of the state and investigating who actually wields political power have provided an important focus for this school of political economy (Panitch 1977).

Historically, one noteworthy feature of the Canadian political system has been a greater degree of state activism when compared to its most common reference point, the United States. In Canada the government, or state, at both federal and provincial levels has been more likely to intervene in economic and social matters than have the equivalent institutions in the United States. Moreover, the Canadian state (political system) played a major role in creating the Canadian state (country). The two senses in which the word "state" are used in political science are, then, more obviously and closely connected than would be the case in many countries that are considered, often incorrectly, to have emerged "naturally" or "historically" (Smiley 1967). Still, Canadian statism is remarkable only in comparison to its southern neighbour. By European standards the Canadian state has played a relatively unobtrusive role, whether considered in economic or social terms (Atkinson and Coleman 1989). One explanation for this state of affairs is the weakness of the subordinate classes (Laxer 1989) and the corresponding relative strength of capital. Yet if capital has been the dominant social group in Canada, it traditionally countenanced a stronger role for the state than its counterpart in the United States. Why?

One standard explanation of this tendency cites a difference in ideologies or values. U.S. values are seen as revolutionary; those informing the construction of the Canadian state are seen as counter-revolutionary, monarchical, conservative and, hence, more tolerant of a strong state (Lipset 1990; Hartz 1964; Horowitz 1968: ch.1). Sometimes described as "Toryism," this component of Canadian political culture led in a certain direction: "The emphasis on *control* of the processes of national development, the element of the collective will of the dominant class expressed through the public institutions of the state ... was crucially relevant to a thinly settled frontier colony struggling on the fringes of a growing economic and political power to the south" (Whitaker 1977: 38).

The emphasis on political culture could easily be linked to a second type of explanation favoured by early staples interpretations of Canada's development. In a context of scarcity of private capital, and the heavy investment in infrastructure required to transport staple products to foreign markets, the state was the only agency capable of building or financing the necessary canals, railways and port facilities (Innis 1975: 400). Such an account implies that in Canada it was "necessary" for the state to intervene more than it was, for example, in the United States. To translate such imperatives into practice, of course, requires human agents. Nothing actually happens as a result of necessity. The efforts came from the participants in the political system—politicians, political parties, interest groups, social reformers and the like—who, through their interactions and conflicts, fashioned a series of "national policies" (Fowke 1967). These policies, in combination with later initiatives in the social and cultural areas, characterized Canada as a "public enterprise culture" (Hardin 1974), in contrast to the bastion of free and private enterprise to the south.

If, as class and elite theory suggests, Canada has always been ruled by a capitalist class or economic elite, that class must have been in favour of state activism over long periods of time. Indeed, business leaders in the post-Confederation period were conservative nationalists who supported a degree of state activism; but their nationalism was not altruistic. Their economic interests were served by having the state contribute to the process of capital accumulation. For Stanley Ryerson (1973: 309), one major source of pressure for Confederation came from "the growth of a native, capitalist industry, with railway transport as its backbone, and expansion of the home market as the prime motive for creating a unified and autonomous state."[3]

In the post-World War II period, a later generation of Canada's economic elite tolerated the expansion of the social functions of the state. The state activities served to legitimate the free enterprise system at a time when it was engaged in "Cold War" with an ideological rival and when its own recent history, in the Great Depression of the 1930s, demonstrated that its performance, in the absence of economic management and social provision by the state, was deeply problematic. Some political economists, though, have pointed to the limits of Canadian capital's endorsement of an active state. Staples theorists have always depicted Canada as a disadvantaged actor in an international economy shaped by others. The country's disadvantages sprang from geography, history and technology. For some, they were compounded by the tendency of the indigenous business elite to act as local representatives of international capital (Laxer 1989). Thus, Naylor (1972) used a class fraction approach to argue that Confederation and subsequent national policies were measures devised by the dominant commercial bourgeoisie to consolidate their dominance of the Canadian economy at the expense of a nascent industrial bourgeoisie.

In Naylor's account, commercial capitalists earned their money through financing extraction of staples and through arranging the transportation of these staples to foreign markets. In comparison to industrial capitalists they were risk-avoiders rather than risk-takers. Their cautious and conservative outlook rendered them unsuitable to lead a nation-building exercise. They tended to rely on U.S. entrepreneurs to get things done, and on British financiers for investment capital. Content to cede manufacturing to foreign investors, the Canadian capitalist class also ceded the commanding heights of the Canadian economy to U.S. multinationals. In turn this doomed the Canadian state to dependency and ultimate disappearance: "A Canadian capitalist state cannot survive because it has neither the material base nor the will to survive" (Naylor 1972: 36). From this perspective, the surprising aspect of continental integration, as represented by the Free Trade Agreement and NAFTA, is that it took so long to consummate.

Naylor's historical interpretation has been widely criticized (McBride 1974; MacDonald 1975; Richardson 1982) by supporters of Ryerson and others who interpreted Confederation, and Macdonald's subsequent National Policy, as an attempt by an indigenous capitalist class to engage in a nation-building exercise (Ryerson 1973; Laxer 1992; Resnick 1990). If this effort at nation-building had been incompletely successful its failure could be attributed to structural difficulties. For example, Canada had the misfortune to be situated next door to the dominant capitalist power in its most expansionary phase of development. Or the failure of subordinate classes, such as farmers in the nineteenth century, to wrest power from business and to make the nation-building project their own might be held responsible (Laxer 1989: ch. 4).

One corollary of this argument is that the policy was remarkably successful in another way: in nurturing a Canadian capitalist class. However, the interest of this class in "nation-building" proved, over the long term, to be contingent on other factors. In the context of financial liberalization and U.S. pressures towards liberal internationalism in the 1980s, this by-now self-confident national capitalist class opted for a policy of liberal continentalism. Its influence proved decisive in moving the state authorities in the same direction and many of the characteristics which shaped the Canadian polity came under sustained assault as a result of this shift (see McBride and Shields 1993, 1997).

Thus the alternative to Naylor's theory posits that in the 1870s, and for decades beyond, a relatively unified capitalist class promoted a National Policy that included tariff protection. Obviously the FTA and NAFTA represented a sea change in this long-standing position, because they were enthusiastically supported by Canadian capital. Rather than being the result of a weakly developed and dependent capitalist class, however, these moves reflect the emergence of a strong, self-confident and continentalist *indigenous* capitalist class.

Nationalist Awakening

By the 1960s it already seemed that Canada's nation-building experiment had gone awry and that continentalism—closer and closer integration with the United States—was the dominant trend in Canadian politics (Grant 1965). A series of government reports drew attention to the extent of foreign, mainly U.S., direct investment in the Canadian economy and challenged the prevailing assumption that this state of affairs was a good thing for Canada.[4] Initially these concerns triggered a degree of popular opposition to foreign investment.

In the aftermath of the Watkins (1968) and Gray (1971) reports, there was an increase of national consciousness in Canada. The prospects for a new national policy to foster greater economic, cultural and political independence from the United States seemed good. It was in response to the new mood that the Trudeau Liberals enacted a foreign investment review agency and created its state-owned oil company, Petro-Canada. Donald Smiley (1975) foresaw a new national policy centred on repatriating control of the Canadian economy. An industrial strategy would form a central component of such a policy. The historical alternative to an industrial strategy was to embrace free trade and further economic integration (Williams 1986: ch. 7). Various neo-corporatist initiatives were launched to induce labour, business and state co-operation in devising new strategies for competitiveness. These included a 1978 attempt to devise an industrial strategy through twenty-three sectoral consultative task forces established to make recommendations to the provincial and federal governments. In addition, a Second Tier Committee was established "to identify and make recommendations about factors and policies that cut across sector lines" (Canada, Department of Industry, Trade and Commerce 1978; Brown and Eastman 1981). Similarly, a Major Projects Task Force reported in 1981. Rianne Mahon (1990: 164) described the process as a series of state initiatives to restore international competitiveness by reducing labour costs, while attempting to maintain labour peace through the establishment of a variety of 'consultative mechanisms.'"

The 1980–84 Trudeau government's embryonic industrial strategy, with the federal government playing a highly interventionist role, included the National Energy Program and various megaprojects initiatives. The strategy aimed to consolidate Canadian ownership in the energy sector and to use the sector as the cornerstone of an economic development strategy. Thus the new industrial and national policy was "staples-based" and was partly a response to a nationalist agenda created by the revival of political economy in the 1960s (Clarkson 1985: ch. 4).

That such policies could be launched might be taken to indicate that a nationalist fraction of Canadian capital had come into existence. Jorge Niosi (1985a) considered one such possibility: that indigenous Canadian capital was pursuing a strategy of "continental nationalism." The strategy consisted of Canadianization of ownership, especially in traditional areas of strength such as the financial-commercial and resource-related sectors, combined with extension of the activity of Canadian multinationals into the United States. Such a strategy would not alter the underlying economic structure, but, rather, would focus largely on expanding Canadian ownership. Conceding that U.S.-owned businesses and large Canadian corporations, including banks, were opposed to the policy, Niosi cautioned: "The continental dimension may take precedence over the nationalist aspect.... Such developments make the Trudeau era an interlude, a short-lived reversal in the dependent development of Canadian society" (Niosi 1985a: 64).

Indeed, an alternative view seemed plausible. This was a period in which the Canadian state enjoyed considerable autonomy, and while its efforts were firmly linked to the interests of private capital accumulation (Pratt 1982: 40–41), it was prepared to promote indigenous over foreign-owned capital. Despite its attachment to private enterprise the Liberal attempt at a third national policy encountered major opposition from the United States and from the Canadian business community, which was itself composed, to a considerable degree, of managers of U.S. branch plants. A contemporary study of capital's attitudes on these issues provided little backing for the notion that any significant portion of Canadian capital supported a nationalist strategy (Ornstein 1985).

The week after the NEP was launched Ronald Reagan was elected president of the United States, and it was predictable that an interventionist and nationalist policy of this type would attract the enmity of the new administration. U.S. opposition was accompanied by hostility in Canada from business and provincial governments. Perhaps if energy prices had remained high the attractiveness of energy self-sufficiency would have enabled the federal government's interventionist wing to build a political base that would have sustained the NEP. As it was, oil prices fell. The National Energy Program had been grounded on the assumption that oil prices would continue to rise. When that scenario did not materialize, the Canadian state was all the more vulnerable to pressures from within and without (see Laxer 1983). The potential material basis for its autonomous and ambitious strategy diminished as oil prices fell, and the NEP was abandoned.[5]

With the election of the Mulroney government the state, reflecting the articulated demands of Canadian business (Langille 1987), adopted a neo-liberal economic strategy. The new strategy removed constraints on foreign investment, dismantled FIRA and the NEP, and opted for continental free trade.[6] The shift to a free-trade strategy was assisted by the conclusions of the Macdonald Report,[7] whose findings appear to have been wholly influenced by orthodox free-market economists (Simeon 1987) and the representations of the business community.[8]

The adoption of this strategy indicated that the existence of a nationalist fraction within Canadian capital had been exaggerated. Either indigenous capital had become thoroughly subservient to transnational corporations, or it had become strong enough, at least in certain sectors, to define its interests in terms of the continental rather than the national economy (Carroll 1986; Layton 1976).

Mature Canadian Capital and the Move to Continental Free Trade

William Carroll's work on the nature of Canadian capitalism tends to support the idea of a strong indigenous capitalist class that defines its interests in terms of a continental economy. Critiquing those who contend that there was a "silent surrender" to foreign capital, Carroll maintains that they underestimated the degree to which Canadian capital gradually matured in the postwar period. In contrast, he argues, "rumours of the Canadian bourgeoisie's demise—or its stillbirth—have been greatly exag-gerated" (Carroll 1986: xvi). At least until the mid-1970s, far from surrendering to U.S. foreign direct investment, Canadian finance capital was well on the road to emerging in a normal, mature monopoly phase. The

Canadian business community was increasingly concentrated, and increasingly Canadian (Carroll 1986, 1989)—but still, in the last quarter of the century, it made the sharp turn towards continentalism.

The sharp change of direction was intimately associated with the shift from Keynesianism to neo-liberalism and the implications of that change for a trading nation such as Canada. Canadian Keynesianism had been grafted onto a pre-existing economic strategy that saw exports as the key to growth and prosperity (Wolfe 1984: 48). However, in the heyday of national Keynesianism, from 1945 to 1975, Canada was less dependent on external trade than before or since (see Table 2.3). Canadian trade ambitions were generally in favour of a liberalized international trading system and largely expressed in multilateral forums such as GATT or in bilateral trade arrangements such as the Auto Pact or defence production agreements. Yet the logic of a Keynesian economic development strategy was based on sustaining economic growth through using the national state to maintain domestic aggregate demand at full-employment levels. This logic led to a focus on the domestic economy. Keynesianism, which had been predicated on a form of state economic management, had provided a rationale for continued "statism" in Canada.

With the abandonment of Keynesianism in the decade after 1975 came a resurgence of interest in export-led and market-driven economic growth—in sharp contrast to the Keynesian tilt towards economic growth based on domestic economic management by the state. Neo-liberalism, premised on a drastic reduction of the state's role, provided little political space for the kind of activities in which the Canadian state had been long engaged. Neo-liberals wanted to transfer many of those activities to the private sector. They also wanted the state to behave more like a business and adopt market principles in its own operations. This was a paradigm shift of some magnitude.

Although Canada had begun the paradigm shift to neo-liberalism as early as 1975 (McBride 1992), the move was contested and incomplete. Other alternatives seemed possible and, as with the National Energy Program, were actually implemented. The turning point in the debates about which economic strategy Canada should pursue was the report of the Macdonald Royal Commission on the Economic Union and Development Prospects for Canada. The Macdonald Report was partly a blueprint for policy direction but, even more importantly, was a legitimation device for a paradigm shift. Over a short period of time in the early 1980s Canadian policy switched dramatically away from multilateral forums to advocacy of bilateral, comprehensive, regional free trade with the United States. The reversal was far-reaching and a departure from over a hundred years of opposition or at least ambivalence about being drawn into such an arrangement with the Americans.

It is worth recalling how open the options seemed prior to this major change of paradigm. As late as 1981, the under-secretary of state for External Affairs, Allan Gotlieb, published an article announcing the rebirth of "the Third Option," which stressed the diversification of trade and a break of dependency on the United States (Doern and Tomlin 1992: 16). Only six years later, as ambassador to the United States, Gotlieb would play an important role in drumming up support for free trade south of the border. Similarly, the day after Donald Macdonald made his famous "leap of faith" comments in favour of free trade, a senior policy adviser to Prime Minister Mulroney argued that the idea was "poorly thought out" and that Canada should focus on expanding trade opportunities with countries like Japan (*Globe and Mail* 20 Nov. 1984: 3).

In the academic world, too, as Clarkson (1991: 103–4) points out:

> As recently as the spring of 1984 few academic experts would have had the temerity to suggest that Canada was poised to abdicate the bulk of its economic and cultural sovereignty. Conservative political scientists were describing how Canada as a "principal power" had followed a path towards greater autonomy on the world stage. Neo Marxist political economists were documenting how Canada's once dependent capitalist class had grown in strength over a quarter of a century to become a normal and mature, if continentally oriented national bourgeoisie.

The great change in state policy was preceded by a consensus among Canadian business organizations around the desirability of free trade with the United States. Within the state, sectors of the bureaucracy, notably those concerned with foreign trade and external affairs, worked hard to engineer a shift to free trade. These efforts received a major boost from the election of the Conservative government and the subsequent pro-free-trade report of the Macdonald Commission. The Commission's chair had been a prominent Liberal politician, associated to some extent with the nationalist wing of the party, which lent an aura of bipartisanship and inevitability that helped to legitimate the move to free trade.

The pivotal domestic political event on the longer road to the FTA was the embrace of free trade by the Canadian business community (Doern and Tomlin 1992: 40). The mature, highly centralized, politically well-organized and increasingly internationally oriented Canadian business community saw free trade with the United States as being in its interests for three commonly advanced reasons: security of access to the U.S. market; improved competitiveness through an increased ability to achieve economies of scale and access to state-of-the-art technology; and as a spur to domestic economic reform (see Winham 1994: 478–86).

The business preference was not a product of weakness but of growing strength. The push to free trade would serve both the material interests of the Canadian capitalist class and its political ambitions to refashion Canada along explicitly pro-market lines.[9] In short, the free trade story really begins not with a "silent surrender" but with the emergence of mature capitalism in Canada. In the lead-up to the free-trade debate Canadian capital, more concentrated and cohesive than ever, was increasingly interested, like capital elsewhere, in pursuing its own international strategy of foreign direct investment and exports; and its organizational capacity was enhanced with the establishment of the Business Council on National Issues (BCNI).

Jack Richardson (1992) suggests that the crucial factor in the push to free trade was the strengthening of the Canadian capitalist class relative to subordinate class interests in Canada.[10] He highlights a number of key developments concerning the nature of Canadian capital in the period leading up to the free trade agreement. Drawing in part on evidence that Carroll collected for the postwar period, Richardson makes a case for the emergence of a mature finance capital in Canada. Based on his own statistical analysis of ownership interlocks, he argues:

> This analysis of recent developments in the proliferation of ownership ties between financials and non-financials extends Carroll's (1989) conclusions concerning the recomposition of Canadian finance capital derived from his analysis of directorship interlock networks. It also indicates a significant increase in both corporate concentration and finance and non-financial integration. These latter developments inevitably produce a new and higher degree of cohesion, unity and strength for the hegemonic group of enterprises which comprise Canadian finance capital.... The concentration and integration of economic institutions is replacing the decisions of hundreds of thousands of independent actors in the Canadian market with decision making by the small group of 17 dominant enterprises, backed up by access to huge financial resources, and a similarly small group of foreign-controlled multinationals. (Richardson 1992: 314)

Indeed, Richardson argues that the extremely concentrated nature of

Canadian capital put it in an almost uniquely powerful position vis-à-vis Canadian society:"This places these economic actors in a position where they can exercise veto power on many government initiatives.... Because of the dense interconnections among the dominant enterprises in the economy, it also becomes easier for this group to perceive their collective interests and to articulate them" (314).

Other research supports the Carroll-Richardson thesis of a mature and highly concentrated capitalism. For example, Niosi (1985), in documenting the rise of Canada's own multinational corporations, also makes the point that Canadian capital had come of age and was increasingly dominated by a handful of leading Canadian-bred multinationals.

The increasing interest of Canadian capital in external markets was due not only to a defensive concern about the threat of renewed protectionism in the United States, but also to the new multinational aspirations of Canadian capital itself. The threat of U.S. protectionism became a real concern especially to companies in the resource/staples sector, which had traditionally been more supportive of the notion of free trade (Richardson 1992: 317; see also Hart 1994: 174). Indeed, virtually all analyses of free trade highlight this concern as a central motivation of the Canadian business community in supporting the move to the FTA. Business and government interests alike saw a free-trade agreement as a way of heading off U.S. protectionism by guaranteeing Canadian firms access to the U.S. market. The parties involved would receive exemptions from U.S. trade harassment in the form of countervailing duties (CVDs) and anti-dumping measures.[11]

As well as an expanded access to world markets both in trade and investment opportunities, Canadian firms also wanted to lock in domestic neo-liberal reform and ensure that episodes of state autonomy like the National Energy Program would not reoccur. If this other motivation had not been present, continued business support for the agreement, given Canada's failure to achieve security from countervail or anti-dumping measures, would indeed have been puzzling (Winham 1994: 480–81).

Investments in the United States by Canadian firms had grown prior to the free-trade initiative. These firms had a structurally determined interest in free trade: "The multinational segment of the Canadian economy includes not only foreign-controlled firms, but also Canadian-controlled multinationals. In fact direct investment by Canadian multinationals in the United States was growing so rapidly that by 1985 it amounted to 60% of American direct investment in Canada" (Richardson 1992: 317). By the early 1980s, "Canadian firms with global operations were increasingly coming to share the view of their U.S. counterparts that nationalistic restrictions only impeded their worldwide growth" (McQuaig 1992: 82).

A growing academic literature tries to explain the waxing and waning of support for protectionism or liberalization in the business community. The dominant approach, which has emerged from what is now called neo-liberal institutionalism (Milner 1988; Keohane and Milner 1994), suggests that the relative support for protectionism and liberalism is connected to the strategic interests of the domestic business community. If a majority of firms have international interests they will have an innate interest in global market liberalization, and a state is likely to move in that direction. If most companies are national in orientation, then support for protectionism will probably follow. This approach corresponds in some ways with a structurally deterministic reading of globalization. The key assumption is that the spectacular move away from protectionism in the 1980s and 1990s can be explained by how an increased market integration led to more firms—or firms accounting for an increasing share of economic activity—having international interests and thus supporting liberalization.

Richardson's data on concentration and cohesion in Canadian capital not only explains why companies in Canada have had an interest in free trade but also leads to an explanation for the business sector's ability to build a consensus in support of free trade. By documenting the extremely concentrated nature of Canadian capital, he hints at the emergence of a leading fraction, more cohesive and co-ordinated in their demands upon the state and dominating the rest of the business community. Structural changes in Canadian capital also produced another characteristic trend just prior to the free-trade agreement by creating "the ideal conditions under which its institutional counterpart—the Business Council on National Issues (BCNI)—could emerge" (Richardson 1992: 316).

Organized Business
Canadian business always did have a close relationship with the government (Panitch 1977) but by the 1980s several conditions related to that relationship had changed. One was the greater centralization and maturity of Canadian capital; another was the degree to which Canadian capital had multinational ambitions; and a third was its greater organizational capacity. The newly created BCNI was able to create a consensus within the business community and, therefore, articulate a unified stance on key policy issues. When business speaks with one voice, as it did on free trade, its power is maximized.

The BCNI, made up of the chief executive officers of the 150 largest companies (see Table 3.1), was one of a number of peak business

Table 3.1
BCNI **Membership (1989)**

	BCNI Memberships
17 dominant enterprises	27
Other Canadian non-financials	40
Foreign-controlled non-financials	41
Government-controlled non-financials	2
Total non-financial	110
Big banks and their subsidiaries	11
Other Canadian financials	11
Foreign-controlled financials	8
Total financial	30
Law, accounting and consulting firms	7
Trade associations	3
Total BCNI membership	150

Source: Richardson 1992: 317.

organizations. The Canadian Manufacturers' Association (CMA) included a much broader range of firms in its membership of over three thousand firms, and the Canadian Chamber of Commerce, with a still broader and more variegated membership of 170,000, was organized into different categories and included many small- and medium-size businesses of all descriptions (see Brooks and Stritch 1991: ch. 7). Support for free trade was understandably higher in the BCNI than in the CMA (which included many smaller firms more oriented to the domestic market) or in the Chamber of Commerce.

The BCNI, dominated by Canada's largest multinational corporations had "internationalist" members that wanted expanded access to foreign markets. But it also included representatives of both the CMA and the Chamber of Commerce and was thus in a position to strive for a business consensus on issues.

In the early 1980s the BCNI expressed concerns about the increasing threat of U.S. protectionism (Finlayson 1985: 30). In the wake of U.S. hostility to Canada's National Energy Program, threats of retaliation, the recession and generally rising protectionist sentiments in the United States, an overwhelming sense had emerged of the need to "get the relationship with the US right" (Doern and Tomlin 1992: 17). So many Canadian businesses relied on exports to the United States that the threat of increased U.S. trade harassment (CVDs and anti-dumping measures) served as a powerful consensus-building mechanism. Indeed it was this fear that the BCNI's Thomas d'Aquino and other free-trade crusaders most often played upon in their calls for business to support free trade.

The BCNI's support for free trade came from the familiar sources: the structural changes within the Canadian business community; the business leaders' concerns about declining productivity and competitiveness in Canada (Rocher 1991: 141); and the felt need of the business community to lock-in domestic neo-liberal reforms. Earlier attempts to pull business on-side behind a different agenda—an activist industrial policy based on a modicum of sectoral planning, major infrastructural investments by government and increased research and development—had been undermined by the government's perception that business lacked a peak level organization that it could deal with (see Brown and Eastman with Robinson 1981). More to the point, perhaps, was the lack of a business consensus around such policy developments. Meanwhile, business was also frustrated at what it viewed as too great autonomy (unresponsiveness to business concerns) on the part of the state (Langille 1987: 47–54).

The formation, in 1976, of the BCNI as a new type of business organization established a voice that was to prove, over time, that it really did "speak for business." The organizational formula chosen by founder W.O. Twaits, the chairman of Imperial Oil, was a copy of the U.S. Business Roundtable (founded in 1974). According to Linda McQuaig (1992: 111):

> The central formula of both organizations was to greatly increase the clout of the largest and most powerful corporations by banding together in an exclusive, by-invitation-only club. The club was made up of a single representative of each of these super-companies—and each representative had to be the chief executive officer. No substitutions allowed. Without a lot of puny vice-presidents cluttering up the club, it would speak with more authority.

The BCNI's strength is derived from both organizational and structural sources. Indeed, it is unlikely that organizational cohesion could have overcome structural division. The BCNI became, then, the organizational expression of mature Canadian finance capital, an organization well designed to lead the Canadian business community. By including not only Canada's largest corporations but also ex-officio members from the other business organizations, including the CMA and Canadian Chamber of Commerce, BCNI spanned the entire business sector, serving as a sort of executive committee of the business community (Langille 1987: 42).

Furthermore, the BCNI's centralization, through the exclusive participation of executives and the strong leadership, made it more effective than "coalition-style" groups such as the CMA (Doern and Tomlin 1992: 46). The BCNI brought almost all of the key players of Canadian business together into one organization, aiding in the development of a business consensus on national issues.

These organizational strengths must be put in the context of the BCNI's enormous potential structural power. Its member corporations, according to data compiled by Brooks and Stritch (1991: 211), employed 1.5 million people and controlled assets of $750 billion, or more than seven times the book value of the federal government's own assets. The top one hundred enterprises alone accounted for "roughly 55 per cent of the total Canadian non financial assets and profits" (Richardson 1992: 343). But the top twenty-five corporations present an even more daunting picture of the centralization of economic power (see Table 3.2).

Directorship interlocks, which created informal links between the executives and directors of leading corporations further enhanced the concentration of economic power in the hands of a relatively few business leaders (Richardson 1992). The highly concentrated economic structure of Canada provides an ideal circumstance for an effective business organization.

Functionally, the BCNI's executive was divided into small task force committees that served as a "shadow cabinet" monitoring various government ministries. Supervised by an overall policy committee, the task forces drew on the expertise of corporate staff and hired consultants, which enabled them to engage state officials with comparable levels of expertise.

The BCNI's influence was further strengthened by its ability to forge a pan-business consensus. Business once had been incoherent in its demands on the state (Bradford 1998: 104). That situation maximized state autonomy and perhaps explains the prolonged battle within state institutions between interventionist-nationalists and liberal continentalists. With the emergence of BCNI, Canadian business effectively organized itself into a serious political force. More to the point, business single-mindedly latched onto the liberal-continentalist tradition in Ottawa policy-making circles and refashioned it into a sweeping critique of state management of the economy (Bradford 1998: 65). From the outset the BCNI had a clear set of "reforms" in mind for Canada. It favoured "the free flow of goods, capital, services and people" and proposed free trade with the United States as a strategy for restraining both the federal and provincial states. Further North American integration would confine the federal government to market-reinforcing reforms (Bradford 1998: 106).

Table 3.2
Non-Financial Enterprises in Canada, 1983

Enterprise characteristics	(Size ranking of enterprise)			
	Top 25	Next 75	Remainder	Total
Number of enterprises:				
Foreign-controlled	9	35	3,355	3,399
Government	4	5	39	48
Canadian private	12	35	387,718	387,765
Total	25	75	391,112	391,212
Financial Data	(mean, in $ millions)			
Assets	8,216.2	1,459.0	0.7	1.5
Profits	431.2	87.3	0.04	0.08
	(per cent of total)			
Assets	34.0	19.7	46.3	100.0
Profits	32.6	22.8	44.6	100.0

Source: Richardson 1992: 344.

The BCNI's most important contribution to free trade was that it spearheaded an "attitude adjustment" within the business community towards support for free trade (Doern and Tomlin 1992: 3). Canadian business prior to the 1980s had little interest in such an agreement, but within a few years a near-total consensus existed on the issue. The CMA also worked hard to promote free trade, although its conversion to that position was not as straightforward. In contrast to the BCNI, the century-old CMA (founded 1871) had a membership consisting mainly of manufacturers producing for the Canadian market—and particularly manufacturers based in Central Ontario. They were simply not as interested in exports.

According to Doern and Tomlin (1992: 46–47), "the CMA was a coalition that contained the many sub-elements of the manufacturing sector, and the structure dictated a more complex decision process than prevailed at BCNI." This institutional complexity led to an initially more ambivalent stance towards free trade. While the BCNI was consistently a vocal proponent of the internationalist agenda, in the late 1970s CMA strategists believed that free trade was a non-starter for them because the majority of their members would oppose such a deal (Doern and Tomlin 1992: 48).

Mirroring the structural trends in the business community, though, the CMA members' attitudes changed. In response to the across-the-board-tariff reductions achieved in the GATT Tokyo Round, CMA members became far more trade-oriented: "The proportion of its member companies that exported had risen from 15 to 40 per cent.... In short, Canadian manufacturers were more engaged in international trade, and would benefit from the removal of barriers to that trade" (Doern and Tomlin 1992: 49). Then, in the wake of the early 1980s recession, which hit CMA members particularly hard, the organization realized that its members had to adjust to greater competition and that the U.S. market offered room for expansion (McQuaig 1992: 49). The anti-interventionist backlash in the business community generated by the Liberal policies of the early 1980s helped sell the notion of free trade as part of an anti-industrial strategy. As well, CMA members that were exporting to the United States, like so many other Canadian businesses, had good reason to fear expanded U.S. protectionism. Thus the BCNI plan for a comprehensive free-trade agreement as a way of protecting Canadian firms from U.S. trade harassment had its attractions for CMA members too. The complex interaction of these concerns produced an "attitude adjustment" at the CMA as it (perhaps as early as 1982) became a leading proponent of free trade. In addition, the BCNI was instrumental in bringing small business into a united front on the free-trade issue.[12]

Enter Macdonald: Opening the Door to Continentalism

Business in Canada wanted a free-trade agreement before Ottawa launched the free-trade initiative. Indeed, a delegation from the BCNI broached the free-trade idea with U.S. officials as early as 1982 and began to promote the idea in Canada publicly from 1983 (Merrett 1996: 33). In early 1984 the Business Council floated the idea of a bilateral "Trade Enhancement Agreement," and in 1985 it noted, "A framework agreement along the lines of TEA was one of four policy options canvassed in both the consultation paper issued by the Minister for International Trade in January [1985], and then in the External Affairs discussion paper released later (BCNI 1985: 7–8).

Developments inside the state facilitated business pressure for free trade. As early as September 1982, a cabinet shuffle diminished the economic role of the nationalists in the Trudeau cabinet while enhancing the influence of more business-friendly members. This move signalled the possibility of a change of course within the state. One of the important changes was the transfer of Herb Gray, a nationalist unpopular with both business and the United States, from Industry, Trade and Commerce to the less influential Treasury Board. He was replaced by Ed Lumley, a more congenial figure from a business point of view. Other changes were made that would prove significant from the perspective of promoting the free-trade agenda, including the appointment of Gerald Regan as international trade minister. More important for the cause of free trade was a reorganization of responsibilities for trade policy, which became integrated into a new Department of Foreign Affairs and International Trade (DFAIT) from 1982.

By 1983 the possibility of a free-trade agreement had emerged into public view. The Liberals tentatively explored a sectoral free-trade agreement with the United States, an initiative that was stillborn, in part because the United States wanted a "big deal" and in part because of a leadership transition within the governing Liberals.

In September 1984 Brian Mulroney's Conservatives were elected in a landslide victory. Almost immediately the business lobby intensified its efforts to place free trade on the national agenda (Doern and Tomlin 1992: 23). The various machinations, trial balloons and other techniques used to advance free trade as official policy have been well described elsewhere (see, for example, Doern and Tomlin 1992; McQuaig 1992). Apart from ongoing business pressure, a small number of state agencies and individuals played a significant role in bridging business demands and state priorities. The Department of Foreign Affairs and International Trade, especially through the person of one of its senior officials, Derek Burney, was most important, followed by the Department of Finance (Molot 1994:517). The decisive public intervention came from Donald Macdonald and his ongoing Royal Commission on the Economic Union and Development Prospects for Canada.

The subject of free trade was within the mandate of the Royal Commission, and in November 1984 Macdonald leaked his "leap of faith" analysis to the media. According to Doern and Tomlin (1992: 24), "Although the Commission had neither completed its studies nor framed its conclusions, Macdonald nevertheless announced that he favoured free trade between Canada and the United States as the principle long-term solution to Canada's economic problems."

Macdonald's reason for supporting free trade was relatively straightforward. He believed that Canada had to increase its exports as the key to future growth. The gains were not likely to be made in either Europe or Asia (*Globe and Mail* 19 Nov. 1984: 8). Macdonald, perhaps sensing the inappropriateness of calling for free trade in the middle of the commission process, chose a very odd set of circumstances to "leak" his personal views to the media. He was one of about forty people invited to speak at a closed conference on trade held in the United States. As Doern and Tomlin (1992: 24) put it: "A few journalists were invited to attend, on condition that they not quote the participants on what they said during the sessions. Mr.

Macdonald agreed, however, to repeat in an interview the substance of what he had said in the sessions."[13] As a former "nationalist-interventionist" in the Liberal cabinets of the 1970s, no one was in a better position to lend intellectual legitimacy to the calls for free trade: "Because the Commission was bipartisan and seemingly authoritative, Macdonald's support provided important momentum to the free trade option at a crucial juncture, as the new government was considering its options" (Doern and Tomlin 1992:24).

The Macdonald Commission's principal argument for why Canada needed a free-trade agreement with the United States was based on a defensive or prudential reasoning. Canada was a trade-dependent nation, particularly reliant on the U.S. market, and the threat of rising protectionism jeopardized that trade. A deal with the United States was a way of guaranteeing Canadian access to the U.S. market.

Built into the Macdonald Report was an implicit theory of export-led growth. This theory held that the route to sustainable economic growth lay through encouraging exports rather than, as in the Keynesian period, attempting to sustain the level of aggregate demand by a variety of measures focused on the domestic economy. Cohen (1991) suggests that an export-led growth stimulus was attractive because, first of all, it enhanced competitiveness and encouraged restructuring by ensuring that only those firms that could competitively sell in other markets would be able to expand. Less efficient producers would not be able to compete. As well, wage levels could lag behind the growth in productivity without undermining demand, because domestic wage levels have little effect on the demand for exports. Some difficult public policy dilemmas could also be avoided: the trade-offs between investment and consumption become blurred when consumption is no longer simply a function of internal demand. Finally, in cases of small domestic markets, the stimulus would promote economies of scale in manufacturing (where real productivity gains can be made) through the export of products.

Underlying this theory is the relatively straightforward assumption that productivity gains are the real key to economic growth. Thus the theory does not simply recommend expanding exports simply for the immediate economic benefits, such as increased earnings abroad, that they bring. Rather, the goal is to successfully export manufactured goods to take advantage of economies of scale and resulting productivity gains. Expanding exports of lower-productivity scarce natural resources may not produce many of the dividends assumed by export-led growth theory.

The Macdonald Commission argued that Canada could no longer rely, as it had done in the past, on the export of resources. Rather:

The real growth in international trade has been in manufactured goods.... If we fail to expand our manufactured exports over the next decade we shall suffer a reduced capacity to import and, with that reduction, a corresponding drop in our standard of living. Britain's poor economic performance shows that the stakes are high in this matter, for with its slow productivity growth and its erosion of international competitiveness over the past 30 years, its standard of living, also, has declined.... Thus, to an important extent, Canada's future trade performance will depend on our country's manufacturing performance. (Canada 1985, vol. 1: 267)

The Commission expressed scepticism as to whether the GATT and Canada's traditional multilateral approach to trade negotiations could serve as vehicle for future expansions of Canada's exports. Rather, the Commission argued that bilateral negotiations promised quicker results (Canada 1985, vol. 1: 293–96); and there was only one realistic partner for bilateral negotiations. The Commission concluded that Canadians were missing out on opportunities in the United States (Canada 1985, vol. 1: ch.6), and it rejected the notion of negotiating with other countries or regions. For example, in the case of a possible "European solution," the Commission argued, "The realities of distance, lack of intra- and inter-corporate links, and the continuing high levels of trade barriers which protect European processing and manufacturing industries all reduce the likelihood of a major expansion in trade" (vol. 1: 250). With respect to Japan, the commissioners expressed interest in exploring freer trade with Japan but ultimately stopped short of recommending that such a policy actually be pursued (vol. 1: 255). As to the rest of the world, they pointed out that Canada's trade with the less developed countries was "small" (vol. 1: 256).

Thus, much like the "leap of faith" speech, the commission ended up offering only one option: Canada must expand its exports; and the only place that it was possible to do so was in the United States. Thus Canada must get a free-trade agreement with the United States. However, in "selling" this argument the commission placed more emphasis on the threat of losing access to the U.S. market than upon the theoretical merits of free trade per se.

When in September 1985 the Macdonald Commission Report was finally released to the public, its message was unambiguous: "Market liberalization, social adjustment, and limited government were the cornerstones of the Macdonald Commission's public philosophy" (Bradford

1998: 113).At the centre of this analysis was the conclusion that free trade with the United States was essential to any Canadian economic strategy. The Commissioners argued,"Our basic international stance complements our domestic stance.We must seek an end to those patterns of government involvement in the economy which may generate disincentives, retard flexibility, and work against the desired allocation of resources" (quoted in Bradford 1998: 114). Clearly, the domestic implications of this stance were as important as the international factors.

The commissioners' recommendations were markedly similar to what many in the business lobby saw as the most desirable element of free trade with the United States—a reduced role for the state backed up by the sanction of international law. The Commission mirrored the business community sentiment identified by McQuaig (1992: 26–27)—that free trade really was a kind of "tough medicine" way of making Canada more efficient. Doern and Tomlin (1992: 34) suggest that:

> It was primarily as an industrial policy, loosely defined, that free trade was advanced as a solution to Canada's economic problems.... According to the commission's analysis, the source of Canada's economic problems could be found in a manufacturing sector that produces at too high a cost for too small a market. Free trade would at once expand the market and remove the protective barriers that insulate inefficient firms from competition.

The business community's submissions had a clear influence on both Macdonald's leap of faith and his final analysis. Business interests led by the BCNI and the CMA had "almost uniformly" told Macdonald and his colleagues that they could compete with the United States if given the chance. Personally impressed by their "entrepreneurial nationalism" and curiously uninterested in any other possible motives on the part of business leaders, Macdonald, according to Doern and Tomlin (1992: 55), told the Commission on more than one occasion, "If these people say they can compete in a free market, who am I to say they cannot?" In addition, Simeon (1987) has suggested that these outcomes were partly the product of the organization of the Commission's research program into separate, functional spheres. A small group of neo-classical economists had a particular influence on the Commission's economic analysis.

Unsurprisingly, business welcomed the report's conclusions. Laurent Thibault, the president of the CMA, claimed, "The commission has made a powerful case for Canada to face the realities of world competition by entering into a free trade agreement with the United States" (*Globe and*

Mail 6 Sept. 1985). Roger Hamel, the president of the Canadian Chamber of Commerce, also supported the free-trade, pro-market components of the report, calling it an excellent "road map," though he rejected the aspects of the report that called for government interventions. Other business associations were equally supportive, calling for a quick move towards negotiations (McQuaig 1992: 26–27). Neil Bradford (1998: 12) found:

> There remained a few dissenters among the so-called corporate nationalists, but the Macdonald Commission consultations revealed a new alignment of business opinion behind the policy agenda elaborated since 1975 by the BCNI. Fears of American protectionism and of further intervention along the lines of the Third National Policy were frequently cited as reasons behind this coalescing of opinion.

The BCNI's influence, already apparent in the policy formulation stage, continued through the negotiations. The BCNI already had its own view on what "a comprehensive agreement might look like" (Doern and Tomlin 1992: 103). Doern and Tomlin's analysis of the negotiations from 1986 on suggests that the BCNI had a major impact, working on its own and through the government in maintaining a "united front" in the business community in support of a deal (Doern and Tomlin 1992: 109–25).

Influence came through two channels: d'Aquino's personal connections with and influence on the cabinet (and negotiators); and the Sectoral Advisory Groups on International Trade (SAGIT). The Sectoral Advisory Groups were designed to build consensus within various sectors of the Canadian economy around the goals that Canadian negotiators should be seeking. An umbrella group, the thirty-eight-member International Trade Advisory Committee (ITAC), was chaired by a former chairman of Northern Telecom (Hart 1994: 130). The SAGIT and ITAC committees were dominated by the BCNI and CMA (Doern and Tomlin 1992: 105). Furthermore, when consensus became difficult, it was the BCNI that intervened to maintain the solidarity of the business community. When the beer industry threatened to "go public" in opposition to the deal, the BCNI urged appeasement and got the breweries special protection under the final agreement (Doern and Tomlin 1992: 107–8). It was of crucial importance for the BCNI to maintain public solidarity while these disputes were worked out behind closed doors. In the end, the only major corporations to oppose the Free Trade Agreement were the Bank of Nova Scotia and McCain Foods. Had groups like the beer industry broken with BCNI over free trade, the passage of the agreement might have been more difficult.

Business support was also crucial to the re-election of the Mulroney government in the "free-trade election" of 1988. When, following the leadership debates, it briefly appeared that the agreement was threatened by a revival in the fortunes of the Liberals, now led by John Turner, a major infusion of funds and support rescued the deal. The primary conduit of this last-minute business rescue was the Canadian Alliance for Trade and Job Opportunities, which the BCNI formed as a vehicle to show wider support for free trade. For much of the organization's existence it was run out of the BCNI offices (Doern and Tomlin 1992: 218), and most of the Alliance's funding came from BCNI members. The Alliance spent $3 million in the final weeks of the election alone on multipage advertising in *Maclean's*, the *Globe and Mail*, and the *Financial Post*, along with buying radio and television spots across the country on eight hundred radio and ninety television stations (Fillmore 1989: 15–17).

Notes

1. See the discussion of Innis in Williams 1986: 133–37.
2. For a good account of the connection between Innisian and Marxian influences in Canadian political economy, see Drache 1991, especially 41–43.
3. The other pressure sprang from "an imperial strategy that required unification not only in order to preserve the colonies from United States absorption, but also to strengthen a link of Empire reaching to the Pacific and hence to the approaches of Asia" (Ryerson 1973: 309). This account should remind us that while we may be living in an age of globalization, there have been others.
4. See Royal Commission on Canada's Economic Prospects, Report (Ottawa 1958), known as the Gordon Report; Task Force on the Structure of Canadian Industry *Foreign Ownership and the Structure of Canadian Industry* (Ottawa 1968), the Watkins Report; and Canadian Forum, *Citizens' Guide to the Gray Report* (Toronto 1971).
5. For a comprehensive analysis of the Trudeau government's retreat from involvement in a "crisis" with the United States and move towards "adjustment," see Clarkson 1985.
6. For a useful account of the economic policy options, see Leslie 1987.
7. Royal Commission on the Economic Union and Development Prospects for Canada, *Report* (Ottawa 1985), the Macdonald Report.
8. The impact of free trade has received detailed analysis in Cameron and Watkins 1993.
9. Linda McQuaig develops a compelling account of how leaders in the Canadian business community saw free trade in part as a vehicle by which they might achieve a massive overhaul of Canadian society. See, for example, McQuaig 1992: 194.
10. Given Gordon Laxer's arguments (1989) regarding the consequences of an earlier imbalance between dominant and subordinate classes in Canada, one conclusion would be that the 1945–75 period represents an exception in the

balance of class power in Canada.

11. As early as July 1985 U.S. Trade Representative Michael Smith told Canadian emissaries that the United States would only be interested in negotiating a "big" comprehensive agreement. He specifically avoided making any promises that the United States would put its CVDs and anti-dumping measures on the table. Ignoring the fact that Smith had been non-committal about Canada's supposed main priority in negotiations (to get secure access to the U.S. market free from trade harassment), Derek Burney from the Department of External Affairs informed Mulroney that the basis for a deal existed and that negotiations should be launched (Doern and Tomlin 1992: 29–30).

12. See the joint press release of Thomas D'Aquino, president and CEO of the BCNI, and John Bulloch, president of the Canadian Federation of Independent Business, Ottawa, 26 June, 1986.

13. The *Globe and Mail*, 19 Nov. 1984: 1. Interestingly the *Globe and Mail* was careful to point out the conditions under which it had obtained the comments from Macdonald, perhaps sensing the unusual circumstances of a Royal Commissioner "shooting from the hip" in such a way.

Chapter Four

Domestic Neo-Liberalism

As long as Keynesian ideas held sway, most people concerned about public policy saw the active involvement of government in achieving goals (such as full employment) as a legitimate function. Although the practice of Keynesianism was less enthusiastic in Canada than in some other countries and, certainly, proved to be imperfect (Campbell 1987), the framework was encouraged by an international economic regime that tended to support national economic management. Everywhere there were strong domestic pressures for more interventionist states to provide economic stability and social security—political goods that differentiated the postwar state from its predecessor before the war.

By the mid-1970s the long postwar economic boom that, in reality, had its shares of ups and downs was widely recognized as being over. A more difficult economic environment was at hand. Two international oil crises drove inflation higher, though in political debates rising prices were often attributed to domestic causes. Prime among the domestic reasons advanced to explain inflation were increased wages stemming from the power of labour under a full-employment regime. The popular interpretation of inflationary pressures became "too much money chasing too few goods"—an explanation that overlooked the possibility that wages were simply chasing externally induced inflation. From this point of view, wage controls became the remedy for inflation.

Some commentators argued that a decline in profits had occurred (Gonick 1987: 341–42; Heap 1982: 81). Others predicted capital flight—that multinational corporations would shift their manufacturing investments to the newly industrializing centres of the Third World, where cheap pools of labour could be readily found. The deregulation of the international monetary system with the termination of Bretton Woods also led to instability. A process of deindustrialization, "a widespread, systematic disinvestment in the nation's basic productive capacity" (Bluestone and Harrison 1982: 6), became apparent in the recession of the 1980s. Whole sectors of the industrial heartlands of North America were dubbed "rustbelts." In Canada, employment in goods-producing industries fell from 34.8 percent of the labour force in 1951 to 26.7 percent in 1981, a pattern replicated in most other OECD nations (Economic Council of Canada 1984: 157, Table 11-5). Accompanying these painful adjustments was a rapid technological change as corporations strove to modernize, cut labour costs and restore profitability.

Unemployment in OECD countries steadily rose from about 3 percent of the labour force in the 1950s and 1960s to much higher levels in the 1970s and 1980s (see McBride 1992). Official unemployment figures in Canada peaked in 1983 at almost 12 percent. Economic assumptions concerning a trade-off between unemployment and inflation proved invalid as the two indicators rose in tandem. Inflation rates climbed steadily during the 1970s, reaching double-digit figures and easing only after 1982 (see, for example, Ruggeri 1987: 297, Table 3). A new phenomenon, "stagflation," the co-existence of economic recession and high inflation, made its appearance in public discourse.

The sense of crisis occasioned by these developments provided an opportunity for long-standing critics of the Keynesian revolution in economic thought to emerge from obscurity. The economics profession, undergoing what amounted to a paradigm shift, returned to a version of neo-classical orthodoxy of the kind that Keynes and like-minded econo-mists had overturned, with the help of the Great Depression, two generations earlier. The revived ideas found powerful backers, mostly in a business sector concerned about increasing state intervention in the economy. This coalition of neo-classical economists and corporate inter-ests pushed right and centre political parties to a decisive break with Keynesianism. The left, as represented by social-democratic parties, was not long in following (see, for example, McBride 1996).

The shift of paradigms between 1975 and 1984 was far from smooth, and other options certainly seemed to be available throughout the period. One example was the Science Council of Canada's advocacy of interven-tionist nationalism. Generally, however, these years also saw an incremental retrenchment of public programs, efforts to minimize the public's expec-tations of government, and advocacy of a reduced role for the state in the economy and social affairs

The fiscal crisis generated by budget deficits contributed to the questioning of the legitimacy of the Keynesian welfare state. A more balanced assessment might have led to the conclusion that major problems of public debt occurred after the abandonment of Keynesianism and the adoption of neo-liberalism. Implementation of that alternative paradigm, with its arsenal of high interest rates that cured inflation by driving the economy into recession, led to government revenue shortfalls on the one hand and growing expenditures on the other.

Nonetheless, it was the social welfare state that came to be seen as a creator of economic distortions. While never as generous in its contributions as opponents suggested, the welfare state did to some degree modify market outcomes.[1] As the Macdonald Commission Report put it, the welfare state is "an embodiment of concepts of sharing which subordinates market results ... to citizenship concerns and community values" (Canada 1985, vol. 1: 45). The welfare state was not all bad news from the perspective of capital. Its defenders argued that social welfare provisions allowed for the creation of a much more secure, healthy and educated labour force: "A comprehensive system of income security may therefore help improve productivity, transform bad jobs into good ones, and hence boost economic growth" (Esping-Andersen 1983: 32). Or, as Bob Russell (2000: 41) put it in describing New Labour in Britain and its Canadian imitators' view of the matter: "The welfare state is optimally an adjunct to capitalist economic development, not an alternative to market-based failure." Still, the ability of the welfare state to decommodify a portion of the potential labour force did enhance the bargaining power of labour, and under conditions in which a fundamental reorientation of economic strategy was on the agenda, social welfare policy became a target. Increasingly critics depicted the welfare state as "a destabilizing influence that has indeed given rise to a new set of economic problems" (Russell 1991: 489).

The Globalization Hypothesis
Globalization sometimes features as an explanation of the changes that began to occur in the 1970s and have intensified since then. Sometimes the argument depends on the interaction of economic globalization with other factors such as "societal pluralization" (Rice and Prince 2000: ch. 1)—defined as the phenomenon of growing diversity within societies. For others, economic and technological factors formed the centrepiece of globalization's influence. Economic forces, and actors such as multinational corporations, were said to have outgrown national boundaries, with the economic basis of national autonomy eroding. Thus, "Keynesian fiscal and monetary policy is rendered largely ineffective in open global financial markets" (Simeon 1991: 47–48, 49). Or, as Thomas Courchene argues, "This situation poses major concerns for national welfare states since they were ... geared to national production machines" (quoted in Simeon and Janigan 1991: 39). Academic interpretations are matched by business organizations' oft-expressed view that state efforts to regulate economic activity not only are ineffective but also act as a barrier to the economic success of the private sector.

Ramesh Mishra (1999: 15) summarizes the full globalization hypothesis as containing three elements: the greater openness of economies has eroded national autonomy, which has been supplanted by supranational authority; capital mobility has curtailed the state's policy options; and the only option for national governments is to move to a residual welfare state—a policy of "competitive austerity."

Mishra (1999: 24) concludes: "There seems to be no compelling logic of globalization that requires the downsizing of government, retrenchment of social programmes and substantial deregulation of labour markets. Such measures are being pursued by English speaking countries but amount to little more than old neo-liberal domestic policies now rationalized and legitimized in the name of globalization."[2]

The neo-liberal agenda was one response to the perceptions in the 1970s and 1980s of economic crisis, some of which originated in the international economy. But much of its early emphasis was domestic and concentrated on clearing the domestic obstacles to international liberalization. In this sense globalization is as much or more of a consequence of neo-liberalism at the national level than the reverse. Neo-liberalism has involved political action aimed at reducing or removing impediments to the operation of market forces, including global market forces. Various justifications, economic and moral, have been advanced for placing markets in this privileged position. An economic argument, for instance, is that markets enhance competitiveness in a global economy and that international competition has beneficial effects on efficiency in the domestic economy. A "moral" argument is that people removed from the discipline of the labour market lose independence and become undesirably dependent on social programs.

The chief impediment to the free operation of markets is the state, and a number of measures have been advanced to reduce its role. Among these are fiscal policy, government employment, privatization, social policy, labour-market policy and health policy.[3]

Fiscal and Monetary Policy

The main neo-liberal themes—that government is too large, deficits unacceptable, the tax system in need of reform, and spending priorities are in need of revision—entered public discourse before the election of the Mulroney government in 1984. But with that event they moved from the status of ideas that might reluctantly be endorsed, out of crisis-driven necessity, to the centre of policy discussions (see Wilson 1984). They have remained at the centre despite a 1993 election in which the successful Liberal campaign promised a different approach. In practice, the Liberal government of Jean Chrétien adopted the neo-liberal fiscal agenda much more vigorously than did its predecessor.

The government justified expenditure restraint by declaring the need to balance the budget. Governments were ideologically committed to the *means* of expenditure restraint (cutting state expenditures) rather than the *end* of a balanced budget (which could also have been achieved by tax increases). This approach was taken up because reduced expenditures typically meant a smaller role for the state, especially in the crucial economic and social areas.[4] The government's primary focus, both rhetorically and in reality, was on the expenditure side of the ledger. According to the *Budget Plan 1995* the ratio of expenditure reductions to tax revenue increases was projected to increase from 4.4:1 in 1995–96 to 8.3:1 in 1997–98. Early signs of this imbalance in successive governments' treatment of expenditures and revenues led some observers to depict the deficit as a "Trojan horse" for a somewhat different agenda: reduction of the state's role (Doern, Maslove and Prince 1988: 28).

Although expenditures, including those on personnel, bore the brunt of neo-liberal policies, considerable evidence suggests that deficits and rising public debt had little to do with profligate expenditures by government. Rather, these phenomena were the product of foregone tax revenues, high interest rates, and recessions that were partly due to the implementation of neo-liberal economic policies. Rather than originating in the Keynesian era, these problems flourished *after* the monetarist economic theories favoured by neo-liberal politicians took root.[5]

A number of writers have drawn attention to the scope and impact of the loopholes, tax breaks, and tax expenditures that led to the shortfall in revenues after 1975 (Maslove 1981; McQuaig 1987; Ternowetsky 1987; Wolfe 1985). Apart from this revenue shortfall, the main cause of increased deficits was high real interest rates resulting from monetary policy (Chorney 1988; McQuaig 1995). A Statistics Canada project—the Mimoto study—attributed 50 percent of the increased deficit incurred between 1975–76 and 1988–89 to revenue shortfalls relative to GDP, 44 percent to an increase in debt charges relative to GDP, and only 6 percent to higher program spending relative to GDP (McIlveen and Mimoto 1990; see also Klein 1996).

Indeed, from negative or low positive rates in the 1970s, real interest rates climbed under the impetus of monetarist policies to average around 6 percent in the 1980s, peaking at 9 percent in 1990. Even in the "low interest rate era" of the late 1990s they remained in the 4 to 6 percent range (Statistics Canada, cat. no. 11-010, 62-001). High real interest rates perform a classic function of redistributing wealth in that they protect and even expand the value of money—a result that particularly benefits creditors

Table 4.1
Federal Budgetary Expenditures as a Percentage of GDP

	Total Expenditures(%)	Prog. Expenditures(%)	Public Debt(%)
1980–81	20.1	16.7	3.4
1981–82	21.1	16.9	4.2
1982–83	23.6	19.2	4.5
1983–84	23.6	19.2	4.4
1984–85	24.4	19.4	5.0
1985–86	23.3	17.7	5.2
1986–87	23.0	17.6	5.2
1987–88	22.5	17.3	5.2
1988–89	21.7	16.3	5.4
1989–90	21.7	15.8	5.9
1990–91	22.3	16.0	6.3
1991–92	22.9	16.9	6.0
1992–93	23.1	17.5	5.6
1993–94	21.8	16.6	5.2
1994–95	20.9	15.5	5.5
1995–96	19.7	13.9	5.8
1996–97	18.0	12.6	5.4
1997–98	17.1	12.4	4.7
1998–99	17.1	12.4	4.6

Source: Public Accounts (various years); Budget Papers.

and the affluent, to the detriment of debtors and the less affluent. High interest rates contributed to economic slowdown and recession in both 1981–82 and 1990–93 (McQuaig 1995: ch. 3; Krehm 1993).

Thus many of the problems associated with fiscal policy, such as the deficit, which provided the pretext for implementing neo-liberal, expenditure-cutting and state-reducing policies, had their origins in neo-liberal political choices made in the monetary policy area.

After 1984 there was a slight reduction in federal expenditures (as a percentage of GDP) until the recession of the early 1990s. The size of the federal state was still greater in the early 1990s than it had been in the early 1980s, indicting the gradualism and limited impact of neo-liberalism; but the total expenditures understate the impact of neo-liberal policies (see Table 4.1). If program expenditures are considered in isolation from debt-servicing costs, the impact is more striking. In the recession of the early 1980s, spending on programs climbed to 19.4 percent of GDP. In the 1990s recession this item accounted for a peak of 17.5 percent of GDP before falling dramatically to 12.4 percent by the end of the decade—the lowest level for decades.

Table 4.2
State Employment, 1990–99

Year	Federal Govt.*	Prov./Terr. Govts.	Local Govt.	Total Govt.	Govt. Business Enterprises	Total Public Sector
1990	406,336	1,387,076	869,170	2,662,582	364,773	3,027,355
1991	415,387	1,401,733	888,733	2,705,853	350,927	3,056,779
1992	411,278	1,409,252	904,250	2,724,780	338,454	3,063,235
1993	404,734	1,397,171	909,991	2,711,896	325,581	3,037,477
1994	394,106	1,375,802	909,161	2,679,069	323,622	3,002,690
1995	371,053	1,370,443	907,405	2,648,900	308,935	2,957,835
1996	356,099	1,335,090	907,147	2,598,335	272,828	2,871,163
1997	337,713	1,315,126	891,483	2,544,322	258,426	2,802,748
1998	330,981	1,314,617	891,560	2,537,188	260,903	2,798,061
1999	330,003	1,312,806	893,709	2,536,519	262,451	2,798,970
% change (1990–99)	-19	-5.5	+3	-5	-28	-7.5

* Federal government employment figures include military personnel.

Source: Statistics Canada, Cansim various.

Government Employment
Another indicator of the shrinking state is the number of people employed by it (see Table 4.2).

The reduction in government employment has been concentrated at the federal and crown corporation (government business enterprises) levels, which is where the state's role in the economy and society has been most reduced. Employment at the provincial/territorial level has declined less, and at the municipal level it even increased in the 1990–99 period. To some extent, however, the statistics covering the entire decade understate employment impacts at those two levels, because provincial/territorial employment in 1992 reached a high for the decade (from which it had declined 7 percent by 1999), and municipal employment peaked in 1994 (after which it had declined by almost 2 percent by 1999). Total government employment declined by 5 percent over the decade, but by 7 percent after its 1992 peak.

But the impact of downsizing was most dramatic at the levels of federal and government business enterprises. The decline in employment in the federal government in particular—19 percent—illustrates the shrinking impact of the central government.

Table 4.3
Largest Privatizations of Federal Crown Corporations

Name	Sector	Year	Sale proceeds $m
CNR	transport	1995	2,079
Petro-Canada	oil and gas	1991	1,747
NavCanada	transport	1996	1,500
Air Canada	transport	1988	474
Teleglobe	telecommunications	1987	441
Canadian Development Corporation	financial	1987	365
Nordion International	manufacturing	1991	161
Telesat	telecommunications	1992	155
de Havilland	manufacturing	1986	155
Canadair	manufacturing	1986	141
TOTAL		1986–96	7,218

Source: Bank of Canada 1997: 30–31.

Privatization and Deregulation

In seeking to roll back the boundaries of the state, neo-liberals in Canada, like elsewhere, have targeted Crown corporations and state regulatory activity (Laux 1991: 289–91). Some analysts argue that the attack has been less rapid and extensive in Canada than elsewhere, perhaps because of the initially small size of the public sector (Bank of Canada 1997: 28). To some extent Canadian neo-liberals were impeded because in this case their doctrines ran counter to a well-established national tradition of public enterprise (Hardin 1989; Smith 1990: 40). Reliance on public enterprise is an historically important Canadian cultural characteristic (Hardin 1989: 104; Stanbury 1988: 120). The public enterprise tradition, which predates Confederation, was the product of necessity in that the state undertook works considered to be beyond the capacity of the private sector and for much of the country's history encountered little ideological resistance in doing so (Taylor: 1991: 97–100).

Despite this long tradition, in recent decades governments have privatized an impressive range of Crown corporations in what can only be described as a sustained attack (see Tables 4.3 and 4.4).

Indeed, much of the employment decline in the government business enterprises sector in the 1980s was the result of privatization, although other factors (efficiency drives, for example) have also had an effect on employment (see Table 4.5). Again, federal privatization has been in the

Table 4.4
Largest Privatizations of Provincial and Municipal Crown Corporations

Name	Sector	Year	Sale proceeds $m
Alberta Government Telephones	telecommunications	1990	1,735
Manitoba Telephone Systems	telecommunications	1996	860
Cameco	mining	1991	855
Nova Scotia Power Corporation	electricity generation	1992	816
Alberta Energy Company	oil and gas	1975	560
Syncrude	oil and gas	1993	502
Edmonton Telephones	telecommunications	1995	468
Potash Corp. of Saskatchewan	mining	1989	388
Suncor	oil and gas	1992	299
Vencap Equities Alberta	financial	1995	174
TOTAL		1975–96	6,657

Source: Bank of Canada 1997: 30–31.

vanguard of this decline. Possibly because there is so little left at the federal level, the big initiatives in the future are expected to come through provincial privatizations, especially of utilities. In addition to the cases of outright privatization, other forms of partial or creeping privatization are prominent in both federal and provincial jurisdictions. Apart from the Canada Communication Group, formerly the Queen's Printer, most of the federal government's plans for privitization after the mid-1990s involved commercialization and joint public-private-sector ventures in areas such as weather services, food inspection, space technology and defence supply (Finance Canada 1995).

Commercializing the Public Sector

Beginning in the 1990s the federal government started to contract out service delivery to private firms (Bank of Canada 1997; McFettridge 1997)—the upkeep of national parks in 1997, and the earlier system of franchising Canada Post outlets, for example. An increased use of contractors came in some core areas of federal jurisdiction, such as employment insurance—with an especially huge increase in contracting out after the new generation of labour-market development agreements came into effect in the late 1990s (interview, public-sector union official, April 1998).

Table 4.5
Government Business Enterprises Employment: Selected Years

	Federal	Provincial/Territorial	Total Government Business Enterprises Employment
1981	225,115	170,910	439,231
1985	215,044	157,869	420,091
1990	154,327	159,876	364,773
1995	135,763	126,371	308,935
2000	89,534	124,176	260,966
% change 1981–2000	−60	−27	−40.5

Source: Cansim D466042,D466397,D466490 (1 Aug. 2000).

The switch included work that was formerly central to the employment service, such as counselling and assessment of clients, and the contractors performed little or no monitoring or quality control over the work. The next stage of contracting out was to be that of "non-decision functions of Employment Insurance" benefits (HRDC 1997), which would include the receipt and review of applications, handling routine enquiries, verification of records of employment, and issuing cheques. In the space of a decade, one union official argued, the ethos of Human Resources Development had altered from that of helping people find work and improving economic conditions through developing the expertise of working Canadians, to a simple routine of cost-saving and processing individuals so that they would remain on the books for as short a period as possible.

This increased use of contracting out of services achieves two neo-liberal goals. Although the state continues to provide funds, it transfers the delivery of services and the profit-making opportunities associated with that function to the private sector. This move, among other things, enables a competitive market to insinuate itself within the state structure (Shields and Evans 1998: 77).

Some provincial governments introduced competitive bidding for services such as highway maintenance and computer support. Municipal garbage collection and snow removal have also been contracted out. The usual rationale for such measures is to increase efficiency and achieve cost-savings. The Canadian Union of Public Employees (CUPE 2000) has documented the growth of partial privatization in a number of areas, including health and education, and links the measures to deteriorating services without, in most cases, compensatory gains in efficiency.

Social Policy

The establishment of the Canadian version of a Keynesian welfare state was largely complete by 1971. Almost immediately the edifice came under attack. Some programs, such as unemployment insurance, were reduced in generosity during the 1970s (McBride 1992: ch. 6), but, for the most part, the main features of the welfare state remained in place when the neo-liberal Mulroney Conservatives took office in 1984.

The precise impact of the Mulroney government on existing programs was a matter of debate in the 1980s and early 1990s. The prevailing view was that change was incremental and consisted of erosion rather than outright dismantling (Banting 1987: 213). In retrospect it appears that incrementalism and "stealth" over a protracted period produced fundamental change. The very means of implementing changes in social programs indicated a cautious approach on the part of Canadian neo-liberals. Common techniques included transforming universal into selective programs, tightening eligibility requirements, and imposition of ceilings on program costs—or, alternatively, attempting to make programs self-financing or subject to "clawbacks" over a certain benefit level (Houle 1990). Stephen Phillips (2000: 5–6) notes that in 1979 universal programs paid out 43 percent of income security benefits, and by 1993, 0 percent. Benefits paid in social insurance programs increased; but the most dramatic increase, from 14.2 percent of total income security benefits to 43 percent, came in selective or targeted programs (see also MacDonald 1999).

Economic initiatives such as the free-trade agreement also played a part, perhaps, in permitting neo-liberal social policy to be introduced "through the back door" (Mishra 1990: 99; Hurtig 1991: ch. 22). But caution was deemed necessary because of continued public support for social programs. The Liberal Party's election campaign in 1993 seemed to recognize the deep-rooted attachment of Canadians to social programs and widespread fears about those programs being under threat (Liberal Party 1993). Again, however, once the Liberals were in office, their implementation of neo-liberal prescriptions proved more energetic even than that of the preceding government.

The 1995 federal budget marked a fundamental shift in the role of the federal state in Canada. This was the point at which erosion of social programs ended and demolition began. Prior to the budget one prominent journalist commented: "All manner of rhetoric will be used to mask Ottawa's decline:'reinventing government','flexible federalism','modernizing Canada'.... The essence of the matter, however, is this: the shrinking of the federal government, attempted by the Conservatives under the guise of fiscal restraint and constitutional reform, will now be accelerated by the

Liberals through non-constitutional means" (Jeffrey Simpson, *Globe and Mail* 27 Jan. 1995). Others defined the budget as an "epiphany in fiscal federalism and national social policy" (Prince 1999: 176) or as the end of an era:"It is now clear that the Minister of Reconstruction's White Paper on Employment and Income of 1945 can be regarded as one bookend on a particular period in Canadian history, and Paul Martin's February [1995] budget as the other" (Kroeger 1996: 21).

The case for 1995 as the termination point of the Keynesian welfare state rests on the primacy of deficit reduction over maintenance of the social safety net. The determination to reduce the deficit through spending reductions in the social policy area quickly resulted in declining federal transfers to provinces and a fundamental redesign of the unemployment benefit system. The reduced federal commitment to social programs was accomplished not only by eroding transfer payments but also by diminished federal conditions attached to the funds transferred. The major change occurred in 1996 with the introduction of the Canada Health and Social Transfer (CHST).

From 1977 to 1996 the federal government had provided funding in two social policy areas—post-secondary education and health care—under a financial arrangement known as Established Programs Financing (EPF). Funding for social assistance and welfare was transferred under the Canada Assistance Plan (CAP). EPF, introduced in 1977, replaced earlier cost-sharing arrangements that had split health and post-secondary education costs on a fifty-fifty basis. The new formula was a block funding arrangement in which the federal contribution was partly cash and partly tax points transferred to the provinces. Its effect was to decentralize funds and therefore political power over these policy areas. It represented a substantial, and historical, devolution of power from the federal to the provincial governments (Taylor 1987: 435).

Under EPF, increases in the federal contribution were tied to the growth of GNP and population rather than, as previously, to increased real costs. Under the "six and five" anti-inflation program, the government limited EPF payments for post-secondary education. It imposed further ceilings on EPF in 1986, 1990–91, and 1991–92; and the 1991 budget extended the freeze until 1994–95, after which it was to revert to the constraint of GNP growth minus 3 percent (Canadian Council on Social Development 1990; Wilson 1991: 70–71). The Canadian Council on Social Development (1990: 2) analyzed the effect of these measures:

> Since the money raised by the tax points continues to grow—it is not limited—all reductions in the growth of the block fund

come out of the federal cash transfers. This means that the cash portion of federal block funding shrinks over time.... Federal cash to the provinces for medicare and higher education will shrink ... to zero by about 2004 under Bill C-69.... Less and less federal money for medicare and colleges and universities puts the financial burden of these programs squarely on the shoulders of the provinces, and he who pays the piper calls the tune. The federal government's ability to influence national standards or guidelines will diminish.

In 1996 the EPF and the Canada Assistance Plan (CAP), which had also been subject to ceilings during the 1990s, were rolled into the Canada Health and Social Transfer, a single block funding scheme. The CHST removed most remaining federal conditions attached to the transfers. No matching expenditures were required of provinces, as had been the case, for example, under CAP. The new scheme eliminated the other conditions attached to CAP, with the exception of a prohibition on residency requirements. The CHST contained no conditions as far as post-secondary education was concerned, and federal enforcement mechanisms were either diminished or less direct than formerly. Moreover, "welfare," traditionally less well regarded in public opinion than either education or health, came into the same funding pool, which placed it at a competitive disadvantage (MacDonald 1999: 77).

Funding reductions under the CHST added to those that had occurred under the earlier funding mechanisms (see Table 4.6). Social policy advocates regarded the erosion of the cash component of the transfer, which fell by 33 percent between 1993 and 1998, as the key indicator. As cash transfers went down, the argument ran, so too did Ottawa's ability to insist on national standards. The federal agenda in this area was certainly driven by the Finance Department, and fiscal motives enjoyed priority. However, as Ken Battle and Sherri Torjman (1996: 64) also point out, the government approach also fitted into a constitutional agenda of decentralization: "Ottawa is seeking ways of 'renewing' itself and its relationship with the provinces—especially in light of the Québec referendum which threatens to break up the country. The Canada Health and Social Transfer has high symbolic value in that it represents a move by the federal government to retreat from provincial territory." The abrogation of the federal capacity to sustain national standards thus had a rationale beyond that of fiscal restraint.

With the return of budget surpluses in the later 1990s, and the approach of another election, the federal government made moves to

Table 4.6
Canada Health and Social Transfer (CHST) (in $billions)

	Cash	Tax Transfers	Total
CAP/EPF*			
1993–94	18.8	10.2	29
1994–95	18.7	10.7	29.4
1995–96	18.5	11.4	29.9
CHST**			
1996–97	14.7	12.2	26.9
1997–98	12.5	13.3	25.8
1998–99	12.5	14.2	26.7
1999–2000	14.5	14.9	29.4
2000–01***	15.5	15.3	30.8

* CAP = Canada Assistance Plan. EPF = Established Program Financing
** CHST = Canada Health and Social Transfer
*** projection

Source: <http://www.fin.gc.ca/budget00/bpe/bpch6_1e.htm#Health>.

restore some of the funding cuts and repair some of the damage inflicted on social programs. Michael J. Prince terms this the "reparation agenda," but notes that it stopped well short of restoring programs to their original levels of financial support. Moreover, reflecting on the period 1980 to 2000 he identifies a "general trend" of "cuts to programs, and challenges to their legitimacy as well as that of their clients.... Some federal social programs are relatively intact and untouched by retrenchment and dismantling, but many programs have been altered in fundamental ways" (Prince 1999: 189). This assessment can serve as a general verdict on the fate of social programs under neo-liberal hegemony. Indeed, some analysts have depicted the fiscal surplus, which was to finance the restoration agenda, as having been largely disbursed to tax cuts and debt repayment, with only a very small proportion truly representing new spending on programs (Stanford 2000). In addition, efforts to decentralize and privatize delivery continued (Russell 2000).

The government's approach to social policy had predictable results including the growth of various types of inequality (Yalnizyan 1998: 127). For example, focusing on market incomes (wages, salaries, self-employment and investment income) of families with children under eighteen, Armine Yalnizyan notes that in 1973 the top 10 percent of such families earned an average income twenty-one times higher than those at the bottom. By 1996, "still near the peak of the business cycle in [the 1990s], and so presumably a 'good' time for reducing disparities—the top 10% made 314 times as much as the families in the bottom 10%" (Yalnizyan 1998:45). She explains this astonishing statistic by noting that almost three-quarters of low-income families still did not have any work, and hence market income, while in 1973 almost two-thirds of low-income families had at least some work. Until the mid-1990s, Yalnizyan argues, government intervention—programs, taxation, income transfers—tended to stabilize after-tax income, notwithstanding the severe increase in market-income inequality. But, she notes, recent changes in the tax and transfer systems were about to change that situation dramatically.

Support for this view comes from recent Statistics Canada data. A study of family income finds that after tax-income in 1998 had risen and now exceeded, by 1.7 percent, average after-tax income in the prerecession peak year of 1989. In itself this speaks volumes about the impact of neo-liberal policies on incomes. Most pertinent is the observation that income inequality increased during the second half of the 1990s. The study notes that in the early part of the decade, "Taxes and transfers held the ratio of highest-to-lowest after-tax incomes at just under five to one. During the second half of the 1990s, as transfers declined, the ratio widened from about 4.8 to one in 1994 to 5.4 to one in 1998" (Statistics Canada, *The Daily* 12 June 2000: 4). A Vanier Institute (2001) study attributes the slight increase in family incomes in the late 1990s almost entirely to an increase in the number of hours worked rather than to increased hourly wages. Average incomes for unattached individuals, who made up one-third of all households in Canada, were down by 2.6 percent over the decade from 1989, with much of decline being concentrated among young adults. For families, 60 percent experienced an after-tax real income decline in the 1990s. The poorest 20 percent of families (average income in 1998— $17,662) had the biggest decline—5.2 percent; the richest 20 percent (average income in 1998—$96,175) experienced a 6.6 percent increase (Vanier Institute 2001: 7–8).

Table 4.7
Income inequality in the 1990s

	Market Income		After-tax and Transfers	
	Top 20 %	Bottom 20%	Top 20%	Bottom 20%
1989	41.9	3.8	37.0	7.6
1998	45.2	3.1	38.8	7.1

Source: Statistics Canada, *The Daily*, 12 June, 2000

While economic and income growth picked up in the late 1990s, the overall picture remained inferior to the postwar Keynesian years. Growth in real disposable income per capita was 1.3 percent in the 1980s and 0.1 percent in the 1990s (though 2.3 percent in the 1997–June 2000 period). This finding compares to figures of 2.2 percent for the 1950s, 3.0 percent for the 1960s, and 4.2 percent for the 1970s (Maxwell 2001: 6).

Behind these income statistics is a job market that delivers a deteriorating stock of jobs. Mike Burke and John Shields (1999) term this the "hour glass" job market, in which significant groups of the population are excluded from employment opportunities, and considerable polarization exists—not just in incomes, but in security of employment and vulnerability to the economic cycle—among those who do manage to find employment.

Health

From time to time studies identify ways in which globalization, or more correctly international agreements such as NAFTA, is having an impact on the Canadian health-care system. Such effects include creeping privatization, primarily through the contracting out of services (CCPA *Monitor* July/ August 1995: 5), and Bill C-22, which anticipated NAFTA provisions on intellectual property rights (Fuller 1996: 18). Under Bill C-22 patent protection for name brand drugs was originally extended from four to ten years. In 1993 the protection was extended to twenty years. The result has been rapidly escalating pharmaceutical costs. Some provincial health plans reduced coverage in order to contain costs (CCPA *Monitor* March 1995: 9). There is also what Burke (2000: 180–81) terms the discourse of efficiency, which is linked in business rhetoric to globalization. When applied to the health-care sector this discourse promotes markets, decentralization and individualism.

Although international conditioning frameworks do have a demonstrable effect, domestic sources, notably the dominance of the neo-liberal paradigm, have been responsible for most of the changes. As with social policy and services generally, it may be that the full effect of the international influences lies in the future.

Earlier funding changes, such as the 1977 change to block funding in the form of Established Programs Financing (EPF), with minimal conditions attached, had the predictable effect of increasing provincial variations in medical coverage and billing practices. In 1984 the federal government responded by passing the Canada Health Act, which reaffirmed the conditions stipulated in the 1967 Medical Care Act—universal coverage, accessibility, portability, comprehensiveness and public administration—

and provided that federal funds would be withheld, on a dollar for dollar basis, for every dollar of extra billing or hospital user fees that provinces permitted. Reflecting on the experience since 1984, Susan Silver (1996: 77) comments that the "'stick' of the CHA has been effective as long as the federal government has the political will and the financial means to enforce it."

The Mulroney Conservative government was constrained from making substantial changes to medicare by the Liberal decision to pass a new Canada Health Act just before the 1984 election and by the immense popularity of the program (Weller 1996: 130). The Conservatives were forced to vote for the Liberal measure or face the prospect of it becoming the main issue in the election. Having voted for it, they were bound by its provisions as long as medicare itself retained its public support. This same constraint also applied to the Liberal successor, though perhaps to a diminishing extent.

Although rhetorically committed to the principles of the Canada Health Act, the Chrétien government undermined the federal government's ability to sustain national standards in the health field. The declining cash portion of federal transfers for health care purposes (see Table 4.5) reduced the federal capacity to oppose user fees, private health clinics, the delisting of covered services, and the variety of other means by which the market is being allowed to creep into a system previously based on quite different principles.

The decline in the public portion of the total health bill (from a normal level of 75 or 76 percent to 69.8 percent in 1997) could be used as an indicator of "passive privatization," characterized as "a generalized retreat of the state from the provision of health care services and an enlargement of the health space occupied by the private sector" (Burke 2000: 182). As Burke (183–85) notes, such indicators are but part of an ongoing and intense commodification of the health system. In a careful analysis of the determinants of the increased private share of health-care costs in Canada, Livio Di Matteo (2000) concludes that the decline in real per capita health transfers from the federal government has eroded the public share in public health expenditures, a factor combined with the effects of changes in the distribution of income. In particular, "Those in the top 20 percent of the income distribution appear to have a preference for greater private health expenditures," Di Matteo (2000: 108) points out, referring to the group that under the neo-liberal paradigm has done rather well in terms of income share.

The retention of a cash component to CHST transfers, announced in the 1996 budget, did appear to ensure continued federal authority. Questions continued to be posed, however, about whether the federal government retained the political will to perform this function.

One leading health policy analyst concluded that the Liberal Party's political will was being exercised in an entirely different direction:

> The Liberals have done an about face.... A government elected on the plank of preserving medicare is governing in a manner that will undermine and then destroy it. The end result for the Canadian health care system will be its eventual return to the private, profit-making market. That will inevitability lead to precisely what the Liberal Party itself said it would in the 1993 election campaign, namely a two-tiered, inequitable system—one that will be far more expensive and less efficient than the current one, and yet will suffer from most of the same problems. (Weller 1996: 143)

Even though the Liberals reached an agreement with the provinces to transfer an additional $23.5 billion over five years for health care, concerns about the nature of their commitment to a public health-care system remained. Reports of the new federal-provincial health deal emphasized that the money came with few strings attached (*Globe and Mail* 12 Sept. 2000). Given the recent Alberta legislation, Bill 11, which extended private, for-profit health care and may have also exposed Canada's hospital sector to the provisions of NAFTA and the GATS (see Evans et al. 2000), this is a remarkable omission.

(Un)Employment Insurance and Labour-Market Policy

Reduced spending on social support has been accompanied by an increased emphasis on "active" measures that would enable individuals to enter or re-enter the labour market rather than remain dependent on social assistance. As social policy's star waned, that of labour-market policy waxed, at least rhetorically. That area entered the process of being transferred from the federal to provincial level, and there it is likely to function, using policies such as workfare (Rehnby and McBride 1997), chiefly as a social control adjunct to residual social programs.

The evolution of Canadian labour-market policy falls into four broad periods. First came a period of rather limited activity, lasting until the mid-1960s. Next was a period of increased state intervention, in which programs multiplied, which lasted through the late 1980s. From the late 1980s to the mid-1990s, an attempt was made to create neo-corporatist training institutions in the name of achieving a high-skills, high-value-added competitive economy. That period has largely been succeeded by the current approach of labour-market deregulation and devolution.

Throughout the earlier periods the active components of labour-market policy were underpinned by a relatively generous system of unemployment insurance—one that was often criticized for its generosity and passivity.[6] In 1996 the federal government announced its withdrawal from the training sphere and began a radical restructuring of the renamed employment insurance system along with the transfer of responsibility for active employment measures to the provinces.

That transfer consisted of a variety of programs funded through the Employment Insurance account. The clientele who could access them was for the first time extended to include people not currently drawing benefits from the unemployment insurance account. Such measures would include wage subsidies, temporary income supplements, support for self-employment initiatives, partnerships for job creation and, where provinces requested, skills loans and grants. Provinces that assumed responsibility for delivery of active measures could also opt to take over the delivery of labour market services—screening, counselling, placement—from the federal government. The federal government was to withdraw from labour-market training over a three-year period, or sooner if provinces wanted. It would no longer be involved in purchase of training, funding apprenticeships, co-op education, workplace-based training or project-based training (HRDC 1996a, 1996b).

Some $2 billion would be available for active measures directed to claimants and some former claimants of unemployment insurance. If EI coverage rates had remained constant, the pool of clients to be served by the devolved programs would expand. Given an actual decline in coverage, however, the pool would shrink, though without providing any great fiscal advantage to the provinces. Those individuals not covered by EI would require provincial social assistance, and a declining pool might stimulate future reductions in federal funding.

Three types of active measure were to be transferred to the provinces immediately: targeted wage subsidies, to aid employers in hiring, and thus providing on-the-job experience; self-employment assistance to help individuals start their own businesses; and job-creation partnerships with provinces, the private sector and communities. Two other programs were to be pretested: targeted earnings—wage top-ups to encourage the unemployed to accept low-paid jobs; and skills loans and grants, which would be implemented only with the consent of a province. Under this program funds would be made available so that individuals could choose the form of training best suited to them. This approach rests on the observation, disputed by some provincial officials (interview, B.C. official,

March 1998) that better results, defined as end-of-program employment, are obtained when people share in the costs of the training they receive (HRDC 1996c: 17–18).

Despite the asymmetrical arrangements that are emerging as a result of devolution to the provinces, some common neo-liberal principles run through the new labour-market development agreements. For example, they typically contain language committing the governments to reduce dependency on public assistance, and they elicit a commitment, on the part of those who do receive assistance under employment benefits and support measures, to take primary responsibility for identifying their own employment needs and locating services necessary to meet those needs. This approach includes, if appropriate, sharing the cost of such assistance (see, for example, the Canada–British Columbia Agreement on Labour Market Development 3.1.h).

Indeed, the "results"-based orientation of the Employment Insurance Act consists precisely of these targets and, measured by these standards, achieved early success. Reporting to the minister on the first year of experience with the new act, the Canada Employment Insurance Commission showed that income benefits had declined by 8.4 percent, the number of initial claimants had dropped by 14.5 percent, and there had been an increase in the number of clients receiving short-term interventions such as information and counselling and a decrease in those receiving longer-term interventions such as training. As a result, "average costs per participant in Employment Benefits and Support measures declined from $7300 to $3900," or by 46.6 percent (HRDC 1998: ii–iii).

The federal authorities retained a limited range of labour-market policy responsibilities—employment insurance benefits, provision of a national system of labour-market information and exchange, support for interprovincial sectoral development and developing responses to national economic crises, and jurisdiction over a one-time Transitional Jobs Fund (HRDC 1996b: 1). But these reforms completed a long-term trend to ending federal Consolidated Revenue funding for employment measures. Any future federal money for these purposes will come from the employment insurance account. On current evidence, many of the services that remain will be contracted out.[7]

The federal government also restructured the unemployment insurance system (HRDC 1995). The program had already ceased to be generous by international standards. The 1996 changes to the system (see HRDC 1996b) included calculating qualification periods in terms of hours worked rather than weeks worked. The department claimed that this would be more equitable for part-time workers and women workers in particular, and that it reflected the labour-market reality of increasing part-time work. Other changes reduced the benefit replacement rate for repeat claimants and introduced a supplement for low-income family claimants, increased the clawback of benefits from high-income earners and reduced premiums and maximum insurable earnings.

Coverage declined sharply. A Canadian Labour Congress (1999) study based on Statistics Canada data shows that in 1997 the percentage of unemployed workers covered by UI was less than half of what it had been in 1989—36 percent as compared to 74 percent. Women, whose coverage had declined from 70 percent in 1987 to 31 percent in 1997,[8] and young people—55 percent to 15 percent—were particularly hard hit (see Table 4.8).

The primary reason for declining coverage seems to be that the number of weekly hours required to qualify jumped from fifteen to thirty-five, with an immediate impact on part-time workers. Women were overrepresented among this group. Young people were also hurt by the change in regulations. In their case an additional factor was the tripling of the total hours required to qualify for benefits, from 300 to 910 hours for new entrants.

A government study (Applied Research Branch, Strategic Policy, HRDC 1998) estimates the decline in the beneficiaries to unemployed ratio at almost 50 percent in the 1989–97 period (83 percent to 42 percent). The report attributes just under half of the decline to policy and program changes. The rest is due to labour-market changes such as increased long-term unemployment. The effects were to increase the number of "exhaustees," produce more unemployed people who lacked previous work experience, and increase the number of people who were "self-employed."

In addition to the coverage issue, benefits are of shorter duration and the benefit rate has fallen steadily from 66.6 percent to 55 percent (under the new system repeat claimants can receive as little as 52 percent). The

Table 4.8
Percentage of Unemployed Receiving Unemployment Benefits

	1989	1990	1991	1992	1993	1994	1995	1996	1997	% change
Men	77	77	72	63	59	52	47	44	39	-49
Women	70	69	63	58	52	47	40	37	31	-55
All	74	73	68	61	56	50	44	41	36	-52

Source: Canadian Labour Congress 1999.

changes not only continue a long-standing process of dismantling the 1971 employment insurance system[9] but also further reduce the individual security formerly provided by the system.

In fitting with the "reparation agenda," in September 2000 the Liberal government announced the reversal of several of its 1996 reforms to the unemployment insurance system. These included removal of penalties for seasonal workers with repeat claims and an extension of the limit at which benefits are clawed back to $48,000 from $39,000 (*Globe and Mail* 29 Sept. 2000).

Made in Canada

Retrenchment of the state has been a chief characteristic of national politics over the last two decades. While the global context—and the rhetoric surrounding the need to be competitive and efficient in a global economy—may have had some bearing on the direction of policy, the available evidence indicates that the causation has been domestic. This tendency may be due to the dominance of neo-liberal policy prescriptions and/or the increased strength of business relative to labour, as power resource theory might suggest.[10] In either event it is not necessary to look beyond national borders for an explanation. Significantly, as the federal deficit came under control and a surplus emerged, speculation grew about how the government might make use of the "fiscal dividend." With an election in the offing there were signs that federal purse strings were loosening—which only seems to confirm that social policy has been driven by domestic rather than global factors.

Notes

1. But only to some degree: Leo Panitch has referred to welfare's redistributive effects as "socialism in one class" (cited in Leys 1980: 52), because the transfers are largely "from younger, employed workers, to retired, unemployed workers, workers' widows and one-parent families."
2. For a somewhat sceptical view of the claims of "strong" versions of globalization theory, see Evans, McBride and Shields 2000.
3. For a fuller, though still incomplete account of neo-liberal policy measures, see McBride and Shields 1997, and the contributions to Burke, Mooers and Shields 2000.
4. As Gamble (1988) points out in his analysis of Thatcherism, the neo-liberal state was far from uniformly weak.
5. For an overview of monetarism, see McBride 1992: ch. 3.
6. For a review and rebuttal of literature suggesting that the unemployment insurance system acted as a disincentive to work and hence raised the unemployment rate, see Jackson 1995: 3–9; see also McBride 1992: ch. 6.

7. Since, at the time of the Charlottetown Accord, the federal authorities contemplated transferring unemployment insurance to the provinces (interview, former HRDC official, July 1996), it is possible that further devolution will occur. Indeed, the posture of HRDC with respect to contracting out of functions would seem well suited to preparing the ground for this eventuality. Such a trajectory has been made more likely by the major shift towards radical decentralization of federalism favoured by Ontario, traditionally an upholder of a strong role for Ottawa. An Ontario position paper on the constitution called for unemployment insurance to be run jointly by the federal and provincial governments or by the provinces alone (*Globe and Mail* 16 Aug. 1996).
8. The CLC's figures refer only to women on lay-off and do not include those on maternity leave.
9. See McBride 1992: ch. 6 for details of earlier rounds of restrictions.
10. For a test and partial confirmation of power resource theory in the social policy area, see S. Phillips 1999.

Chapter Five

Trade Is Trump
International Conditioning Frameworks and the State

In many nation-states neo-liberal restructuring has been associated with a new generation of international economic agreements. Ricardo Grinspun and Robert Kreklewich (1994: 33) argue that free-trade agreements, for instance, "serve as a restructuring tool or, put differently, as a conditioning institutional framework that promotes and consolidates neo-liberal re-structuring. These international treaties serve as a mechanism whereby domestic ruling groups, with the encouragement of the United States government, can advance economic and social reforms that are inherently anti-democratic." International conditioning frameworks are, then, rooted in the societies to which they apply.

The international agreements are "anti-democratic" in the sense that their provisions foreclose certain options that the populations of nation-states may want to preserve or adopt in the future; and the governments that have agreed to these provisions reflect the interests of domestic and international economic elites. The agreements are intended to tie the hands of successor governments and to make neo-liberal changes perma-nent. It is in this sense that Stephen Gill (1995) uses the term "new constitutionalism" to refer to a system of "disciplinary neoliberalism." The object is "the insulation of key aspects of the economy from the influence of politicians or the mass of citizens by imposing, internally and externally, 'binding constraints' on the conduct of fiscal, monetary, trade and invest-ment policies" (Gill 1995: 412). The system disciplines public institutions and protects private property rights.

In similar vein, Stephen Clarkson (1993) considers that the Canada–U.S. Free Trade Agreement should be best understood, in Ronald Reagan's phrase, as "a new economic constitution for North America." In Clarkson's view, this constitution is asymmetrical; it constrains the exercise of autonomy in Canada (and, since NAFTA, in Mexico as well) far more than in the United States.

Conditioning frameworks can be informal and relatively invisible. For example, policies of financial deregulation can make states vulnerable to international financial markets. That vulnerability often appears to be a structural problem because its political origins (financial deregulation) are unacknowledged and thus relatively invisible, but it is instead the product of political choices.

Grinspun and Kreklewich focus primarily on conditioning frameworks that are formal and visible, such as free-trade agreements, even if they are highly technical and poorly understood. The frameworks may well be global, as with the World Trade Organization (WTO), or regional, as with the North American Free Trade Agreement or the European Union (EU). They may also be bilateral. David Schneiderman (2000) uses the lens of new constitutionalism to analyze Canada's role as a participant in a number of bilateral investment treaties. He finds that Canadian policy has adopted stringent standards that have been characteristic of U.S. trade and investment policy. Noting, in passing, that Canadian trade negotiators have emerged as "fervent advocates of US trade policy" (Schneiderman 2000: 761), he explores the degree to which the bilateral investment treaty between Canada and South Africa incorporates NAFTA principles. Schneiderman demonstrates how the agreement has constitutional implications for the Republic of South Africa because its provisions are discordant with the South African constitution's provisions pertaining to property rights.

Whether such agreements are described as trade or investment agreements, their provisions increasingly reach into areas of investment, services and intellectual property rights. In so doing, they "condition" a large part of what was previously considered to be "domestic" policy. Certainly, the term "trade" is a misnomer, and the idea that these are simply free-trade agreements, as the term "trade" has traditionally been understood, is an illusion. In Grinspun and Kreklewich's (1994: 48) account, these developments are linked to the interests and preferences of an emerging transnational business class.

As the cases of the WTO on the one hand and FTA–NAFTA on the other demonstrate, conditioning frameworks can assume a multilateral, bilateral or trilateral guise. The historical multilateralist orientation in Canadian foreign policy, including foreign economic policy (see Keating 1993: 19–20), was partly designed to act as a counterweight to continentalist pressures. Canada's "creeping continentalism" of 1945 to the mid-1970s, as reflected in trade and investment patterns, found expression in the 1980s and 1990s through the bilateral FTA and trilateral NAFTA. Notwithstanding such deviations,[1] Canada's influence in constructing the post–World War II international economic regime had originally been exercised in favour of a multilateral, liberalized international economic system that policy-makers believed would offset the continental embrace of the United States (Keating 1993: 53). Canadian policy appears to have had a significant influence on these developments (Muirhead 1999).

Canada's preference for a "liberalized" international economic system highlights another condition: for Canada, multilateralism was not just a process; it also had a substance stemming from the dominant liberal ideology. How long the depiction of multilateralism as an *alternative* to continentalism remained valid in Canadian foreign policy is a matter of debate. Certainly, post-FTA multilateralism, as represented, for example, by Canadian enthusiasm for the revamped World Trade Organization, or acting as cheerleader for a Free Trade Area of the Americas (FTAA), can be depicted as an *extension* of continentalism rather than as an alternative to it. By the 1990s, Canadian policy in this area had become an enthusiastic echo of U.S. policy (Keating 1993: ch. 10).

The key element of the postwar international economic regime was the Bretton Woods international monetary system. Its leading international institutions were the International Monetary Fund (IMF) and International Bank for Reconstruction and Development, or World Bank, together with the General Agreement on Tariffs and Trade (GATT), which later evolved into the WTO. Today many of the institutions of this conditioning framework are still "under construction" and have implications that are only beginning to become apparent. Much of their impact still lies in the future. Undoubtedly such organizations did condition national choices in the postwar period, especially choices in developing countries. But they did so in a less intrusive manner than in the later period. Originally the institutions were more tolerant of politically diverse choices at the national level, especially as far as the advanced industrial countries were concerned. Liberalism, for these were undoubtedly liberal and liberalizing institutions, was more accepting of the state and state economic interventionism in the immediate postwar period than it later became. Still, as the case of the proposed International Trade Organization indicates, tolerance, especially on the part of the United States, has always stopped short of endorsation.

From the GATT to the WTO

The origins and subsequent evolution of the General Agreement on Trade and Tariffs (GATT) highlight the argument that the intrusiveness of the conditioning frameworks and the content of liberalism changed dramatically over the postwar period. The GATT, an agreement to lower tariffs, was originally proposed as one chapter in a broader conception of international trade that called for the creation of an International Trade Organization (ITO). The ITO Charter, proposed but subsequently not ratified by the United States, encouraged economic development, full employment and investment and provided for an international structure and enforcement mechanisms (Cohn 2000: 205–6). For Jean-Christophe Graz (2000: 21) it represents an effort to reconcile, on an international basis, "the historic antagonisms of capitalism between an open international economy and the socio-economic functions of the state." Its statutes "acknowledged a conception of trade regulation that shielded substantial economic and social functions of the state: heavy agricultural support, quotas on a discriminatory basis for development or balance of payment purposes, a wide range of safeguards to avoid international propagation of recessions, intergovernmental agreements for primary commodities and recognition of the legitimate right of expropriation for capital-importing countries" (Graz 2000: 22).

While isolationist fears played some role in its non-ratification, economic liberals and interests such as the International Chamber of Commerce, hostile to the broad goals and state interventionism conveyed by the ITO charter, were more important (O'Brien, Goetz, Scholte and Williams 2000: 69). In reality, there were conflicting interests within the United States, and it was easy to forge agreement there that the country should not limit its own policy options: "Congress certainly did not intend to delegate authority to anonymous international bureaucrats at the ITO rather than a president subject to political pressures and horse trading" (Schwartz 1994: 282).

Yet the GATT itself was not intrusive in the cause of economic liberalism. Originally the agreement focused on tariff reduction, for the most part as applied to manufactured goods. It remained in existence for almost fifty years, but its small staff and budget emphasized its consultative and decentralized characteristics. When countries joined the GATT—134 had done so by 1999—they agreed to a number of rules that the organization itself had no power to enforce. Enforcement rested in the hands of "injured parties" (states) that could retaliate against an offender. The major rules—still operative under GATT's successor, the World Trade Organization—provided most-favoured-nation status for all members, national treatment, prohibition of import quotas, and commitments to consult on trade problems and to submit disputes to GATT panels.

The organization permitted certain exceptions to these rules (see Brown and Hogendorn 2000: 250–52), which enabled the GATT system to balance the liberalization of trading rules against a considerable degree of policy autonomy for states (Brown and Hogendorn 2000: 68). To a degree, therefore, the tacit postwar compromise that in many Western states led to domestic Keynesianism was integrated into the GATT (Ruggie 1983).

The GATT underwent several revisions, each involving a "round" of negotiations. The Uruguay Round of GATT negotiations, which began in 1986 and concluded in 1994, was protracted and on several occasions seemed on the verge of failure. However, the end result was an intensification of the liberalization of world trade, the extension of trade to new areas, and a greater capacity for enforcement. The changes were in response to the increased resort to non-tariff barriers, continued protection in agriculture, textiles and services, and perceptions that enforcement mechanisms were inadequate (Cohn 2000: 214). Robert Wolfe (1996: 692–93) describes a transformation from a system of shallow or negative integration based on reciprocal reduction of border measures (GATT) into "'deeper,' positive or 'behind the border' integration which can require analysis of almost any national policy likely to have spillover or external effects across borders."[2]

The driving force behind the enhanced agreement was the United States, which had resorted to aggressive trade tactics in the 1980s in response to a persistent trade deficit.[3] A desire to overcome U.S. unilateralism and secure access to the U.S. market was one of the principal motivations behind the Canadian proposal to negotiate a FTA. From the U.S. perspective, the conclusion of regional trade agreements, FTA and then NAFTA, not only was partly born of frustration with the slow pace of GATT negotiations, but also presented an opportunity to establish precedents in the regional trade agreements that could then be extended to the GATT level.

NAFTA

In some ways the North American Free Trade Agreement and its precursor, the Canada-U.S. Free Trade Agreement, anticipated the contents of the World Trade Organization. In other respects NAFTA continues to "go beyond" the WTO provisions and hence serves as an indicator of the probable future direction of liberalization measures, especially of those pertaining to investment. Although by mid-2001 little hard information was still available about the text of the Free Trade Area of the Americas draft agreement, it seemed likely to attempt to extend liberalization measures in the investment and services areas beyond the level already achieved in NAFTA and the WTO (see Lee 2001).

The NAFTA objectives include the elimination of barriers to trade and encouraging the cross-border movement of goods and services between the signatories.[4] It also seeks to substantially increase investment opportunities, protect intellectual property rights and create an effective framework for disputes resolution (Article 102). The incorporation of the national-treatment and most-favoured-nation principles and inclusion of investment, services and intellectual property rights indicate not only the consistency of the (U.S.-inspired) architecture with other international trade agreements but also the dominance of the U.S. trade agenda. Article 103 provides that "in the event of any inconsistency with this Agreement" and other agreements such as GATT, "this agreement shall prevail to the extent of the inconsistency." Article 104 provides that *specific trade obligations* in a number of international environmental agreements shall prevail over NAFTA, with the proviso that NAFTA signatories will use any alternative that is "least inconsistent" with its provisions. This is a very limited nod in the direction of environmental protection.

This agreement imposes a variety of obligations upon signatories. These obligations include the application of national treatment to trade in goods (chapter 3 of the agreement), government procurement (chapter 10), investment (chapter 11), cross-border trade in services (chapter 12), financial services (chapter 14), and intellectual property rights (chapter 17); and most-favoured-nation status for investment (chapter 11), cross-border trade in services (chapter 12), and financial services (chapter 14). Reservations to the various obligations are contained in annexes. The degree of obligation varies by topic, but to a greater or lesser extent all of the provisions operate to reduce a nation's discretion to discriminate in favour of domestic industries.

With some exceptions (including, for Canada, export of logs and unprocessed fish)[5] each party agrees to accord national treatment to the goods of other signatories. Article 105 commits the signatories to "ensure that all necessary measures are taken in order to give effect to the provisions of this agreement ... including their observance ... by state and provincial governments." Subject to certain conditions (such as size of contract)[6] federal government procurement contracts for goods and services are also subject to national-treatment rules. Nor may a government discriminate against a local supplier on the basis of foreign affiliation or ownership or on the basis that its goods or services are imported from another NAFTA signatory (Article 1003). The agreement's Chapter 11 covers, subject to certain reservations, all forms of investment interests. With respect to provinces and states the principle of "best in Province" treatment is to be applied (Article 1102.3). A noteworthy aspect of this article is its prohibition of a wide range of performance requirements and the creation of investor rights in dispute resolution. The lengthy list of prohibited performance requirement measures include requirements to export a certain proportion of goods or services produced, or achieve any specified level or balance of foreign exchange earnings, or target specific export markets. The agreement bars domestic content or purchasing requirements, as well as provisions that would insist on transfers of technology.

Jim Stanford (1993: 166–67) points out that restrictions on performance requirements make it difficult for Canadians to channel types of investment and use investment for long-range reasons of national or regional industrial strategy. As a result investors will focus on areas of "natural" comparative advantage—in Canada's case, natural resources. In addition, NAFTA effectively "prevents governments from imposing these performance requirements on domestic investors" (Stanford 1993: 160). In some cases the national-treatment language in NAFTA outlaws these requirements. In other cases requirements would place domestic firms at a disadvantage in competing with foreign firms. The possibilities that foreign investors might be treated better than domestic investors and that investor rights provisions could undo carefully worked out compromises between states have begun to attract the attention even of proponents of trade and investment agreements (Grady and Macmillan 1999: 93).

In these respects, NAFTA sets up a much more deregulated investment regime than other regional blocs such as the EU. The type of regime created is far more consistent with traditional U.S. approaches to economic policy than it is to either Canadian or Mexican traditions.

Under certain NAFTA articles (for example, Article 1116), investors can directly submit a claim without "their" government acting as an intermediary. Such provisions confer rights on multinational corporations, in particular, that strengthen their hand vis-à-vis states and also privilege "corporate citizens." "Natural" or human citizens have no specific rights under this particular conditioning framework. The investor rights provision was a breakthrough for U.S. policy and the interests of multinationals. It established a precedent in international economic agreements by giving corporations, for certain purposes, equal status with states.

Governments may enter reservations so that certain sectors are removed from the NAFTA provisions. Canada's chief reservations in the investment areas (see Annex II of the agreement) pertain to Aboriginal affairs (other investors might be denied rights or privileges accorded to Aboriginal peoples); communications (ownership restrictions and corporate governance, and market entry and other measures), trade in government, securities, rights or preferences to socially and economically disadvantaged minorities, and any measure pertaining to public law and "the following services to the extent that they are social services established or maintained for a public purpose: income security or insurance, social security or insurance, social welfare, public education, public training, health and child care."This language echoes Articles 11.01.4 (investment) and 12.01.3 (cross-border trade in services), which provide that these articles shall not be construed to "prevent a Party from providing a service or performing a function such as" those listed above.

Despite the apparent protection for public services, some limitations, actual and potential, are in place on the exemptions (Sanger 1993:189–92). First, NAFTA treats public services as commodities. Those declared exempt from other NAFTA provisions are "non-conforming" (Article 1206) and, in a sense, odd or anomalous from the natural state, which is presumed to be market competition and private enterprise.[7] Second, there may be conflict within the requirement that publicly provided services be consistent with the rest of the rules in the services sector (which are commercially oriented). This requirement could apply to public services that are subcontracted to local private providers. There may be strong cultural grounds for protecting local providers of, say, educational services. But the services sector, which might trump the social services exemption in this context, requires national treatment and most-favoured-nation. Thus it may prohibit restricting the bids to local providers.

Third, the protection to public services applies only "to the extent that they are social services established or maintained for a public purpose." Ancillary functions of public services (janitorial, food, maintenance) could be challenged along with partially privatized services such as seniors' homes and day cares.

The inclusion of intellectual property rights in NAFTA represented a first for U.S. economic policy. It was the first time national treatment and most-favoured-nation were extended to intellectual property rights in a comprehensive international trade agreement. The inclusion was a victory for U.S. policies and the U.S. multinational corporations in research-intensive areas such as computer software and pharmaceuticals. For the Americans, it also established an important precedent for the GATT talks, in which the U.S. government was pursuing similar goals.

Article 1902 reserves a country's rights to "apply its own anti-dumping law and countervailing duty law to goods imported from the territory" of other parties to the agreement. It was the desire to escape precisely this exercise of (U.S.) national autonomy that motivated many to support the original FTA with the United States (though that agreement failed to deliver on the goal of rendering Canada exempt from the aggressive use of those measures by the United States). Article 1902 guarantees that dispute panels will be applying *national* laws in these areas. Consequently, it embeds whatever asymmetries of power that may exist between the signatories. The provision (Article 1902.2) that "each party reserve the right to change or modify its anti-dumping law or countervailing duty law" provided it is made explicit that it applies to a fellow NAFTA member emphasized this point. The search for a rules-based trading arrangement in this case seems to have made little difference to power differentials. Indeed, they are embedded within the text of the agreement.

As well, Article 605 provides that any restrictions applied to energy exports do "not reduce the proportion of the total export shipments of the specific energy or basic petrochemical good made available to that other Party relative to the total supply of that good of the Party maintaining the restriction as compared to the proportion prevailing in the most recent 36-month period." Nor can the regulations alter the mix of products. Similarly, the agreement prohibits a two-price system—for example, when export prices are higher than those charged domestically. This element effectively prevents any future Canadian government from repeating anything like the National Energy Program. For the Americans, it locks in supplies of Canadian energy and provides security of supply. For Canadian business, it is an important limitation on the interventionist powers of the Canadian state. For the government of the day it was a "desirable loss of sovereignty" (Doern and Tomlin 1992: 258). From a long-term point of view it restricts a major source of competitive advantage that could easily feature in an interventionist industrial policy.

Finally, the chapter on Competition Policy, Monopolies and State Enterprises permits states to designate a monopoly that can be either private or public, but places an injunction on such a monopoly to act "in accordance with commercial considerations in its purchase or sale of the monopoly good or service in the relevant market, including with regard to price, quality, availability, marketability, transportation and other terms and conditions of purchase or sale." That kind of injunction is clearly likely to undermine the public policy purposes that have often led to the creation of Crown corporations.

Sample Cases under NAFTA
NAFTA contains not only a number of provisions that restrict state capacity but also a number of sections that provide for settlement of disputes. For example, Chapter 20 outlines the procedures for settling disagreements over interpretations of the agreement itself, and Chapter 19 provides a resolution procedure for disputes on issues of anti-dumping and countervailing duty matters (see Herman 1998; Valihora 1998; Winham 1994). Although Chapter 19 disputes have drawn considerable public and academic attention, the panels under that chapter are simply reviewing

whether a country's administrative agencies have correctly interpreted its own laws. There is certainly a sovereignty or autonomy dimension to this practice—the determination would otherwise be made by national courts—but it leaves the ultimate determination of the substance of the law itself at the national level.

A number of cases under the innovative Chapter 11 procedures, however, appear to strike at the heart of member countries' ability, short of withdrawing from NAFTA itself, to enact health and environmental, and potentially other legislation. Chapter 11 is the section of NAFTA that enables investors to challenge government actions directly. In brief, the implications of four cases—Ethyl, Myers, Methanex and Metalclad—indicate how state capacity has been changed and could change further as a result of these provisions.

In the Ethyl case, Canada banned a gasoline additive, MMT, on the grounds that its primary ingredient, manganese, constituted a public health risk. The Ethyl corporation countered that the ban amounted to expropriation because it would eliminate anticipated sales (and resultant profits) of its product in Canada, and the company sued the Canadian government for $250 million. The outcome, in an "out of court" settlement, was that Canada agreed to pay Ethyl $13 million in damages plus costs, to publicly proclaim that MMT was "safe" and to repeal its ban on the substance.

A week after that settlement S.D. Myers Inc. launched a lawsuit against the Canadian government for profits lost during a period, 1995–97, when Canada banned the export of PCB-contaminated waste. A decision to revoke the ban was made after U.S. firms announced they would challenge it under NAFTA provisions.

Methanex, a Canadian corporation that manufactures a gasoline additive, MTBE, is suing the U. S. government for $970 million for losses claimed to be incurred as a result as a result of California's 1999 decision to phase out use of the additive. The state's decision followed a series of studies linking the substance to cancer. In this case a corporation is attempting to hold a national government liable for the actions of a subnational government acting within its area of jurisdiction. The case of Metalclad also includes the intergovernmental dimension. Metalclad Corporation had acquired a waste-disposal plant in Mexico and undertaken to clean up pre-existing contaminants, but an environmental impact study revealed that the site was located in an environmentally sensitive area. A Mexican state governor decided to prevent the company from opening the plant. The NAFTA tribunal adjudicating the case found in favour of Metalclad and awarded $16.7 million damages as compensation for "expropriation." Mexico attempted to have the award set aside on the grounds that the tribunal's three findings of breaches of Articles 1105 and 1110 of NAFTA were beyond the scope of the submission to arbitration. When the case was heard in the Supreme Court of British Columbia,[8] Judge D.F. Tysoe found that Mexico had successfully established that two of the findings of breaches of NAFTA did involve decisions on matters beyond the scope of the submission to arbitration. The court did, however, sustain the third finding, and while the value of the award was reduced somewhat, it remained in effect.[9] In addition Metalclad was awarded 75 percent of its costs in the case.

The World Trade Organization (WTO)

The WTO comprises a group of agreements, including the GATT, which contain the essential principles of the liberalized trading system. According to the WTO itself the first principle is that the trading system should operate without discrimination. This means no discrimination in a country between its own and foreign products, services or nationals, all of whom are given "national treatment." Any benefit given to one is extended to all. All enjoy most-favoured-nation status. Other principles include achievement of freer trade through lowering trade barriers, guaranteeing predictability through "binding" states' commitments on issues like tariffs, and promoting fair competition through working towards elimination of subsidies and dumping (selling overseas below cost in order to gain market share).

Like GATT, the WTO also involves agreements on various traded goods such as agricultural products, textiles and clothing, and, in addition, agreements on sanitary and phytosanitary measures, technical barriers to trade, trade-related investment measures, anti-dumping, customs valuation, pre-shipment inspection, rules of origin, input licensing, subsidies and countervailing measures and safeguards. Yet other agreements cover services, intellectual property rights, trade policy review mechanisms, dispute settlement processes, government procurement, civil aircraft, and dairy and beef products. [10]

In contrast to the GATT, which balanced trade liberalization with policy autonomy, the WTO is intended to be more prescriptive—as witnessed in the strengthened (as compared to GATT) disputes resolution procedures, measures to increase transparency (such as the trade policy review mechanism) and achieve better co-ordination, and the agreement to hold biannual ministerial meetings. In an unintended consequence these measures also serve as a focal point for those opposed to the diminution of national autonomy that is a feature of the new WTO. Another significant aspect is that the WTO is a single undertaking in the sense that countries must sign on to all the agreements under its umbrella (Wolfe 1996). Under the GATT, compliance with dispute settlement rulings was largely the result of moral suasion and consensus, and countries could delay or avoid compliance (Brown and Hogendorn 2000:251–52). Indeed, since panel decisions had to achieve consensus in the GATT Council, in effect they could be vetoed by the country that lost its case. The impact of this practice was limited, however. Virtually the only entities to exercise this right were the United States and the European Union.

Still, under the WTO there was a significant change in procedures. A member country can initiate a panel hearing to determine if another country had contravened a WTO agreement. Panels act quickly, and decisions can be appealed to an appeal body; but, once confirmed, the panel's decision must be implemented or compensation paid. Turning down a panel decision now requires a consensus. In the event that a country does not comply, the WTO can authorize retaliatory action (see Das 1998: ch. 21; Valihora: 1998).

In practice, the procedures may be more intrusive for small and medium states that are less able to bear the costs of retaliation. Not all states are created equal. Certainly the procedures are more intrusive for states that are less committed to the neo-liberal view of the proper relationship between states and markets. This is because two themes emerge from WTO panel decisions: "The first is the expansive reading given to rules that limit government options that might (even indirectly) interfere with trade. The second, the exceedingly narrow interpretation given trade provisions that might create space for environmental, cultural or conservation exceptions to the free trade orthodoxy" (Shrybman 1999: 17–18). These decisions express a hostility to state intervention in the economy that is characteristic of neo-liberal understandings of the proper sphere for state action.

The key concepts that make up the "conditioning framework" for Canadian policy, which are part of NAFTA and were to have played a crucial role in MAI, will also be a feature of negotiations on the FTAA.[11] A survey of selected WTO agreements indicates that there is scope for much greater intrusion than has yet occurred.

Non-discrimination, expressed in the concepts of "most-favoured-nation" (MFN) and national treatment, is a basic principle of the WTO global trading regime. Most-favoured-nation (Das 1998: ch. 3) simply means that any benefit relating to trade in goods (imports or exports) extended by one member to any country must also be extended to all other members. Certain exceptions exist, including the capacity to establish regional free-trade areas such as NAFTA and custom unions such as the EU. As Marc Lee (2001:3) notes, this type of agreement is permitted on a sort of "WTO-plus" basis—that is, such agreements must at least meet WTO standards and, in reality, there would be little point to negotiating them unless they exceeded WTO standards of liberalization or coverage. National treatment (Das 1998: ch. 4) requires that imported products, once they have entered the importing country, must be treated no less favourably than domestic products. Again, certain exceptions can apply, such as government procurement and payment of subsidies exclusively to the domestic producers of a product. Theodore Cohn (2000: 210–11) argues that reciprocity—the concept that a country benefiting from another country's trade concessions should provide roughly equal benefits in return—is another central concept because it "limits free riding under the unconditional MFN principle." In practice, the advanced states with large markets and extensive trade relations have greater power because they have the greatest concessions to offer.

A third crucial principle, freer trade, includes the elimination of quantitative restrictions (import and export controls) and has potentially far-reaching consequences for various areas of economic and environmental policy, including industrial policy. Historically, in Canada, the government placed conditions on the export of raw logs and unprocessed fish (see Shrybman 1999: ch. 6). The effect was to stimulate domestic processing industries, value-added production, and jobs. Environmental factors—for example, the energy and transportation impacts of exporting unprocessed raw materials—could militate towards similar provisions affecting other commodities. These provisions would undoubtedly be subject to challenge.

The impact of GATT trade rules becomes far-reaching especially when extended from trade in goods to trade in services and, especially, to investment under the WTO. For one thing, the WTO includes an agreement on Trade Related Investment Measures (TRIMS) (Das 1998: ch. 16). This agreement applies only to trade in goods, not investment and it does not prohibit restrictions on repatriation of profits and foreign ownership rules. However, the TRIMS agreement does identify a number of measures that are inconsistent with GATT. These include so-called domestic content provisions, such that an enterprise must use or buy a particular quantity or proportion of domestically sourced products in its operations. The agreement similarly outlaws the linking of a quantity of domestically supplied products to the export or foreign-exchange earnings performance of the enterprise. This removes one of several "performance requirements" (domestic content) that countries often used before authorizing foreign investments. Others were unaffected, and so from the standpoint of international capital, TRIMS failed to produce the kind of investor-rights regime it was seeking. NAFTA and the MAI proposals are much closer to prototype agreements in the investment area (Shrybman 1999: 15).

Under the WTO an agreement on State Trading Enterprises limits the industrial policy potential of state-owned corporations by stipulating that they must act in a non-discriminatory manner, as this is defined in the GATT agreements, and that their sales and purchasing policy must be solely based on commercial conditions. Additionally, enterprises of other WTO members must receive adequate opportunity to participate in purchases and sales.

The Agreement on Technical Barriers to Trade (Das 1998: ch. 12) deals with government regulations of products for security, health or environmental reasons. It applies to both federal and provincial or state levels of government. The agreement contains a Code of Good Practice for the Preparation, Adoption and Application of Standards, and provides for advanced notice to be given of new regulations that differ from international regulations on a subject, or that cover areas not covered by international regulations. Beyond that, the agreement lays down a number of general principles for mandatory technical regulations. Government regulation of matters such as national security, prevention of deceptive practices, and protection of human health and safety, animal or plant life or health and the environment are deemed legitimate provided the regulations are not more trade-restrictive than necessary, are non-discriminatory, and respect the national-treatment principle. The provision that regulations should not be more trade-restrictive than necessary opens the door to a variety of challenges to national systems of regulations. The text privileges trade above other legitimate policy goals. For example, the least trade-restrictive health or environmental regulations may not be the best regulations as viewed from health or environmental value systems.

The Trade Related Intellectual Property Rights (TRIPS) agreement covers areas such as copyrights, trademarks and patents. Winning such an agreement was a central goal of U.S. trade negotiators and of the transnational corporations that are so influential in setting U.S. trade policy. Steven Shrybman (1999: 14) describes the impact of the TRIPS agreement:

> By conveniently attaching the term "trade-related" as a prefix ... this WTO agreement transforms an entire domain of domestic policy and law into one ostensibly suited to WTO regulation. The TRIPS agreement compels all WTO member nations to adopt and implement U.S. style patent protection regimes. The effect is to provide both U.S and European transnationals with global patent rights enforceable by retaliation trade sanctions.

TRIPS has had a notable impact in the pharmaceuticals area. Multinational corporations holding drug patents, in some cases the product of government rather than corporate research,[12] have vigorously and successfully opposed the production of, or trade in, generic substitute drugs. This has the effect of denying drugs at affordable prices to poor nations; and increasing the costs of health care in other nations. Canada extended its patent protection for brand-name drugs from four to ten years prior to NAFTA, and prior to the conclusion of the WTO agreement, it extended this protection to twenty years (Fuller 1996: 18).

The Agreement on Sanitary and Phytosanitary Measures makes explicit the notion that laws and regulations dealing with food and food safety may be considered unjustifiable barriers to trade.

The WTO agreements also include the General Agreement on Trade and Service (GATS), sometimes referred to as a bottom-up or opt-in agreement because many of its provisions apply only to services that national governments agree to "put on the table." However, some GATS provisions apply to all services regardless of whether a government has made commitments to have them included. In this sense the GATS is partially a "top-down" international agreement. Scott Sinclair (2000: 22) points out that GATS affects all government measures that have an impact on services. Certain GATS rules, like the most-favoured-nation and transparency conditions, apply to all services, delivered by any of four modes of service delivery identified in the agreement, regardless of whether a government has made specific commitments in those sectors. The GATS applies to provincial and local governments, state enterprises and even non-governmental organizations, if acting on delegated authority from government (Sinclair 2000: 24). It commits member governments to try to ensure that subnational governments comply with the agreement (Article I.1, I.3a).

In addition, there are crossovers between GATS and GATT, which mean that—unless governments have correctly anticipated the crossover and lodged a timely statement of exemption—services related to particular goods may unexpectedly turn out to be covered. Canada discovered this in losing a case involving magazines. In essence, Canadian measures directed at advertising services, about which no specific commitments had been made under GATS (this service had not been "opted-in") were ruled invalid because of their impact on goods, magazines in this case, which are covered by the GATT (Sinclair 2000: 36–37). Such protections or exclusions as GATS does extend are often very narrowly defined. For example, the agreement excludes services provided in the "exercise of government authority" (Article I.3b). But the excluded service must meet two conditions. It must not be provided on a commercial basis or in competition with another or other service supplier(s). Sinclair (2000: 25) comments:"Because most public health care, education and social service systems involve a mix of public and private funding and public, private not-for-profit, and private, for-profit delivery, it is hard to see how they would benefit from this exclusion." From the perspective of national autonomy, then, GATS has several troubling aspects.

The WTO Secretariat (1999a: 1) is open about the agreement's capacity to intrude into national decision-making. The Secretariat states:

> The reach of the GATS rules extends to all forms of international trade in services. This means that the GATS agreement represents a major new factor for a large sector of world economic activity. It also means, because such a large share of trade in services takes place *inside* national economies, that its requirements will from the beginning necessarily influence national domestic laws and regulations in a way that has been true of the GATT only in recent years.

In a related document (WTO 1999b: 1) the Secretariat cited as advantages the ability of bindings, once undertaken, to "lock in a currently liberal regime or map out a future liberalization path" while overcoming domestic resistance to change.

The WTO has a "built-in" agenda from the Uruguay Round that promotes further liberalization of trade in services (Das 1998: 110). Thus for trade liberalizers the very broad scope of the GATS is in essence a "wish list," with the process tilted towards progressive "opting-in." Indeed, the process is a little more stringent than that:"In committing governments to repeated efforts to enlarge opportunities for international trade in services, it [Article XIX of GATS] ... is a guarantee that the present GATS package is only the first fruit of a continuing enterprise, to be undertaken jointly by all WTO members, to raise the level of their services commitment towards one another" (WTO Secretariat 1999a: 10).

The agreement itself does not define "services." In itself this could be construed as an effort not to restrict the scope of the agreement. *Trade* in services, though, is construed very broadly as delivery of services in any way. This trade could be from the territory of one country to the territory of another (for example, a calling centre maintained in the United States but directed at Canadian customers); it could be in one country but serving visitors from another (as with tourism); it could involve a service supplier based in one country establishing a presence in another (for example, a branch operation of a health-care provider); or it could be "by a service supplier of a member, through presence of natural persons of a member in the territory of any other member" (Article I.2). This condition comprises right of temporary entry visas for personnel involved in provision of services and, as such, makes the GATS a labour-mobility agreement as well as a trade agreement. Since services may also be provided from foreign branches established in the host country, this condition also provides for an investment agreement.

If the definition of "trade in services" is broad, so too is the sector to which it pertains. An estimated 75 percent of jobs in Canada are in services (Canada, DFAIT 2000). The sector includes health, education and other services that in Canada are part of the public domain and have often been regarded as part of Canada's national identity (see McBride and Shields 1993, 1997). By mid-2001 Canada had not made commitments to open these areas to GATS provisions, but a general danger exists that pressures in future rounds of negotiations, possibly combined with pressure from those sectors of Canadian business that see export opportunities in the service sectors, may induce it to do so, in whole or in part. Given that the WTO is a "single undertaking," in which the provisions of all the agreements comprising it must be accepted by member states, the likelihood of cross-pressures from other arenas being brought to bear is increased. Canada's inclusion of "life, accident and health insurance services" in its GATS commitments could arguably trigger future challenges from foreign health-care providers.[13]

Once the door is opened, critics fear, the door to deregulation and privatization of health and education will be impossible to close. This is partly because the operation of the national-treatment and most-favoured-nation principles will quickly erode the legislated discriminatory mechanisms on which public services have been built. For example, Shrybman (1999: 16) argues, "National treatment would require governments to provide the same subsidies and funding support to private hospitals and schools as it makes available to non-profit institutions in the public sector."

It is true that under GATS, when countries enter into specific commitments to open access to their service sectors, or extend national treatment to service-providers from other members, they can prescribe limitations and conditions. But later changes or additions to the exemptions require the approval of three-quarters of the WTO membership—a high threshold. Should a country discover it has made a mistake and needs to modify its commitments, it may have to offer compensation, on a most-favoured-nation basis, or face sanctioned retaliatory measures.

Thus conditionally opting in to GATS puts a premium on the state's negotiators "getting it right" the first time. Even with the best of intentions this will prove to be a difficult endeavour. The decisions of GATS panels will be unpredictable, except to the extent that they will be systemically biased in the direction of liberalization. Moreover, measures that a government believes are valid because of exemptions filed under GATS may still be found to be in violation of other WTO agreements, such as GATT— particularly because the boundary between services and goods will in some cases be unclear.

Continued national autonomy in relation to services, including social services such as health and education, therefore depends on the existence of the political will to resist pressures to opt in to GATT, or the technical competence to devise conditions and exemptions to protect the public interest. Critics consider that neither of these necessities has been sufficiently evident to induce confidence in the protection of Canada's public services. Reflecting on the complexities of the trade agreements, Scott Sinclair (2000: 81) comments: "It is also sobering to recognize that the 1995 Canadian magazine legislation was designed by Canada's top government trade experts specifically to withstand WTO challenge. These experts repeatedly reassured the Canadian cultural community that the proposed policies were 'WTO-proofed.' Nevertheless, Canada lost on every count."

Sample Cases under the WTO

Lawrence Herman (1998) identifies two trends in WTO panel decisions. The first is to construe exemptions from WTO obligations narrowly, and the second is to apply a strict approach to the issue of national treatment. The periodicals case illustrates the latter trend.

Canadian cultural protection efforts have not fared well under the WTO dispute-settlement process. In pursuit of protection of cultural industries and identity, Canada enacted legislation giving tax breaks to Canadian advertisers using domestic magazines and reduced postage rates for some Canadian periodicals. Following a U.S. challenge, these measures were ruled to be in violation of GATT (Shrybman 1999: 37–43). The Canadian case partly rested on the argument that the legislation covered advertising *services*, not a "good," and therefore that these services were not covered by GATT. Since Canada had made no commitments to advertising under GATS, its representatives believed that the action would be upheld. The essence of the U.S. case was that Canadian cultural protection denied "national treatment" to U.S. *products*, in this case magazines. The WTO decided that Canadian and U.S. magazines were "like goods," not unlike different varieties of beer that would compete with each other. The panel dismissed arguments about the cultural distinctiveness of Canadian magazines. Rather, the market view that magazines and their contents are simply tradable commodities prevailed, and the Canadian measure was ruled to violate national treatment by subjecting foreign split-run magazines to a tax not incurred by domestic magazines (see Herman 1998; Sinclair 2000).

In response Canada attempted to use the criminal law (Bill C-55) to discourage prospective Canadian advertisers in U.S. magazines. The Americans responded, this time under NAFTA provisions, threatening $300 million in trade sanctions unless the legislation was withdrawn. Steel products were to bear the brunt of the sanctions. (The minister responsible for Bill C-55, Sheila Copps, represented Hamilton East, a constituency heavily dependent for its prosperity on the steel industry.) The legislation was withdrawn and U.S. magazines would now have access to Canadian advertising markets. In addition, the Canadian government relaxed Canadian ownership requirements on magazines.

However, Canada has also used the WTO to challenge regulatory efforts by other states. Canada was a party, with the United States, to a challenge to the EU ban on meat imports from livestock that had been treated with growth-promoting hormones. Canada conducted its own scientific assessment of the growth-promoting hormones in question and concluded they were safe if used in accordance with good veterinary practices. The European ban on beef raised with growth hormone was based on a precautionary scientific principle: the hormone had not been proven to be safe, and the WTO required absolute proof. The EU lost its case when the WTO overturned the precautionary principle on which it was based. The United States and Canada have taken steps to retaliate against the EU given the EU's subsequent failure to implement the WTO ruling.

Despite its unwillingness to implement the WTO's decision on hormone-treated meat, there are signs that the EU is backing off in other health protection cases. Press reports in the summer of 2000 indicated that the European Commission had become convinced that a European moratorium on approval of new types of genetically modified foods was unsustainable. Environmental and consumer activists, responsible for the moratorium in the first place, will oppose the move, which is fast-tracked to avoid debate at the national level: "In an unprecedented step the commission is lobbying for the new directive to became law as soon as it is endorsed in Brussels, and thinks it cannot afford to wait for individual countries to implement its provisions, a process that could take as long as two years" (Osborne 2000).

Another WTO ruling declared the Canada-U.S. Auto Pact to be in violation of Canada's WTO obligations (see Sinclair 2000: 42–43). Measures designed to promote investment, purchasing and employment commitments on the part of automakers aiming to sell products in Canada were ruled in violation of various sections of GATT. Moreover, some of the measures were ruled in violation of GATS' national-treatment and most-favoured-nation obligations (on appeal, the GATS most-favoured-nation decision was reversed, but the national-treatment decision was not appealed).

Clearly these examples indicate that WTO provisions have the potential to trump a variety of other policy areas in which governments have been active, such as food safety, industrial policy and culture.

The Proposed Multilateral Agreement on Investment

The draft Multilateral Agreement on Investment expanded upon many of the intrusions upon national autonomy that appear in the WTO and NAFTA agreements. The scope of the proposed MAI was extremely broad, because it was designed to cover "every kind of asset owned or controlled, directly or indirectly, by an investor."[14] While some items might be exempted by a country making "reservations," such reservations were to be subject to "standstill" (meaning existing laws could not be strengthened or extended) and "rollback" provisions. The rollback provisions would involve periodic reviews of reservations with the clear intent of inducing further liberalization: "Combined with standstill, it [rollback] would produce a 'rachet effect,' where any new liberalization measures would be 'locked-in' so they could not be extended over time" (OECD 1997: 153). The breadth of the definition of investment (which includes real estate, natural resources, portfolio investments and stocks, all forms of intellectual property and the products of an investment) created a correspondingly broad basis on which a country's regulations or laws could have been challenged.

The MAI established various rights for investors. First, under the national-treatment and most-favoured-nation rules, investors were to be treated equally in relation to other investors. As Public Citizen (1998) notes, however, while these are "the bedrock principles of economic integration in international law," in one respect the MAI did represent a "stunning departure." This was the MAI's application of those concepts to the market-entry phase of foreign investment: "The vast majority of bilateral investment treaties apply national treatment only after an investor has been granted market access—the right to establish an investment—the MAI confers upon investors a general right of entry in all economic sectors. This feature essentially eliminates the border of the nation-state for the purposes of investors."

Second, the MAI would have imposed *absolute* obligations on governments in their treatment of investors (Lalumiere, Landau and Glimet

1998).The prohibition on performance requirements, for example, would apply to domestic firms as well as foreign investors. The prohibitions included domestic content or purchasing requirements, import-export balancing, local sales and mandatory exporting requirements (OECD 1997: ch. III). Chapter IV of the proposed MAI guaranteed investors "security or protection from a variety of risks such as expropriation without adequate compensation or losses incurred as a result of war or civil strife." In addition, signatory countries would guarantee that "all payments relating to investors of another party may be freely transferred into and out of its territory without delay and in a freely convertible currency" (OECD 1997: ch. IV.4).

Third, investors received the right to take governments to one of several international tribunals, with the choice of tribunal lying with the investor (OECD 1997: ch. V). One of these options was the arbitration services of the International Chamber of Commerce—an astonishing option, given that it would have subordinated sovereign states to the decision-making of a private agency and one of the most vigorous supporters of neo-liberal trade liberalization. A factor cited in the French government's eventual move to withdraw from the MAI negotiations was the imbalance between the rights of "investors" (that is, corporations) and the rights of nations (Lalumiere et al. 1998).

Finally, countries would have been committed to a twenty-year "lock-in" if they had signed the MAI. After five years they could give notice of withdrawal, but they would still be bound to honour all MAI obligations for a future fifteen years—a "unique" provision among international agreements (Public Citizen 1998: 14).

Constraining the State, Freeing Investors
The Uruguay Round of GATT negotiations produced "deeper" integration of member countries whose reach into each other's affairs was extended far beyond the tariff issues of earlier agreements. In pursuit of the elimination of indirect barriers to trade, more areas of domestic policy-making became subject to scrutiny and challenge.

A number of policies that can be important ingredients of industrial strategy, such as domestic content regulations on foreign investment or the use of Crown corporations for non-commercial, public policy reasons, are now prohibited or rendered much more difficult to use. Measures regulating national security, health, or the environment may be permitted as long as they are the least trade-restrictive measures that could accomplish their purpose. The WTO agreements apply to provincial and local governments, and the federal government undertakes to pursue reasonable measures to secure compliance, even where these are matters of provincial jurisdiction.

Certain provisions of the General Agreement on Trade in Services apply to all services, regardless of whether the federal government has made a commitment to have them covered by the GATS. Other provisions apply only when a government has made commitments to list a given service. Apparent exemptions under GATS, such as services delivered under the exercise of government authority, are narrowly circumscribed by other conditions that must apply if the exemption is to hold. The GATS agreement is lodged in a framework that includes a commitment to successive rounds of further liberalization of trade in services. Thus the boast of the WTO (1999: 1) that "its requirements will from the beginning necessarily influence national domestic laws and regulations" appears all too likely to be true. Since the GATS covers service delivery in any one of a number of modes it effectively serves as a labour-mobility agreement with guaranteed right of entry for certain service personnel. It is also an investment treaty that grants right of entry to establish branches, from which services may be delivered.

The North American Free Trade Agreement inhibits the development of an industrial policy in Canada, other than free trade, by prohibiting a wide range of performance requirements that might be imposed on foreign or even domestic investors. These include domestic content, domestic purchasing, export or foreign exchange quotas, and technology transfer requirements. In addition, the agreement outlaws the use of a two-price system in energy products to stimulate domestic economic activity and curtails the ability to restrict energy exports. The ability of crown corporations to pursue non-commercial behaviour is eliminated by language requiring them to follow commercial considerations. Granting private corporations the ability to sue governments for perceived expropriation of profit-making opportunities threatens to unleash ongoing harassment against governments' efforts to regulate industrial activity for health or environmental reasons, among others. The proposed Multilateral Agreement on Investment unveiled a far-reaching agenda to further cripple regulatory actions by the state and enhance investor rights provisions that had made a debut in NAFTA. The MAI also revealed sophisticated measures to lock in place any liberalization that had occurred and to extend the obligations of governments to absolute guarantees to offset risk. Existing obligations—national-treatment and most-favoured-nation status—could be viewed as relative obligations, a commitment to treat investors alike in procedural terms.

The architecture of the international agreements reflects the neo-liberal concern with constraining the state and freeing investors and markets from state intervention. The agreements can only serve to sustain and enhance neo-liberal measures taken at the domestic level. As part of international law, they have a quasi-judicial and quasi-constitutional aura. Thus their impact is harder to challenge. Yet they are as political in construction as any domestic policy.

Notes

1. Certainly, bilateral deviations from multilateral norms existed in the shape of the Defence Production Sharing Arrangements and the Auto Pact Agreement between Canada and the United States. Under the former, Canadian firms were exempted from the Buy America Act and had other avenues into the U.S. military market. These arrangements were made in 1959 after the cancellation of the Avro Arrow program and the resultant abandonment of an independent military advanced-technology effort. Clarkson (1985: 259) comments that this "was part of the price the U.S. was willing to pay for Canadian adherence to continental defence planning." The Auto Pact, 1965, was a shared production and managed trade agreement designed to establish a proportionate relationship between production and sales shares in the auto industry and thus facilitate an integrated, continentally rationalized industry.
2. Wolfe (1996: 693) notes the familiar lineup of social forces around this issue. Business groups are supporters of deep integration, social and environmental groups oppose it.
3. It was Canada, however, which proposed a more formal institutional structure to replace the GATT (Cohn 2000: 214).
4. The NAFTA text can be found in CCH 1994.
5. See NAFTA text, Annex 301.3.
6. See Article 1001.
7. This legal assumption is, from a historical point of view, outlandish. In many countries it was the absence of market provision that led to the construction of widely accessible public services.
8. *United Mexican States* v. *Metalclad Corporation* 2001 BCSC 664 (2 May 2001).
9. According to the *Vancouver Sun*, 4 May 2001, the effect of the judge's ruling was to reduce the award by about $1 million.
10. For accessible accounts, see Shrybman (1999: ch. II); Das 1998.
11. It is still too soon to speculate on the outcome of negotiations for a Free Trade Area of the Americas (FTAA). Ministers attending the Summit of the Americas in Quebec City in April 2001 were scheduled to consider an initial draft of the agreement. Critics of existing trade agreements believed that the draft agreement would replicate and extend the problematic contents of agreements already in place. See Maude Barlow "The Free Trade Area of the Americas," circulated by <ftaa-l@lists.tao.ca>.
12. See the discussion of anti-HIV patents owned by Glaxco corporation in Palast 2000.
13. The argument is contained in a Canadian Centre for Policy Alternatives study,

authored by Matthew Sanger, and reported in the *Globe and Mail* 19 Feb. 2001.

14. This assessment is based on the May 1997 text and commentary (OECD 1997); the quote is from Chapter II.2.

Chapter Six

Canadian Politics 101 Revisited

The parliamentary and federal systems and, since 1982, the Charter of Rights and Freedoms are often considered the three pillars of the Canadian constitution. An exploration of the functions and ramifications of these institutions makes up the core of most introductory courses and texts in Canadian politics. In most cases the complexities of international interdependence and external pressures on domestic political space are left to be introduced in subsequent courses or texts, to be taken up once the basics of Canada's political system have been mastered. For the most part, then, a preliminary analysis of Canadian politics, like that of domestic politics elsewhere, focuses on the idea of a relatively closed political system that enjoys national sovereignty. Pedagogically this has always seemed an unobjectionable manner of proceeding with the study.

Perhaps, though, the existence of "conditioning frameworks" has now advanced to the point where the provisions of international agreements should be integrated into discussions of the Canadian political system from the beginning. Then, too, federal-provincial agreements, such as the Agreement on Internal Trade (AIT), which parallel the international agreements, also have to be taken into account. A key, and related, issue is the extent to which the implementation of neo-liberalism, domestically as well as internationally, has altered the operation of Canadian institutions in ways that require not only a significant modification of how they are addressed in study, but also an explicit recognition of the ideological roots of institutional change.[1]

The Parliamentary System

The inclusion in the British North America (BNA) Act of the statement that Canada was to have a system of government "similar in principle" to that of Britain symbolized the incorporation of a host of practices and constitutional doctrines that continue to mark the Canadian polity. Not the least of these is the parliamentary system, which, in its British iteration, included the doctrine of parliamentary supremacy. Simply put, this doctrine implied that there was no higher political authority than Parliament; hence, within the limits of the physically possible, Parliament could do anything within the territory over which it was sovereign. The concept meant that the courts could only interpret but could not challenge the validity of laws passed by Parliament; that no Parliament could bind its successor; and that an Act of Parliament could override any court decision, if necessary with retroactive effect (Wade and Phillips 1965: ch. 4). In the Canadian case this constitutional principle was modified by federalism, and it became an issue as to which legislature, federal or provincial, was possessed of supremacy in particular cases (Gall 1990:40). In that regard the role of the courts, which must decide this issue, was enhanced in comparison to Britain.

In practice the parliamentary system is characterized by executive dominance (Savoie 1999; Smith 1995: ch. 4), which is, again, due to the constitutional legacy of the British parliamentary system (see Wade and Phillips 1965: ch. 2, 3), as well as to the conventions[2] under which the institutional system actually operates (Heard 1991) and the practice of party discipline, which normally ensures that the cabinet dominates Parliament. The (institutionally misleading) doctrine of parliamentary supremacy is matched by what C.E.S. Franks (1987: 30) calls "parliament centred rhetoric" but "an executive centred structure of political power."

The entanglement of federal and provincial jurisdictions and the development of co-operative and executive federalism—in essence nego- tiations between the executive branches of the federal and provincial governments—further enhanced tendencies to executive dominance. Once intricate agreements were worked out at intergovernmental meet- ings, they were very difficult to alter after the negotiators returned to home base. The lines of accountability became quite blurred under this system, which further diminished the possibility for effective legislative scrutiny of the executive.

Indeed, some analysts have noted an even further concentration of power within the executive. In this view the cabinet is almost as redundant as Parliament in terms of real decision-making power, which now resides overwhelmingly with the prime minister.[3] According to Donald J. Savoie (1999: 362), the full picture is:

> Cabinet has now joined Parliament as an institution being bypassed. Real political debate and decision-making are increas- ingly elsewhere—in federal-provincial meetings of first ministers, on Team Canada flights, where first ministers can hold informal meetings, in the Prime Minister's Office, in the Privy Council Office, in the Department of Finance, and in international organizations and international summits. There is no sign that the

one person who holds all the cards, the prime minister, and the central agencies which enable him to bring effective political authority to the centre, are about to change things.

The Charter

The addition, in 1982, of the Charter of Rights and Freedoms to Canada's constitutional structure considerably expanded the reach of judicial review. As Peter W. Hogg (1992: 627) notes:

> The addition of the Charter's grounds of judicial review has proved to be a substantial expansion of judicial review. Not only are Charter cases much more numerous than federalism cases, they are also more policy-laden. This is because many of the Charter rights are expressed in exceedingly vague terms, and all of the rights come into conflict with other values respected in Canadian society. The result is that judicial review under the Charter involves a much higher component of policy than any other line of judicial work.

The Charter itself is neutral regarding federal and provincial authority, and limits the powers of both in certain respects. But it may be centralizing in the indirect sense of serving as a focus of national identity.[4] The diminution of legislative power is offset by Article 33, which provides that certain of the Charter rights (expression, legal and equality) may be overridden provided that Parliament or a provincial legislature enacts a law containing an express declaration that, notwithstanding the Charter, the law applies. However, for democratic rights, mobility, language rights and sexual equality there is no override provision. Parliamentary supremacy is thus removed from a limited range of rights; it continues, but subject to certain procedural guidelines, in others.

As a result of the Charter the judicial branch—the Supreme Court of Canada in particular—certainly expanded its role. Supporters of the Charter welcome the protection of minority rights that it brings; sceptics and critics bemoan the legalization of Canadian politics that has resulted and suspect that in the end the rich, who, as John A. Macdonald once said in justifying property qualifications for Senate membership, have always been a minority, will benefit the most from its provisions (see Mandel 1994).

Even given their increased role as a result of the Charter, the role of the courts has been diminished by the new generation of international economic agreements as important issues have been transferred to the jurisdiction of international trade panels under various agreements. Under NAFTA, for example a binational review panel has displaced judicial review of most issues concerned with dumping and anti-dumping, at least for disputes between NAFTA members. The investment chapter of the agreement gives foreign investors the option of pursuing disputes through domestic courts or arbitration panels. Whereas under the anti-dumping and countervailing subsidies provisions the panels are applying domestic law, under the investment chapter they apply international law and are able to award damages and impose other sanctions (Lemieux and Stuhec 1999: 146).

The courts would seem, then, to be losing authority in an important area of property rights. Investors increasingly have access to special disputes procedures; and questions of whether a government is acting in accordance with its treaty obligations, and whether it is applying Canadian law and regulations appropriately, are matters on which the courts will be bypassed.

Similarly, the WTO refers disputes arising under its jurisdiction to panels when attempts at consultation and mediation fail to produce a mutually acceptable resolution—and the scope of regulations under the WTO expanded dramatically as a result of the Uruguay Round. The organization also strengthened its dispute resolution mechanisms to eliminate delays and the right of the "guilty" party to eventually veto decisions. Enforcement mechanisms include elimination of the regulation or legislation found to be in breach of WTO provisions, payment of compensation or, should the offending party fail to implement panel findings, sanctioned retaliation by the injured party. The WTO has already deemed both Canadian magazine legislation, promoted as defence of Canadian culture, and the Auto Pact to be contrary to WTO provisions. These examples alone indicate the scope of the WTO and its extraterritorial adjudication mechanisms.

In certain respects, though, international economic agreements have expanded the role of (some) Canadian courts and have thus contributed to the increased legalization of Canadian politics. With government procurement now covered by NAFTA, a set of procedures had to be established to apply the rules. Prior to the FTA no formal procedures had existed for dealing with procurement complaints: "Traditionally, Canadian courts have regarded government procurement procedures and decisions as substantially immune from judicial review" (Lemieux and Stuhec 1999: 147). In the creation of a procurement review mechanism, pursuant to FTA/NAFTA provisions, the jurisdiction of the courts was expanded, because the Federal Court could now review decisions of the procurement review mechanisms. This practice contributes to the "legalization" or "judicialization" of the Canadian political system. Also, in cases in which domestic law refers to NAFTA, or is an expression of the NAFTA agreement's provisions, the Federal Court's role will be enhanced (Lemieux and Stuhec 1999: 154).

The Federal System

If the parliamentary aspect of Canada's constitutional system represents a fusion of powers under executive dominance, the federal aspect represents a territorial division of those powers. The two aspects have always involved a degree of tension. In Canada as compared to Britain conflicts over which legislature, federal or provincial, enjoyed supremacy produced a stronger role for the courts, which must settle such issues in the absence of political agreement. However, because *some* legislature must be presumed to have the authority to act, and because the Constitution has never been a watertight instrument that clearly allocates responsibilities to one or the other order of government, the courts, at least until the advent of the Charter of Rights and Freedoms, were always less intrusive than in the United States, where the Constitution can be interpreted as forbidding to any legislature the exercise of certain powers.

The British North America Act of 1867, reflecting the centralist views of its drafters, and notably John A. Macdonald, together with the need of the economic elite of the day for a developmental state, created a strong central government. In particular:

> The division of powers in sections 91 to 95 of the British North America Act gave the federal government control of the great apparatus of development—the massive capital equipment which formed the bones of the economy, from canals and railroads to lighthouses and harbours. With it went the two sovereign functions of government—defence and the currency. Thus the full armed power of the state was centralized (with the obvious lesson of the American civil war in mind) and, what is more important in peacetime, the control of banking, credit, currency and bankruptcy, in fact the whole range of the relationships central to the formation of capital was given to the federal government. The rigid exclusion of the provinces from this field and the use of the power of disallowance to protect the security of contract in the years before 1890 show how important this step was. Its effect was to exclude the provinces from interfering with the direction, control and operation of the economy. (Mallory 1954: 25)

Except for periods of wartime, however, the trend in the development of Canadian federalism has been mostly in a decentralist direction. There are multiple reasons for this, and somewhat different ones for the period after World War II than for the period before it. From the start, the very idea of Canadian federation was contested. The centralist view, which saw the provinces as colonies of the imperial centre in Ottawa, was opposed by those who saw the country as the product of a compact between its provinces. In that view the provinces were prior. They had for various reasons ceded certain powers to a federal government that, however, held them only by discretion of the provinces. Still others saw Confederation as a solemn pact between the two founding (European) nations of Canada. Later versions of this view held that either nation had the right to terminate the arrangement (see Black 1975; Resnick 1991).

Judicial action, in the shape of the decisions of the (U.K.) Judicial Committee of the Privy Council (JCPC), radically decentralized jurisdictions. Some commentators argued that the JCPC gave Canada a "living constitution" and preserved the country (Cairns 1971). For if Canada was a federal society, composed of distinct regions, ethnic groups and provincial identities, the centralist interpretation of the 1867 BNA Act clearly did not express that reality. Others have argued that the JCPC, in tune with the liberal certainties of the age, opposed government intervention in the economy and allocated power to the level of government least likely to be interventionist (Mallory 1954: ch. III). The cases in which they restricted the scope of the "Peace Order and Government" (S.91.1 of the BNA ACT) and trade and commerce (91.2) clauses involved challenges by private-sector interests against government regulation (principally the federal government).[5]

The one exception to the unremitting transfer of power to the provinces was taxation. Financial capacity therefore remained tilted to the federal level. Jurisdiction tended increasingly to be provincial. This is especially true when one takes into account the items of education, health and local government. The significance of these items grew as an urban and industrial society took root, but in 1867 they were considered comparatively unimportant and allotted to the provinces. The potential tension between one level of government having the jurisdiction and the other the potential resources to act came to a head in the Great Depression.

The issue was not resolved during the 1930s. However, the classic bargaining situation between the two levels of government, which the JCPC had inadvertently set up, did take off in the postwar era. The Keynesianism version of national economic management necessarily involved an enhanced role for the federal government. The Supreme Court of Canada, which had replaced the JCPC as Canada's final court of appeal in 1949, began to take a somewhat more sympathetic view of the federal case and of governmental activism in general. The conjunction of these factors created a favourable environment for what became known as "co-operative federalism." This practice involved the use of federal "spending power," through the use of conditional grants, in areas of provincial jurisdiction. The two levels of government agreed on cost-sharing and the details of programs. In effect, though not in formal constitutional terms, a system emerged of shared jurisdiction over many policy areas.

Decentralist trends were not long in reasserting themselves. They found reflection in a declining ratio of federal to provincial spending and some use of opt-outs by provinces, such as Quebec's refusal to participate in the Canada Pension Plan. Among the factors behind these developments was the resurgence of Quebec nationalism and the demand for greater autonomy or even independence, an issue that dominated federal-provincial relations from the Quiet Revolution onwards (see McRoberts: 1997). To this issue was added regional tensions. Often Quebec found common cause with unlikely allies, including Alberta and its demands for greater autonomy. Alberta's dissatisfaction with federalism had old roots—most of Western Canada had a lasting sense of grievance about the effects of the National Policy, such as high transportation costs and high tariffs. When Alberta became the centre of a vibrant oil industry, a policy of "province building" conflicted with Ottawa's attempts to exert some control and extract benefits from energy resources. The clash was apparent even before the National Energy Program led to an escalated and intense conflict that waned only after the Mulroney Conservative government rapidly reduced or abandoned the federal role in the area of energy resources. More generally, some commentators argue that the Alberta case was only an example of a broader phenomenon: strong resource interests were dominant in a number of provinces but had a relatively weak influence in Ottawa. Consequently, devolution of power to the provinces became a major objective of a number of powerful economic interests (Stevenson 1982: ch. 4).

Neo-Liberal Globalization and the Parliamentary System

Canada's state is no longer available to take up as wide a range of purposes as formerly.[6] Neo-liberal globalization, in the shape of involvement in the new generation of multilateral and bilateral trade and investment agreements, has significantly modified the doctrine of parliamentary supremacy.

It is true that Parliament could pass legislation withdrawing from these agreements. In Stephen Krasner's (1999: 9) terms the state does retain international legal sovereignty. Short of that, however, its reach is circum-scribed and constrained in ways that would hardly have been imagined even two decades ago. Specifically, other forms of sovereignty have been diminished. According to Krasner, these forms would seem to include "domestic sovereignty, referring to the organization of public authority within a state and to the level of effective control exercised by those holding authority; interdependence sovereignty, referring to the ability of public authorities to control transborder movements; ... and Westphalian sovereignty, referring to the exclusion of external actors from domestic authority configurations."

This diminishment amounts to a significant if informal constitutional change. But, unlike other rounds of constitutional proposals, the change in the capacity for action of government institutions has largely escaped public attention. Clearly, the Free Trade Agreement and the entry to NAFTA attracted widespread public debate. But the concept that these trade agreements would permanently alter the country's institutional character-istics did not receive a high profile at the time. The accountability and scrutiny of the executive, the powers exercised by Parliament and provin-cial legislatures, and the organization of government and public adminis-tration have been altered.

In a book on NAFTA, international trade lawyer Barry Appleton (1994: 207) concludes:

> The NAFTA represents the supremacy of a classical liberal concep-tion of the state with its imposition of significant restraints upon the role of government. All international trade agreements entail some self-imposed limitation on government authority, for exam-ple governments regularly agree not to increase their tariff rates. However, the NAFTA appears to approach an extreme. It does this by the extensiveness of its obligations which attempt to lock-in one perspective of governmental role for all successive North American governments.

Scrutiny

Within the operation of the parliamentary system, executive dominance continues and may even have been enhanced. Executive participation in international negotiations produces policies that, as far as domestic interests are concerned, are in the realm of "take it or leave it," given the difficulty of altering internationally agreed draft agreements. Essentially this approach is a form of "executive federalism writ large." Like the original version of executive federalism, the practice reduces the account-ability of decision-making to Parliament and the public.

But other forms of scrutiny and accountability are emerging. The international organizations to which the country belongs continuously monitor domestic policy. Conducted in the name of "transparency," this monitoring function exercises a strong "moral suasion" effect—for compliance not only with the letter, but also with the neo-liberal spirit, of the agreements to which Canada is a signatory.

GATT's Uruguay Round established a Trade Policy Review Mechanism (TPRM) under which the trade policies of member nations would be regularly reviewed. The TPRM would "contribute to adherence by all members to rules, disciplines and commitments made … by achieving greater transparency" (Laird 1999: 742). Opinion among scholars is divided on whether this is an enforcement mechanism or simply a tool aimed at improving public policy through providing transparency and information about each state's practices. In general the latter seems more plausible as a legal interpretation, though the impact of moral suasion should not be underestimated.

As a member of the Quad, the inner group of trade ministers representing the United States, the European Union, Japan and Canada—a group that co-operates to set the WTO agenda—Canada is reviewed every two years. For the rest of the WTO members the period between reviews varies from four to six years depending on the member's size as a trading entity. The rule of thumb is that the more important a country is in terms of trade, the more regularly it will be reviewed. A review involves questionnaires sent out by the WTO Secretariat and a site visit by a WTO team. Trade policy reviews were among the first to identify increased use of anti-dumping measures, to detect the use of subsidies, state aids and tax concessions in support of industrial and regional development policies, to draw attention to the importance of domestic deregulation to ensure that the effects of trade reforms were not offset by domestic firms' strategies, and to highlight information regarding services and intellectual property. Through its monitoring role, the trade policy review process has "not only contributed to the fulfilment of commitments in the multilateral trading system but has also contributed to the development of national policies" (Laird 1999: 760).

NAFTA Article 105 furnishes another example of constraint through scrutiny. It provides that each party to the agreement "shall ensure that all necessary measures are taken in order to give effect to provisions … including their observance … by state and provincial governments." This item goes well beyond the equivalent article in the GATT, which calls for all "reasonable measures" to be taken. Further, NAFTA's Chapter 18 contains a number of transparency provisions that open up the policy process to the early intervention of NAFTA partners. Contact points must be established to facilitate communications and provide information regarding matters covered by the agreement. All measures affecting the agreement are to be made public in a timely manner. Under Articles 1802 and 1803, to the maximum extent possible, each party has to provide notification of any proposed domestic measure that might affect the agreement and provide opportunities for a reasonable opportunity to comment. Similarly, whether or not advance notification has been provided, parties must promptly provide information and respond to questions regarding any proposed or actual measure.

Powers

The international agreements, as we have seen (Chapter 5), impose significant restrictions on state capacity. For the most part these restrictions play on the state's capacity to engage in industrial policy. Under the provisions of the treaties, many of the key instruments that might be used— such as performance requirements on foreign investment, discrimination in favour of domestic producers, or using energy resources to support domestic industry—are prohibited. Unexpectedly, as a result of the magazines case, Canada is also prevented from applying some of the measures it has used to promote Canadian culture.

Steps that might be contemplated to protect public health or the environment must now meet the test of being the "least trade-restrictive" possible, and the test will be applied by dispute resolution mechanisms established under the international agreements. Even though social policy retrenchment has been driven by domestic factors, there is a constant danger that control over social services will slip out of national jurisdiction because of the investment provisions under NAFTA and the danger that GATS exemptions, even if the political will exists to sustain them, will be bypassed because of the content of other WTO agreements or NAFTA articles. In a wide range of policy areas, Canadian law-makers must now factor in the terms of complex international agreements or face the possibility that their work will be challenged from outside the Canadian political system. These constraints apply just as much to provincial decision-makers, who have had no control over the negotiation of the international economic agreements, as to Ottawa decision-makers, who have had some control.

The contents of international agreements, ostensibly dealing with trade, have become part of the constitutional system. The agreements function to constrain, direct and "condition" decision-making in areas far removed from trade as traditionally understood.

Public Administration
The institutions of the state have been shrunk, reshaped and redirected. Reducing the role of government generally, and in particular reducing the role of the welfare state, have been central features of neo-liberalism (Marchak 1991: ch. 5; Shields 1990). Economic and social interventionism has been curtailed. But in certain spheres of activity a "strong state" has been retained. Strong government is necessary to uphold authority in society—which clearly implies a role for the state in defence of the institution of private property and, perhaps, of institutions such as the family (see Gamble 1988: 35–36).

   In a useful analysis of the effects of neo-liberalism on the British state, Bob Jessop and a number of collaborators argue that the state machinery had been "Thatcherized" (Jessop et al. 1988). Not all the specifics they discuss apply to the Canadian case, but here too there is a sense in which the state has been "neo-liberalized" to an extent that adds up to a quasi-constitutional or informal constitutional change.

   Peter Aucoin (1995, 1996) notes the centralization of budgetary control, the simultaneous decentralization of operations to maximize efficiency. The professional public service has been circumvented as a source of policy advice in favour of private, often corporate-funded, sources such as think tanks and polling firms. Indeed, the partial privatization of state functions has been a feature of neo-liberal administrative reform. Often described in technocratic terms as the "New Public Management," these techniques have served as a conduit for neo-liberal ideology and transmitted its values and practices into the public sector (Shields and Evans 1998). As Daniel Cohn (1997) argues, the doctrine of new public management not only represents an elite consensus on a changed role for the state, but also carries with it the potential to be a technique for the avoidance of blame for the costs incurred in the transition to a new policy paradigm. Other examples of the paradigm in operation are the tendency to go outside the public service for appointments to key public service positions (Savoie 1995); the contracting out of government services to private suppliers; and the general intrusion of commercial principles into government operations (Pierre 1995; Russell 2000: 43–46).

   These practices have been linked to globalization (Doern, Pal and Tomlin 1996a: 1–2) as well as to domestic neo-liberalism. Summing up these trends, John Shields and B. Mitchell Evans (1998: 81) propose: "The new state being constructed is not simply a leaner state but a state with an entirely different purpose. The redistributive market-controlling dimensions of the Keynesian welfare state are being replaced by a focus on market flexibility and wealth accumulation. The apparatus of the state is being redesigned to facilitate this transition from a regime of national economic management to one of global competitiveness." The public administration of the new "lean state" (Sears 1999) has thus been calibrated with the purposes of neo-liberalism.

Some of the changes produce a different configuration of power and influence among state agencies and government departments. For example, the Department of Foreign Affairs and International Trade (DFAIT) has gained power as a result of the growing international influences on the content of public policy (Doern and Kirton 1996), which is at least partly because it acquired international trade as part of its portfolio in 1982 (see Keenes 1992). That addition established the department in a lead role during the negotiation of the FTA and NAFTA. But the department is also in a position of power because it has always had and continues to have a close relationship with the prime minister, who stands at the centre of the power structure. The prime minister is a participant in many of the more important international meetings and negotiations, and maintains a watching brief over others. DFAIT's ability to maintain a key role in the preparations for such events enhances its position.[7] To some extent DFAIT's need to access the expertise, legislative mandate and resources of other (functional) departments offsets this position, therefore implying a degree of power-sharing. Overall, however, DFAIT, together with other key economic ministries such as Finance, has seen its power grow.

Neo-Liberal Globalization and the Federal System

The operation of the federal system has also been altered by the terms of international agreements. Indeed, the conjunction of domestic neo-liberalism, which has tended to decentralize Confederation, and international economic agreements (themselves infused with neo-liberal content), which tend to enhance the role of the federal government, has been somewhat contradictory.

Some activities, such as placing export restrictions on energy resources, are now denied to either the federal or provincial governments. That these limitations on government were negotiated by the federal authorities, which consulted the provinces (though without treating them as full partners) could be taken as tilting the constitutional balance towards the federal level. The agreements essentially legislate, at least "negatively," in areas of provincial jurisdiction.

As well, the terms of the agreements cast the federal government in a supervisory role vis-à-vis the provinces through the injunction to take "all necessary measures" (NAFTA) or all "reasonable" measures (WTO) to obtain the compliance of subnational governments. The international agreements thus put the federal government in the position of acting as "the domestic enforcer of an international system that reduces the scope and effectiveness of provincial policy instruments" (Robinson 1995: 251).

As a number of analysts have noted, the growing power of transnational corporations and of the markets in which they operate poses a challenge to all nation-states (for example, see Simeon 1991: 47–49). In light of Canada's free-trade "solution" to these pressures, it is worth noting the widespread perception that North American integration and Canadian disintegration are directly correlated (for example, see Simeon 1991: 51; and Mel Watkins, quoted in Norman 1991: 27). The argument essentially is that north-south market integration undermines the carefully (and politically) constructed east-west ties that previously characterized the Canadian political economy. As the bonds loosen, support erodes for mechanisms such as regional economic equalization (Courchene 1992: 127). This shift weakens the already fragile unity of the Canadian state and thereby decentralizes the federation. In that sense, the impact of globalization on Canada's political system has been to increase the constitutional strains generated by Canada's internal and idiosyncratic cleavages based on nations, language and region.[8]

The very process of negotiating the economic agreements further illustrates the contradictory nature of these effects. Despite the impact that free-trade agreements would have on them, the provinces were excluded from the negotiating tables (for example, see Doern and Tomlin 1992: 126–51). However, there were consultations between the federal government and the provinces (see Brown 1991). This particular dimension—consultations—could be read as representing an increase in provincial involvement in international trade—a sort of informal intrastate federalism. Certainly, there was virtually no consultation with the provinces prior to the Tokyo Round of GATT negotiations. In that sense, consultation does represent something new. After Tokyo, as international trade agreements began to bear on topics under provincial jurisdiction, the federal representatives made greater efforts to involve the provinces. However, provincial involvement remains incommensurate with the impact of the agreements, whose greater intrusiveness into services and public-sector programs covers the core activities of provincial states. Despite an increased role through consultations, the provinces are increasingly bound by outcomes into which they had little input. This tendency represents an enhancement of federal power.

There is some debate about the legal ability of the federal government to "speak for" and commit the provinces in this way. In the *Labour Conventions* case of 1937 the JCPC "refused to accept the (federal) treaty implementation power as a constitutional support for interfering in provincial powers. However, this case conflicts with another one, the *Radio* case of 1932, which did seem to give authorities such powers for the purposes of international treaties" (Russell, Knopff and Morton 1989: 104–10). Significantly, no provincial government has sought to challenge federal authority over the implementation of the FTA, NAFTA or WTO. Presumably, in those cases in which provinces are opposed to the neo-liberal globalization agenda pursued by the federal government, the reticence is because the provinces believe the Supreme Court would lean to the *Radio* rather than the *Labour Conventions* precedent. Added to these concerns, of course, is the desire of provincial governments to maintain a welcoming image for investment. To this extent the structural power of capital may also explain provincial hesitancy. The Supreme Court's decisions regarding the "trade and commerce" power, in *Crown Zellerbach* (1988) and *CN Transportation* (1983), indicate some basis for the view that the Supreme Court might overturn or, much more likely, significantly modify the outcome of the *Labour Conventions* case should the opportunity arise (see Richards 1991). In conditions in which trade agreements are based on deep integration, the reach of the federal trade and commerce power might be interpreted as a much more substantial foundation for federal power than was formerly the case.

Reflecting on the willingness of the Canadian government to enter into obligations of this type, Donald S. Macdonald (1998) notes that this tendency is indeed a departure. After the *Labour Conventions* case, federal governments were reluctant to conclude international agreements that would require enforcement within provincial areas of jurisdiction. He argues that, in the NAFTA case, the government was prepared to take that risk because of the inclusion of investment and other provisions within the agreement. Section 91(2) of the BNA Act gave the Parliament of Canada the power to make laws in relation to the "regulation of trade and commerce." To the best of Macdonald's knowledge, no trade agreement had ever been subject to an effective challenge. Given the interdependence of investment and trade, investment measures should withstand challenge. This argument raises the spectre of the "trade and commerce " power becoming the de facto residual clause of the Canadian constitution, though it would be premature to even speculate about the likelihood of that coming to pass.

More generally, some commentators have criticized the argument that globalization and international agreements are leading to decentralization. Ian Robinson (1995), who refers to the agreements as "free-capital" rather than "free-trade," considers that their major impact has fallen on provincial jurisdictions as they have come to focus less on tariffs and more on non-tariff barriers. He notes a progression from pre-Tokyo GATT through Tokyo GATT, the FTA, NAFTA and Uruguay GATT with areas of provincial jurisdiction increasingly invaded. However, given the overlapping jurisdiction for many policy areas in Canada, most of these restrictions have also applied to the federal level of government as well. This fits the case for a diminution of all state power rather than a trend to increased federal authority.

Indeed, the federal authority that has been exercised in recent years has often been of a negative kind. Federal "spending power" built up Canada's welfare state and, with it, federal influence over broad areas of social life. Certainly, the "negative" spending power represented by Ottawa's retrenchment in pursuit of deficit reduction has had an impact. In a sense, such negative power means that the federal government could be influencing the shape of the country just as much as it did with positive spending power in an earlier era. But that power is negatively exercised in that it reduces the capacity of all governments and does not particularly strengthen Ottawa's position vis-à-vis the provinces. Indeed, the power has been used in conjunction with the devolution of jurisdictions, such as active labour-market policy, to the provinces. To be sure, these measures were partly driven by an interpretation of the Quebec referendum that led the federal government to the conclusion that devolution of power would reduce the drive to independence. But they also fitted into neo-liberal notions that, in general, power divided and devolved typically means less exercise of power.

The approach of power-sharing with the provinces, in the shape of a new Social Union, also nicely fits the decentralization model. In Thomas Courchene's (1998) assessment: "Intergovernmentalism/co-determination is here to stay. In our increasingly decentralized federal system we need new instruments.... Unilateral federalism on the socio-economic front is dead. If Ottawa fails to embrace the provinces' initiatives, it may have to deal with unilateral provincialism."

The Agreement on Internal Trade

Proposals to strengthen the economic union have a long history, and they seemed to gather momentum in the 1970s and 1980s (Safarian 1974; Canada 1979; Courchene 1986) when they featured in early rounds of constitutional negotiations. To some extent the idea of a stronger economic union had symbolic status as a building block of national unity (see Chrétien 1980). Although Section 121 of the British North America Act created a free-trade area, it did not prevent the creation of barriers to interprovincial trade. Usually the barriers were the handiwork of provincial governments using devices such as marketing boards or preferential procurement schemes. While these devices are contrary to strict notions of economic efficiency, many provinces saw them as desirable in their efforts to achieve a broad-based, diversified economy. They saw the measures as useful instruments to help achieve that goal. In any case, the inefficiencies that can be attributed to interprovincial trade barriers are minimal (Canada 1985, vol. 3: 135; Lee 2000).

Business groups like the BCNI have been vocal advocates of a stronger Canadian economic union:

> Competitiveness is the foundation upon which an improved social, economic, and environmental order will be built. In the quest for competitiveness, the Canadian political system must be an ally and not an impediment. First and foremost, the reforms to our federal system must ensure that the Canadian common market is established in fact and that the Canadian economic union is strengthened. The free movement of labour, capital, goods and services must be guaranteed under any new constitutional arrangement, and in this area, we see the federal government having a strengthened role. (BCNI 1991: 8)

The federal government took advantage of renewed constitutional discussions in 1991 (in what eventually became the Charlottetown talks) to pursue the issue. In its original 1991 constitutional proposals, the federal government adopted a stance similar to the BCNI's. In the government's view, one of the key ingredients of future competitiveness rested in strengthening the free-market basis of the economic union (Canada 1991: 9).

With some defined exceptions, the core of a proposed article on a stronger Canadian Economic Union was clear: the principle that *no* government can legitimately interfere with market relations would be constitutionally entrenched. After the failure of Charlottetown, the government, urged on by business (*Globe and Mail*, 5 Dec. 1992: B3), but largely ignored by the general public, began trying to achieve a stronger economic union through a new approach to intergovernmental negotiations (Doern and MacDonald 1998: 4).

The influence of pre-existing international trade agreements was felt from the outset. A formal set of negotiation rules for the AIT rested on the GATT, FTA and NAFTA precedents:

> In particular, the most-favoured nation and national treatment provisions of GATT, and the importance of dispute-settlement procedures from the FTA, proved to be most influential in negotiating the Agreement on Internal Trade. The agreement institutes a 'most-favoured-province' provision whereby equivalent treatment for all Canadian persons, goods, services, and investments is established with respect to a 'best-in-Canada' measurement ... and a comprehensive provision for dispute resolution. These provisos mirror those found in the GATT and FTA arrangements and form a significant part of the backbone of the AIT. Indeed, it is clear that the experience with GATT and FTA not only had an impact on the structural aspects of the agreement, but also drove much of the philosophical and rules debate in the negotiations regarding the elimination of barriers to trade. (Doern and MacDonald 1998: 4)

Similarly, these authors observe that what they call "the inward tentacles of NAFTA and GATT and their attendant liberal trade ideas" were in evidence at the sectoral negotiating tables (160).

Despite this impressive ancestry, for some the Agreement on Internal Trade, signed on 1 July 1995, turned out to be a damp squib—a nonbinding political accord that provided little enforcement to back up the stated goals of removing internal trade barriers in Canada (see Howse 1996). This was certainly the position of business groups such as the Canadian Chamber of Commerce (Doern and MacDonald: 1998: 152). Big business pressure had, of course, been a major impetus behind the negotiations (55) and business and neo-liberals expressed some disappointment at the limited results. The weakness of the enforcement mechanisms—the result of provincial resistance to any supervisory powers for Ottawa—stands at odds with the provisions of international trade agreements to which Canada is signatory. According to trade consultant Peter Clark, "The more and more we get into international trade agreements, the onus falls on the federal government to ensure that the provinces play by the rules" (*Globe and Mail* 13 Nov. 1995).

Yet the Agreement on Internal Trade is not without institutional or even constitutional import. Proponents of the AIT tend to depict it as part of the government's "trade agenda" and as having no constitutional implications. The preamble to the agreement itself proclaimed its lack of constitutional effect. Yet opponents, including several provinces, tended to view it in governance terms (see Doern and MacDonald 1998: ch. 1). G. Bruce Doern and Mark MacDonald (1998: 152) observe that the existence of the agreement shapes the decisions of policy-makers. It may enhance the federal government's trade and commerce powers, they say, because its anti-discriminatory provisions have the greatest impact on provincial governments (162–63).

Nor have its results been negligible. Reviewing the agreement after five years, Daniel Schwanen (2000) concludes that while its record in dismantling many internal barriers to trade had been disappointing, the agreement had brought some progress. Negotiations towards mutual recognition agreements regarding qualifications in many professions had made headway, and advances had been made by including the MASH sector (municipalities, academe, schools and hospitals) in the government procurement provisions.

Although many provincial barriers were still in place, Schwanen (2000: 53–54) outlines a number of institutional mechanisms that might gradually advance internal free trade. These include a Code of Conduct on Incentives, designed to prevent one province from attracting or poaching away an industry from another by offering subsidies or incentives; and greater transparency in making provinces report and justify measures taken to promote, for example, regional development. The agreement had also led to the creation of some institutional infrastructure: a cabinet-level Committee on Internal Trade, operating on the consensus model, a secretariat, and a dispute settlement mechanism. Investors can have standing in pursuing complaints against governments subject to certain restrictions, including a screening device to weed out illegitimate complaints.

Pressure for a new round of negotiations to improve the AIT is partly driven by the goal of achieving consistency with the provisions of international trade agreements (Doern and MacDonald 1998: 164). Proponents of a strengthened AIT focus on broader coverage, stronger enforcement and improved investor standing to facilitate the corporate challenge of regulations (Lee 2000: 1, 10–11). In its present non-binding condition the AIT has limited impact on the operation of federalism. Marc Lee (2000) argues, though, that changes such as including health and education in the agreement could weaken existing exemptions in NAFTA and the WTO through the operation of the provincial equivalent of national treatment.

National Policies and International Agreements

Many state capacities used in the national policies under which Canada developed are now beyond the reach of governments. Others are under threat from the intrusion of international economic agreements that reach further and further into the realm of domestic policy. Tempting as it is to attribute these developments to forces that states cannot resist, it seems all too apparent that the resort to international agreements to reinforce domestic neo-liberalism was a political strategy that found favour with capital.

Some states, notably the United States and Britain, pushed this agenda vigorously. Given the preferences of Canadian capital it is unsurprising that the Canadian state has been a willing participant in constructing the new architecture of the global economy. To cast Canada as a victim or unwilling participant in these processes is simply incorrect. If the new institutional mechanisms remain in place long enough there will, of course, be an air of inevitability in retrospective accounts of the final quarter of the twentieth century. However, the victory of neo-liberalism did not seem assured until the late 1980s or early 1990s. Its hegemony so far has been of quite short duration, a factor that may explain the great desire by its adherents to lock it into place as thoroughly and quickly as possible.

Resort to these methods can be seen as a sign of weakness rather than a sign of strength—especially given the clear signs of significant resistance to neo-liberal globalization and the initial victories that have been won by its opponents.

Notes

1. Neo-liberal influence is expressed in three ways: in the content of the key international agreements (chapter 5); in the Agreement on Internal Trade (AIT), which has been referred to as the fifth pillar of Canada's constitutional system (Doern and MacDonald 1998); and in NAFTA, which constitutes the fourth pillar, in its role of shrinking the Canadian state (see Shields and Evans 1998) or drastically redefining it (see McBride and Shields 1993, 1997).
2. Rules and understandings of constitutional behaviour, which are considered binding by and upon those in the political system, which may be recognized but not enforced by the courts.
3. Savoie (1999: ch. 4), playing with the old concept of the prime minister as first among equals or *primus inter pares,* heads his chapter on Prime Ministerial Power "*Primus:* There Is No Longer Any *Inter* or *Pares.*"
4. For a critical review of this argument, see Knopff and Morton 1992.
5. In the 1980s the Supreme Court moved to qualify or modify the results of the JCPC with respect to the "Peace Order and Good Government" and trade and commerce clauses. See Richards 1991.
6. It is important not to exaggerate the purposes for which the state was used in

the past. Nevertheless, its constitutional room for action was wider in the past than it has recently become.

7. Doern and Kirton (1996: 262) refer to this as the "sherpa" role. "Sherpas" are the staff who prepare the way and do the necessary groundwork for summit meetings of political leaders (see Putnam and Bayne 1987).

8. For an insightful review of the interconnections between continentalism and the constitution, see Laxer 1992.

Chapter Seven

Paris to Seattle and Beyond

"The most insidious doctrine of our age is that we have no choices."
—Will Hutton (1997: 54)

Although some supporters of neo-liberal continue to refer to it in triumphalist tones, there is no doubt that its air of inevitability and invincibility has been shaken in recent years. A series of economic crises have drawn attention to its volatility, and a number of political challenges have exposed a potential Achilles' heel—neo-liberal globalization's lack of legitimacy.

The forces promoting neo-liberal globalization have enjoyed remarkable success. Domestic retrenchment has seen a reduction of the state's impact on society. In Canada this is especially true of the federal state's visibility. The welfare state has become increasingly residual in nature. The effectiveness of a number of Keynesian-era "automatic stabilizers" for the economy has been drastically reduced. The prime example is the shrunken employment insurance system. Privatization and deregulation have transferred a number of important industries to the private sector. And private-sector rhetoric and practices either infuse or are creeping into what remains of the public sector. Even the health-care system, long a source of social support and national pride, has seen its funding erode and the presence of private health-care provision expand.

These victories, though, may well prove to be pyrrhic in the event of a downturn in the U.S. economy, on whose prosperity the Canadian economy is more reliant than ever before. Should the neo-liberal chickens come home to roost as a result of such a turn of events, they will find fewer perches in the shape of domestic stabilizers or supports available to moderate the impact of global volatility.

Nor will the capacity of the state to devise new strategies be as available as in the past. In the 1930s a constitutional impasse between federal and provincial jurisdictions contributed to the country's inability to respond to the impact of economic depression. Given the content of the international economic agreements in which Canada is an enthusiastic participant, it is not fanciful to suggest that they may play a similar role in any future economic downturn. The FTA and NAFTA were successful in kick-starting languishing negotiations for a new GATT agreement. The resulting agreement was designed to produce deeper integration of member countries, enhancing their ability to challenge other states' initiatives that do not conform to market criteria. For the first time, services were exposed to these pressures. One of the most important features of the GATS was a continuing commitment to negotiations aimed at producing progressive liberalization of the service sector. Despite the damage caused to the broader World Trade Organization agenda in Seattle, the GATS negotiations are proceeding as planned. And other negotiations, like those for a Free Trade Area of the Americas, also continue. The capacity of the state has been reduced by the impact of these quasi-constitutional international agreements. The effects in a future crisis, whether economic, ecological or political, remain to be seen.

Globalization and the Discontented

In Canada, and increasingly elsewhere, the rise of domestic and global neo-liberal policies was always contested. There are some indications, such as successful opposition to the proposed Multilateral Agreement on Investment and the postponement of a new round of World Trade Organization negotiations following the Seattle events of 1999, that opposition is increasing and becoming more effective. In April 2001 the Quebec City Summit of the Americas was the scene of further confrontations. The summit took place behind a four kilometre concrete and steel fence "wall." Entry into "Fortress Québec" was strictly controlled, and the perimeter was protected by the use of tear gas, rubber and plastic bullets, water cannons and arrests and detention. Despite the increasing familiarity of these scenes, they can still bring a sense of shock to peaceful demonstrators. One of them, Jessica Johnston, wrote:

> When I left for Quebec City, I did not know what to expect from the experience. I did not expect to be repeatedly attacked by my own government. I did not expect to see friends (both those I know and those I don't) arrested for no reason. I did not expect to be stalked by tear gas-wielding storm troopers for three days. I did not expect to develop a fear of police. I did not expect to feel, at the end of the weekend that I had been through a war.... On Saturday afternoon, we were involved in a peaceful protest where people sat in an intersection facing rows of riot police who were positioned at the mouth of an alley. The protestors had their masks

off and were talking to the police, trying to tell them that they were not our enemy, that we were all on the same side. Then, after a while, the storm troopers advanced without warning and threw tear gas canisters into the sitting crowd. I sincerely did not expect them to do this. It was shocking to me that they would open fire on a group of people who were not only peaceful, but who had also deliberately made themselves vulnerable to display their peaceful intent.[1]

Sinclair Stevens, a former Conservative cabinet minister under Brian Mulroney, provided a similar view. In a *Globe and Mail* article (24 April 2001), "A Police State in the Making," Stevens reported incidents he had witnessed of police firing tear gas and rubber bullets at peaceful protestors. He concluded: "Some will say that a handful of demonstrators got out of hand and forced the police to take collective action. I can't agree. The police action in Quebec City, under orders from our government, was a provocation itself—an assault on all our freedoms."

Popular protest against free-trade agreements has a lengthy history in Canada. The Free Trade Agreement stimulated a coalition of new and old social movements, a "popular sector," which, despite its defeat on that issue, remained a forceful opponent of new globalization initiatives. Over the years national coalitions in many countries have found ways to form international networks that exchange information, ideas and strategies and co-ordinate their efforts.

The emergence of the popular sector as a significant actor in Canadian politics has been well chronicled (see Ayres 1998: ch. 2, 3). The activity drew upon organizing traditions developed in the peace, women's, labour and nationalist movements of the 1960s and 1970s. The free-trade issue, which in the Canadian context signified that globalization would take a continentalist form, meant that an ostensibly economic program was infused with issues of national identity. This enabled opposition to a host of U.S. policies and images to spill over into the economic arena. Hostility to continental integration, at least in an overt form, has had a long and respectable tradition in the Canadian polity. In addition, these were the years of the Reagan-induced arms race. Memories of U.S. policy in the Vietnam War were still fresh. Under Reagan, the Americans were experimenting with neo-liberal economic policies and social conservatism. For many Canadians it was an unattractive mixture. Provincial versions of this approach, such as the B.C. Social Credit government's restraint program (see Magnusson 1984), led to a major mobilization of opposition forces and the development of a cross-sectoral coalition. Labour at the national level was also becoming more interested in economic nationalism and coalition-building (Smith 1992).

The new popular-sector coalitions were unable to prevent the enactment of the Free Trade Agreement or NAFTA,[2] but still the movement and its component organizations survived. For example, the Council of Canadians grew in the 1990s to a membership of well over 100,000. In the process it moved from a centre-left position to "a much more radical critique of the prevailing forces of globalization and of government straightjacketing because of the unregulated power of transnational corporations" (Ayres 1998: 139). The Canadian Centre for Policy Alternatives, a research organization that provided a number of useful reports during the struggle over free trade, went from strength to strength, establishing a number of provincial branches in addition to its national office.

An important asset derived from the unsuccessful campaigns of the 1980s and 1990s was knowledge of trade and investment issues. Trade and investment treaties are complicated documents. Normally the advantages of expertise would be on the side of the architects of the treaties. Because of their prior experience, Canadian anti-globalization activists were able, for example, to move quickly and provide almost instant analyses of the draft Multilateral Agreement on Investment, when its contents became known. The Internet provided a communications mechanism that was similarly fast and effective (Cohen 2000: 202). A series of events, full-page advertisements and press conferences focused public attention on the issue. But, as Elizabeth May (1998: 33) described it, after pointing out the effectiveness of groups like the Council of Canadians and Polaris Institute in publicizing and forging a coalition against the MAI: "It was the essence of the agreement itself which spawned its own opposition. No amount of funding or organizing could have prompted the virtually spontaneous uprising of public opposition to the MAI which has swept Canada in the last year." In short, the secrecy surrounding the MAI and its contents, once known, were widely viewed as illegitimate.

That aspect points to a weakness in the entire neo-liberal globalization project. For thinkers like Max Weber, legitimacy in modern societies is derived principally from the operation of legal-rational rules and procedures. Decisions and rules are viewed as legitimate, and are therefore obeyed and accepted, based on the nature of the procedures used in making them. To confer legitimacy the procedures must be seen as binding on both rulers and ruled and as carrying no necessary implications in terms of outcomes. The international organizations responsible for implementing neo-liberal globalization lack legitimacy in this sense. They are remote, secretive and technocratic. Outcomes are written into the text of the agreements they administer. Their membership consists of national states that are only presumed to be speaking for their societies. The extension of an aura of democratic control from the national level to the international level is problematic.

Indeed, the contents of the agreements that international organizations administer increasingly diminish national states' autonomy. This exposes the emptiness of democratic control—more and more aspects of decision-making are excluded from the purview of national (and democratic) politics. This leaves the concepts of state and, behind it, popular sovereignty, increasingly threadbare. Sovereignty, for many states, seems confined to the formal legal right to withdraw from the international economic agreements that have diminished state (and democratic) capacity.

Moreover, the neo-liberal ideology that underpins international economic agreements has long depicted states as creatures of "special interests." States are seen as impediments to the expression of the consumer sovereignty that would be expressed in free markets, but for the intrusions and distortions produced by state policy. The domestic and international components of neo-liberalism thus stand in a state of tension. The principal building block from which international organizations must derive legitimacy is diminished by the provisions of international economic agreements, and undermined by the content of the ideology on which the organizations are built. Having delegitimized the state the actors then find it difficult to draw upon the state, as the signatory of the international agreements, to legitimize the agreements themselves. In this sense neo-liberal globalization suffers from a legitimacy deficit.

Recognition of this dilemma has prompted several important international organizations to try to establish direct links with non-governmental organizations. For their own purposes, many non-governmental organizations (NGOs) are interested in trying to influence international organizations, and engagement is one possible route to influence. For their part, the international organizations find NGO involvement useful for two reasons: they are a source of detailed knowledge that might usefully influence policy implementation decisions, and in some cases they might even be recruited as delivery agents; and involving NGOs might serve to consolidate public support behind organizational goals (see O'Brien et al. 2000:18–22; Goodman 2000:49). International organizations are attempting to reach out into international civil society to create legitimacy for themselves through consultation and incorporation procedures.

Faced with opportunities to interact directly with international organizations, NGOs themselves are considering their options and alternatives. For some the invitation to be consulted may be unproblematic. For others the invitation brings further dilemmas. Engagement may lead to influence ... or co-optation; rejectionism may lead to effective opposition ... or marginality. These dilemmas are not unlike those faced by labour movements in contemplating involvement in neo-corporatist institutions (see McBride 1995).

One option that some NGOs are pursuing is the inclusion in international agreements of social, labour or environmental charters or side agreements designed to moderate the market-centred liberalization characteristic of the agreements.[3] The efforts of the International Confederation of Free Trade Unions (ICFTU) to incorporate a labour rights clause in the World Trade Organization provides a noteworthy example (see O'Brien et al. 2000: ch. 3). The attraction for the ICFTU seems to be that the WTO has enforcement capability, while the International Labour Organization, where traditionally such efforts have been focused, does not. Michelle Swenarchuk (2000) provides a detailed critique of the likely ineffectiveness of this strategy and the muddled thinking that lies behind it. Nonetheless, the basic concept continues to exert an attraction for some NGOs, and the possibilities for co-option in pursuit of such initiatives, with legitimacy-building effects for some international organizations, are obvious.

The enhanced ability of anti-globalization NGOs to communicate, educate and organize was made apparent in Seattle in November/December 1999. Major street demonstrations took place there, in the face of police violence. A variety of teach-ins, street theatre events, rallies and educational activities accompanied the demonstrations and attempted blockades of the WTO's meeting places. Some NGOs operated on the "inside," meeting with, briefing and lobbying officials and delegations. The target was the biannual ministerial meeting of the World Trade Organization, and the aim was to prevent a new round of trade liberalization negotiations from being launched. The imagery of the colourful street events, of the impressive unity between tens of thousands of protestors from many countries, drawn from a wide variety of sectors of society—labour, environmentalists, women, students, seniors—and of the police violence was carried worldwide on television. The symbolic importance was heightened by the location from which the images were coming: the global heartland. The opening session of the WTO was shut down, the meetings were disrupted and no agreement was reached on the launch of a new round of negotiations.

WTO officials were quick to claim that the demonstrations had no impact on the failure to launch a new round (Bleyer 2000; Clarke 2000).

Rather, they attributed the failure to divisions between North and South delegates and between the United States and the European Union. There were in fact serious cleavages along these fault lines, and these might have been sufficient in themselves to postpone the launch of a new round. However, the suggestion that civil disobedience and disruption on such a scale had no impact appeared to be an ill-advised public relations strategy. Anti-globalization forces claimed a victory in Seattle, a victory all the more sweet because of the location and because it followed so fast upon the heels of the successful campaign against the Paris-based OECD's MAI initiative.

Further large demonstrations and events followed in Washington D.C. in April 2000 (meeting of the World Bank and International Monetary Fund); Melbourne in September 2000 (World Economic Forum's Asia Pacific Economic Summit); Prague (IMF/World Bank summit); and Quebec City (Summit of the Americas). All were large and involved aggressive policing, arrests and confrontations. These events represent one of many faces of opposition to globalization.

In a review of the alternatives to globalization, Wiseman (2000a: 214) notes:

> Globalization involves a range of contradictory and contested processes which provide new possibilities as well as threats to communities concerned with promoting relationships of diversity, solidarity and sustainability. The central challenge is to recognize the connections between action at different levels of geographical space and political governance and to think and act at a range of levels without losing our grounding in the particularity of our own home place.[4]

This point leads to discussion of a range of activities, some of them active and underway and others that require activation. Not all international organizations are deeply implicated in neo-liberal globalization. Some, such as the United Nations and some of its specialized agencies, play a countervailing role and could certainly do so more effectively if reformed and revitalized (see Weiss and Carayannis 2001). An impressive international civil society has already arisen. Its possibilities for challenging the certainties and rigidities of neo-liberalism may still be in their infancy. In any event they are far from exhausted. Many examples of local initiatives exist and can be built upon, including efforts at community economic development involving co-operatives and community enterprises. Resistance often emerges locally—in peace, environmental, consumer protests, and assertions of rights by First Nations peoples (Goodman 2000; Wiseman

2000a).The resistance is often focused on single targets, but can have global implications. Labour has an often-underestimated capacity for challenging the forces of globalism (see Lipsig-Mummé 2000;Wiseman 2000b). Some of the participants in the anti-globalization movements dismiss the state as a possible source of solutions to current problems. For some this is a result of acceptance of the globalization thesis: that the state has lost power in upward, downward and sideways directions. As a consequence of this belief, some activists and critics see the best sites for action as being supranational or local, and in the sphere of civil society rather than public institutions. Others focus on the deeply disappointing record of reformist governments in the global era. For some, the example of Blair's "Third Way" in Britain indicates the limits of state action under social-democratic leadership.[5]

States have contributed to this perception. They have been implicated in the construction of neo-liberal globalization and have undermined their own legitimacy through reducing their relevance to citizens. This is most noticeable in the domestic area, where welfare state cutbacks, privatization and deregulation and associated policies have shrunk the state in comparison to markets and corporations. It is increasingly obvious in the international arena, where states have sacrificed sovereignty on the altar of free trade.

Nonetheless, states continue to matter. They remain the largest political units in which any semblance of democracy can be practised. Any loss of power by the state is therefore a lost opportunity for democratic decision-making. As the action of France indicated, when it terminated its involvement in the MAI negotiations and brought the whole process to a halt, states can sometimes function as allies of and on behalf of civil society—global or national—though admittedly such examples are, to date, few and far between. After all, states, in collaboration with business interests (which are an element of civil society), were architects of neo-liberal globalization, and the road from Paris to Seattle and beyond was constructed by state as well as NGO action.

The state's role as "a midwife for globalization" was above all else driven by domestic actors—a point that is equally true of the Anglo-U.S. role in engineering the liberalization of capital movements (Helleiner 1996: 194) and of the paradigm shift in Canada that involved embracing the domestic neo-liberalism and continental integration that emanated from Canadian capital. To alter the Canadian state's role as a booster of globalization requires political action that would reduce the influence of the domestic power bloc that has promoted the globalization agenda. While this is no easy task, it would seem to be a necessary step. It could not occur in isolation from the variety of existing anti-globalization activities and forces nor would it seem that these forces could substitute for action at the national level.

Within living memory two major paradigm shifts in the Western liberal democracies have managed to change state policies, in dramatic fashion. The first was the rise of Keynesianism; the second was the shift to neo-liberalism, first domestically and later in the global arena. Undoubtedly many factors are involved in paradigm shifts of this magnitude. One necessity would seem to be a crisis or sense of crisis[6] that undermines confidence in the dominant approach; another would be the existence of an alternative paradigm within which the problem can be framed differently and alternative solutions developed; and a third would be a period of political struggle whose outcome determines which paradigm emerges victorious. Neil Bradford (1999: 53) argues that already "the economic failures of neo-liberalism and the continued political opportunism of governing parties are creating space for questioning Canada's authoritative policy ideas." He notes that neo-liberalism lacks the solid base of "cross-class or inter-regional accommodation that underpinned Keynesianism." This shortcoming renders it vulnerable to other forces and may well account for the powerholders' project of institutionalizing it through incorporation in international agreements.

Certainly, the neo-liberal globalization paradigm delivers a more volatile economic environment than its predecessor. The 1990s saw deep recessions and several financial crises. One does not have to be a purveyor of doom and gloom to predict that other, perhaps more serious, conditions will arise in the future. In Canada the most likely scenario is that a significant and prolonged downturn in the U.S. economy will trigger a period of re-assessment and provide an opening for a substantial paradigmatic debate. Mindful of the adage that economic forecasting was invented to make astrology look respectable, I will make no attempt to predict exactly when this state of affairs might come to pass. But unless the laws of economics have indeed been overcome by the revolution in technology, it is safe to say that a pressing downturn will occur in the not-too-distant future—though with unpredictable duration and length. The key question is: when this scenario does materialize, will there also be in place an alternative paradigm capable of structuring policy options and political choices?

Alternatives: A Different Paradigm

According to Bradford (1999: 51–52) a considerable amount of the work to build an alternative economic paradigm has already been done. In his view the paradigm must also be connected to a program of institutional changes to democratize decision-making. Institutions that have permitted the implementation of neo-liberalism "by stealth" require modification. Among the contributions to an alternative paradigm, Bradford lists the alternative budgets that at the federal level (for example, Cho!ces/CCPA 2000), and increasingly also in the provinces, have been providing detailed economic policies in recent years. The key policy goal in this work is full employment, and the researchers and activists involved propose a range of innovative policy and institutional instruments to achieve that goal.

Alternative priorities in the context of the international economic agreements—in which nation-states are induced to follow common rules based on neo-liberal priorities, with the centrality of "trade" and anything that might be "trade-related" (surrogate terms for the pursuit of profit)— would also include full employment, as well as goals of equality, equity, ecological sustainability, support for national culture, public or collective provision of key services such as education or health or future concerns that have yet to emerge. The policy changes of domestic neo-liberalism have already dismantled the broad welfare states that responded to the desire for security and stability, and they have promoted privatization and the primacy of the market in place of public institutions that reflected a desire for some "goods" to be provided publicly and collectively. Arguably, the dismantling exercise was made easier by the bureaucratic characteristics of the welfare states that were established in the postwar period (see Albo 1993).

At least two big issues need to be challenged if we are to shake off the constraints of politically constructed globalization. The first is the notion of a common set of rules, that "one size fits all." The second is the nature of those rules. Marjorie Cohen (2000: 207) notes: "Uniform economic policies greatly aid the mobility of capital, but they also greatly undermine the power of people to shape societies in their own interests." In essence two principles are in conflict: democracy and the capacity for people to collectively choose alternative futures; and the right of capital to an ideal profit-maximization environment. So far, the former has given way to the latter. Of course, neo-liberal globalization does not abolish democracy entirely; it merely confines it to areas that, from the point of view of international capital, are inconsequential. Reasserting the right of people to make choices in areas of consequence implies a recognition of economic pluralism (see Cohen 2000: 206–7).[7]

There is no shortage of possible alternative models. To take just one example, Arthur McEwan (1999) outlines the main features of an alternative strategy for *democratic* economic development and demonstrates at length that such a program could be realized, based on solid assumptions.

The elements of McEwan's program includes expanded social programs, especially in health, education and environmental preservation. The measures he proposes would be financed primarily by increased progressive taxes. Reallocation of resources from military and wasteful spending would also make a contribution. While McEwan believes that the room for differential tax rates is greater than the conventional wisdom would concede, the program he proposes would require the establishment of financial and capital controls that would deprive private investors of easy-exit options and enable the market to be harnessed to the needs of society. The controls would provide incentives for private investors to operate in socially useful ways. Other fundamental aspects of the package are greater recognition of the value of local production and, in some countries, land reform. The state would play an important role; but McEwan places an emphasis on democracy—stressing that in the absence of effective pressure from civil society, state commitment might falter. The public commitment to the project could also fall by the wayside if an overly bureaucratic delivery on the part of the state were to alienate the population from a package of policies designed to further social needs.

Any firm move to restore democratic capacity and achieve economic pluralism must include the re-regulation of capital; and while the opposition to globalization is manifest at all levels from the local to the global, any tendency to bypass the national level in the effort to re-regulate capital would be counterproductive. James Crotty and Gerald Epstein (1996) make the case that postwar capital controls were an essential ingredient of prosperity. The replacement of Keynesianism by neo-liberalism has involved substantial deregulation, not least as far as capital mobility is concerned. The rise of globalization, following the Keynesian era, was accompanied, Crotty and Epstein (1996: 129) argue, by uncertainty and volatility that

> was fuelled by waves of global hot money flooding into and then out of different countries, dramatically raising exchange rate instability. This ocean of hot money has grown ever wider and deeper as financial sectors inflate, technological and organizational innovation accelerates, and most importantly, the ability and the desire of governments to control these flows erodes.

Since the demise of Bretton Woods the pressure from finance capital for financial deregulation has been unremitting. It amounts, as William Greider (1997: 33) describes it, "to the politics of escape. Transnational commerce, either to defend against price competition or to maximize the potential returns of globalization, has aggressively campaigned over three of four decades to free itself from various social controls imposed by home governments." Greider's explanation, though, leaves out one vital component of this successful campaign—it was heavily dependent on the support of important states, particularly the United States and Britain (Helleiner 1996, 1994).

When discussion of capital controls occurs, a number of questions usually arise. Are they necessary to achieve alternative economic ends? Are they technically feasible? Are they politically achievable?

The main reason for thinking that the reimposition of capital controls is necessary in an alternative economic approach is that capital mobility alters the domestic balance of power to the disadvantage of labour and the state. Capital undercuts labour's ability to apply pressure in certain situations to the extent that capital can plausibly threaten disinvestment. The state's ability to play even a relatively autonomous role is diminished to the extent that policy can be held hostage to currency speculation, adverse comment by international credit rating agencies like Moody's and Standard and Poor's, and capital flight. Capital controls are really about reducing the power of capital.

Those who consider that some re-regulation of capital would be a good thing hold different opinions regarding its feasibility—technical or political. Ideally, such controls should operate in an internationally co-ordinated way, but the push to achieve the consensus to implement such controls faces major obstacles. By default, the next most likely option is for individual nation-states or groups of nations to take action co-operatively. The difficulties of that course, under the prevailing political climate, are significant but arguably not insuperable. Certainly Malaysia, in the midst of an international financial crisis, seems to have used capital controls to good effect.

In the context of proposals to regulate or tax financial flows, critics most often raise technical objections. Among measures advanced to reduce the vulnerability of states to volatility in financial flows is the so-called Tobin tax. Named for Nobel laureate James Tobin, who advanced the idea in the 1970s, it is actually one of a range of measures that would have the effect of subjecting international financial flows to greater control and hence augmenting the capacity of national governments to pursue economic policies suitable to their own circumstances. The original idea was for a tax on all foreign-currency exchange transactions, but further discussions in the literature have led to the expansion of the concept to cover all forms of financial transactions occurring in global markets (see Michalos 1997: 15–22 for a review). Computer technology, in a context of financial liberalization has created enforcement problems for such a tax as far as financial flows are concerned. Companies could evade the tax and enforcement would probably not reach 100 percent effectiveness. But much the same can be said about domestic taxes, and they continue to be levied. Even in this area, as Alex C. Michalos's (1997) review concludes, the obstacles may be more political than technical. Nor would complete international unanimity be necessary. A Tobin-type tax, if agreed to by most of the world's largest economies, could certainly be imposed on the rest. Other ingredients of a package of measures to control financial flows could be enacted nationally—including withholding taxes to discourage specu-lative investment, stronger disclosure requirements, better accounting standards and a variety of prudential measures (Langmore 1995; Akyuz 1995). Separate exchange rates for trade and capital purposes and quanti-tative restrictions are other possibilities (Crotty and Epstein 1996:139–42).

In the area of direct investment the political factors loom largest. By definition investments in the real economy are less mobile than financial transactions. But in particular places a wide variety of possible measures exist or have existed, ranging from ownership restrictions to protected sectors, imposition of performance requirements and review mechanisms to assess the public benefit if any. Most of them are targeted by investment treaties, or treaties containing investment measures such as NAFTA and GATS. Implementation of capital controls would involve halting further extensions of such treaties, and rolling back provisions already in existence. This would require a renegotiation or withdrawal from the most intrusive of these agreements, which would no doubt be a difficult task. But because the logic of deregulated capital mobility is clearly incompatible with the realization of a variety of other economic and social priorities, the task is a necessary one.

All paradigms must popularize "big" ideas and counterpose them to the tendencies that have dominated political discourse in recent decades. Such ideas need to be attractively presented, at various levels of sophisti-cation for various audiences, and speak to people's real needs. Neo-liberal discourse stresses efficiency, flexibility and freedom. The reality for all too many people has been insecurity and stress. And, as we have seen, freedom has been constrained by the democracy-limiting provisions of interna-tional economic agreements.

Human security, broadly defined, should serve the alternative para-digm as an antidote to the insecurity characteristic of neo-liberalism. At its core, human security implies that the well-being of people—expressed through employment, social welfare, political democracy, health, culture and education—should be the prime objective of political life. While the means by which its various expressions might be achieved may be imperfectly understood, it is clear that different means can be used in different places and at different times. No single ideological straitjacket—like the one represented by neo-liberalism—can fit all situations. As a result, it is important to counterpose democratic decision-making, and the opportunity to make different choices, to the restrictive certainties of the global trade and investment regime that is now taking shape. Nor can the narrow self-interest of any one sector of society—like the affluent beneficiaries of neo-liberal globalization—be privileged over the general well-being of the population.

Espousing the goal of human security does not imply a rejection of change. Indeed, negotiated change and adaptability may be the price of achieving security, just as security forms the best foundation for change. Since the logic of neo-liberal globalization is to provide security and risk-avoidance—for investors only—one major difference between neo-liberalism and an alternative paradigm centres around "who" will be secure and protected from risk.

The promise of security and greater equality was at the core of the full-employment and welfare state policies of the postwar era. No evidence existed that significant numbers of people rejected these goals. Rather, in the conditions of the 1970s it became unclear as to how the goals could be met. In those circumstances a concerted ideological offensive against the Keynesian old order gradually succeeded in convincing enough people that Keynesianism was unsustainable. The available evidence indicates that the ideological offensive was less successful in convincing Canadians that the goals were invalid. An important part of an alternative paradigm would consist of demonstrating—to the criterion of plausibility rather than absolute proof, since the adoption of all paradigms requires some kind of "leap of faith"—that security and greater equality are still attainable goals. They are certainly goals that cannot be met through the free market, which by its very nature must produce uneven, irregular results and thus insecurity and greater inequality. This means in turn that markets will have to be regulated and controlled to produce security/equality outcomes rather than efficiency/flexibility outcomes. Strong government at the nation-state level is an absolute essential if such regulatory measures are to be set in place.

The other "big idea" that is central to the alternative paradigm is democracy in its fullest sense. The assertion that one narrowly defined set of social values should prevail over any alternative and the attempts to constitutionalize that preference by foreclosing future options render neo-liberal globalization deeply suspect in its attachment to democracy.

The themes of economic pluralism and capital controls must be central to any efforts to reversing the prevailing power relationships, to establish human security and entrench democratic choice. Other means, in brief, would include implementing new forms of protectionism designed to ensure that inferior social and environmental standards do not lead to employment insecurity in countries with higher standards (see Albo 1996: 273–75; Lang and Hines 1993). The possibilities inherent in the Keynesian notion of the "socialization of investment" (Seccareccia 1995)—an approach never implemented in the Keynesian era—point to another avenue of ensuring that adequate social benefits flow from investment. Measures to redistribute work may also be useful in achieving full employment (Albo 1996: 277–79).

All of these measures would not only involve confrontations with the preferred policies of capital but also require the renegotiation of existing international trade agreements. But in one sense this would simply return Canada to its traditional role of using a modicum of state activism to offset the least acceptable outcomes of unregulated markets. The step would also provide Canada with the opportunity to grow into the actual middle-power foreign policy role that many have long tried to invent for it. This time the role could be exercised not on the margins of world politics, as a helpful fixer for dominant powers but, rather, in a crucial area for improving the human condition—as an advocate of democracy, choice and economic pluralism that promotes human security and equality for all peoples. In this vision, markets must conform to social and political priorities—and not the reverse.

Notes

1. Jessica Johnston, writing in *The Peak* (Simon Fraser University) 7 May 2001.
2. On NAFTA, see Ayres 1998: ch. 6.
3. See O'Brien, Goetz, Scholte and Williams 2000 for a number of other examples of these initiatives.
4. Wiseman is careful to include the nation-state as an important site of anti-globalization action.
5. For an excellent analysis putting Blairism into its recent historical context, see Panitch and Leys 1997. In Canada, the failures of NDP provincial governments, particularly that in Ontario (see McBride 1996) have had a discouraging impact on those who might formerly have favoured reformist political parties as contributors to social change.
6. I use the term "sense of crisis" because I find it difficult to believe that the inflation "crisis" of the 1970s was truly comparable to the events of the 1930s.
7. As Cohen (2000: 207) notes, a case for economic pluralism can be made from within the logic of orthodox trade theory, as well as from outside it.

References

Akyuz, Yilmaz. 1995. "Taming International Finance." In Michie and Grieve Smith 1995.

Albo, Gregory. 1993. "Democratic Citizenship and the Future of Public Management." In Albo, Langille and Panitch 1993.

_____. 1996. "Canadian Unemployment and Socialist Employment Policy." In Dunk, McBride and Nelsen 1996.

Albo, Gregory, and Jane Jenson. 1997. "Remapping Canada: The State in an Era of Globalization." In Clement 1997.

Albo, Gregory, David Langille and Leo Panitch (eds.). 1993. *A Different Kind of State? Popular Power and Democratic Administration*. Toronto: Oxford University Press.

Allen, Bob. 1999. *Why Kosovo? Anatomy of a Needless War*. Ottawa: Canadian Centre for Policy Alternatives.

Appleton, Barry. 1994. *Navigating NAFTA: A Concise User's Guide to the North American Free Trade Agreement*. Scarborough, Ont: Carswell.

Applied Research Branch, Strategic Policy, Human Resources Development Canada. 1998. *An Analysis of Employment Insurance Benefit Coverage*. Ottawa: HRDC.

Archer, Keith, Roger Gibbins, Rainer Knopff and Leslie A. Pal. 1995. *Parameters of Power*. Toronto: Nelson.

Armit, Amelita, and Jacques Bourgault (eds.). 1996. *Hard Choices or No Choices: Assessing Program Review*. Toronto: Institute of Public Administration of Canada.

Atkinson, Michael M., and William D. Coleman. 1989. *The State, Business and Industrial Change in Canada*. Toronto: University of Toronto Press.

Aucoin, Peter. 1995. *The New Public Management: Canada in Comparative Perspective*. Montreal: Institute for Research on Public Policy.

_____. 1996. "Political Science and Democratic Governance." *Canadian Journal of Political Science* (December).

Axford, Barrie. 1995. *The Global System: Economics, Politics, Culture*. Oxford: Polity.

Axworthy, Lloyd. 1997. "Canada and Human Security: The Need for Leadership." *International Journal* 52, 2.

Ayres, Jeffrey M. 1998. *Defying Conventional Wisdom: Political Movements and Popular Contention against North American Free Trade*. Toronto: University of Toronto Press.

Bairoch, Paul. 1996. "Globalization Myths and Realities." In Boyer and Drache 1996.

Bank of Canada. 1997. *Review.* Ottawa (Summer).

Banting, Keith G. 1987. *The Welfare State and Canadian Federalism.* 2nd ed. Montreal: McGill-Queen's University Press.

Banting, Keith, George Hoberg and Richard Simeon (eds.). 1997a. *Degrees of Freedom: Canada and the United States in a Changing World.* Montreal: McGill-Queen's University Press.

_____. 1997b. "Introduction." In Banting, Hoberg and Simeon 1997a.

Battle, Ken, and Sherri Torjman. 1996. "Desperately Seeking Substance: A Commentary on the Social Security Review." In Pulkingham and Ternowetsky 1996.

Bennett, Colin J. 1991. "What is Policy Convergence and What Causes It?" *British Journal of Political Science* 21,2.

Bercuson, David Jay (ed.). 1977. *Canada and the Burden of Canadian Unity.* Toronto: Macmillan.

Berger, Suzanne. 1996. "Introduction." In Berger and Dore 1996.

Berger, Suzanne, and Ronald Dore (eds.). 1996. *National Diversity and Global Capitalism.* Ithaca, N.Y.: Cornell University Press.

Black, David, and Claire Turenne Sjolander. 1996. "Multilateralism Re-constituted and the Discourse of Canadian Foreign Policy." *Studies in Political Economy* (Spring).

Black, David, and Heather Smith. 1993. "Notable Exceptions? New and Arrested Directions in Canadian Foreign Policy Literature." *Canadian Journal of Political Science* (December).

Black, Edwin. 1975. *Divided Loyalties: Canadian Concepts of Federalism.* Montreal: McGill-Queen's University Press.

Bleyer, Peter. 2000. "The Other Battle in Seattle." *Studies in Political Economy* (Summer).

Bliss, Michael. 1972. "Dyspepsia of the Mind." In Macmillan 1972.

Bluestone, Barry, and Bennett Harrison. 1982. *The Deindustrialization of America.* New York: Basic Books.

Bolaria, B. Singh (ed.). 1991. *Social Issues and Contradictions in Canadian Society.* Toronto: Harcourt Brace Jovanovich.

Boltho, Andrea. 1996. "Has France Converged on Germany? Policies and Institutions Since 1958." In Berger and Dore 1996.

Bottomore, Tom, and Robert J. Brym (eds.). 1989. *The Capitalist Class: An International Study.* New York: Harvester Wheatsheaf.

Boyer, Robert. 1996. "The Convergence Hypothesis Revisited: Globalization but Still the Century of Nations?" In Berger and Dore 1996.

Boyer, Robert, and Daniel Drache (eds.). 1996. *States Against Markets: The Limits of Globalization.* London: Routledge.

Bradford, Neil. 1998. *Commissioning Ideas: Canadian National Policy Innovation in Comparative Perspective.* Toronto: Oxford University Press.

_____. 1999. "The Policy Influence of Economic Ideas: Interests, Institutions and Innovation in Canada." *Studies in Political Economy* (Summer).

Brebner, John Bartlet. 1947. *North Atlantic Triangle: The Interplay of Canada, the United States and Great Britain.* New Haven, Conn.: Yale University Press.

Britton, John, and James Gilmour. 1978. *The Weakest Link.* Ottawa: Science Council of Canada.

Brodie, Janine. 1989. "The 'Free Trade' Election." *Studies in Political Economy* 28 (Spring).

_____. 1990. *The Political Economy of Canadian Regionalism.* Toronto: Harcourt Brace Jovanovitch.

_____. 1996. "New State Forms, New Political Spaces." In Boyer and Drache 1996.

Brodie, Janine, and Jane Jenson. 1988. *Crisis, Challenge and Change: Party and Class in Canada Revisited.* Ottawa: Carleton University Press.

Brooks, Stephen, and Alain-G. Gagnon (eds.) 1990. *Social Scientists, Policy, and the State.* New York: Praeger.

Brooks, Stephen, and Andrew Stritch. 1991. *Business and Government in Canada.* Scarborough, Ont.: Prentice-Hall.

Brown, Douglas M. 1991. "The Evolving Role of the Provinces in Canadian Trade Policy." In Brown and Smith 1991.

Brown, Douglas, and Julia Eastman with Ian Robinson. 1981. *The Limits of Consultation: A Debate Among Ottawa, the Provinces and the Private Sector on Industrial Strategy.* Ottawa: Science Council of Canada.

Brown, Douglas, Earl H. Fry and James Groen (eds.). 1993. "States and Provinces in the International Economy Project." In *States and Provinces in the International Economy.* San Francisco, Calif. and Kingston, Ont.: Institute of Governmental Studies Press, University of California, and Institute of Intergovernmental Relations, Queen's University.

Brown, Douglas M., and Murray G. Smith (eds.). 1991. *Canadian Federalism: Meeting Global Challenges?* Kingston: Queen's University Institute of Intergovernmental Relations.

Brown, Wilson B., and Jan S. Hogendorn. 2000. *International Economics in the Age of Globalization.* Peterborough, Ont.: Broadview.

Brym, Robert J. (ed.). 1985. *The Structure of the Canadian Capitalist Class.* Toronto: Garamond Press.

_____. 1989a. "Canada." In Bottomore and Brym 1989.

_____. 1989b. "The Great Canadian Identity Trap: Implications for the Comparative Study of Class and Power." *Canadian Journal of Sociology* 14, 4.

Bull, Hedley. 1977. *The Anarchical Society.* New York: Columbia University Press.

Burbach, Roger, and William I. Robinson. 1999. "Globalization as Epochal Shift." *Science and Society* 63, 1.

Burke, Mike. 2000. "Efficiency and the Erosion of Health Care in Canada." In Burke, Mooers and Shields 2000.

Burke, Mike, Colin Mooers and John Shields (eds.). 2000. *Restructuring and Resistance: Canadian Public Policy in an Age of Global Capitalism.* Halifax: Fernwood.

Burke, Mike, and John Shields. 1999. *The Job-Poor Recovery: Social Cohesion and the Canadian Labour Market.* Toronto: Ryerson Social Reporting Network.

Business Council on National Issues (BCNI). 1985. *Canadian Trade, Competitiveness and Sovereignty: The Prospect of New Trade Agreements with the United States.*

Ottawa.

_____. 1991. *Canada and the 21st Century: Towards a More Effective Federalism and a Stronger Economy*. Ottawa.

Cairns, Alan. 1971. "The Judicial Committee and Its Critics." *Canadian Journal of Political Science* 4.

Cameron, Duncan, and Daniel Drache. 1988. "Outside the Macdonald Commission: Reply to Richard Simeon." *Studies in Political Economy* 26 (Summer).

Cameron, Duncan, and Mel Watkins (eds.). 1993. *Canada under Free Trade*. Toronto: Lorimer.

Campbell, Robert M. 1987. *Grand Illusions: The Politics of the Keynesian Experience in Canada, 1945–75*. Peterborough, Ont.: Broadview.

Canada. 1945. Department of Reconstruction. *Employment and Income with Special Reference to the Initial Period of Reconstruction*. Ottawa: Queen's Printer.

_____. 1979. Task Force on Canadian Unity. *A Future Together*. Ottawa: Minister of Supply and Services

_____. 1985. *Report: Royal Commission on the Economic Union and Development Prospects for Canada*. 3 vols. Ottawa: Minister of Supply and Services.

_____. 1991. *Canadian Federalism and Economic Union: Partnership for Prosperity*. Ottawa: Minister of Supply and Services.

Canada. Department of Industry, Trade and Commerce. 1978. *A Report by the Second Tier Committee on Policies to Improve Canadian Competitiveness*. Ottawa.

Canada. DFAIT. 2000. *Opening Doors to the World: Canada's International Market Access Priorities*. Ottawa.

Canada 21 Council. 1994. *Canada and Common Security in the Twenty-First Century*. Toronto: Centre for International Studies.

Canadian Council on Social Development. 1990. *Canada's Social Programs Are in Trouble*. Ottawa.

Canadian Labour Congress (CLC). 1999. *Left out in the Cold: The End of UI for Canadian Workers*. Ottawa.

Canadian Union of Public Employees (CUPE). 2000. *Who's Pushing Privatization*. Ottawa.

Carroll, William K. 1986. *Corporate Power and Canadian Capitalism*. Vancouver: University of British Columbia Press.

_____. 1989. "Neoliberalism and the Recomposition of Finance Capital in Canada." *Capital and Class* 38.

CCH. 1994. NAFTA Text. Chicago.

Cerny, Philip. 2000. "Globalization and the Competition State." In Stubbs and Underhill 2000.

Chase-Dunn, Christopher, Yukio Kawano and Benjamin D. Brewer. 2000. "Trade Globalization since 1795: Waves of Integration in the World System." *American Sociological Review* February

CHO!CES/Canadian Centre for Policy Alternatives. 2000. *Alternative Federal Budget 2000*. Ottawa: Canadian Centre for Policy Alternatives.

Chorney, Harold. 1988. *Sound Finance and Other Delusions: Deficit and Debt Management in the Age of Neo-Liberal Economics*. Montreal: Concordia University.

Chossudovsky, Michel. 1997. *The Globalization of Poverty: Impacts of IMF and World Bank Reforms.* Penang, Malaysia: TWN.

Chrétien, Jean. 1980. *Securing the Economic Union in the Constitution.* Ottawa.

Clarke, Tony. 2000. "Taking on the WTO: Lessons from the Battle of Seattle." *Studies in Political Economy* (Summer).

Clarkson, Stephen (ed.). 1968. *An Independent Foreign Policy for Canada?* Toronto: McClelland and Stewart.

_____. 1985. *Canada and the Reagan Challenge.* Toronto: Lorimer.

_____. 1991. "Disjunctions: Free Trade and the Paradox of Canadian Development." In D. Drache and M. S. Gertler (eds.), *The New Era of Global Competition: State Policy and Market Power.* Montreal: McGill-Queens University Press.

_____. 1993. "Constitutionalizing the Canadian–American Relationship." In Cameron and Watkins 1993.

Clarkson, Stephen, and Christina McCall. 1990. *Trudeau and Our Times. Vol. 1. The Magnificent Obsession.* Toronto: McClelland and Stewart

_____. 1994. *Trudeau and Our Times. Vol. 2. The Heroic Delusion.* Toronto: McClelland and Stewart

Clement Wallace. 1975. *The Canadian Corporate Elite: An Analysis of Economic Power.* Toronto: McClelland and Stewart.

_____. 1989. "Debates and Directions: A Political Economy of Resources." In Clement and Williams 1989.

_____ (ed.). 1997. *Understanding Canada: Building on the New Canadian Political Economy.* Montreal: McGill Queen's University Press

Clement, Wallace, and Glen Williams. 1989a. "Introduction." In Clement and Williams 1989b.

_____ (eds.). 1989b. *The New Canadian Political Economy.* Montreal: McGill-Queen's University Press.

Coburn, David, Carl D'Arcy, Peter New and George Torrance (eds.). 1987. *Health and Canadian Society: Sociological Perspectives.* 2nd ed. Markham, Ont.: Fitzhenry and Whiteside.

Cohen, Marjorie. 1991. "Exports, Unemployment, and Regional Inequality: Economic Policy and Trade Theory." In Drache and Gertler 1991.

_____. 2000. "Rethinking Global Strategies." In McBride and Wiseman 2000

Cohn, Daniel. 1997. "Creating Crises and Avoiding Blame: The Politics of Public Service Reform and the New Public Management in Great Britain and the United States." *Administration and Society* 29, 5.

Cohn, Theodore H. 1992. "Canada and the Ongoing Impasse over Agricultural Protectionism." In Cutler and Zacher 1992b.

_____. 2000. *Global Political Economy: Theory and Practice.* New York: Longman.

Cohn, Theodore H., Stephen McBride and John Wiseman (eds.). 2000. *Power in a Global Era.* London: Macmillan.

Cooper, Andrew F. 1997. *Canadian Foreign Policy.* Scarborough, Ont.: Prentice-Hall.

Cooper, Andrew, Richard Higgot and Kim Richard Nossal. 1993. *Relocating Middle Powers: Australia and Canada in a Changing World Order.* Vancouver:

University of British Columbia Press.

Courchene, Thomas J. 1986. *Economic Management and the Division of Powers. Studies of the Royal Commission on the Economic Union and Development Prospects for Canada.* Vol. 67. Toronto: University of Toronto Press.

———. 1992. *Rearrangements.* Oakville, Ont.: Mosaic Press.

———. 1998. *Renegotiating Equalization: National Polity, Federal State, International Economy.* Toronto: C.D. Howe Institute.

———. 2000. "A Mission Statement for Canada." *Policy Options* (July/August).

Cowling, Keith, and Roger Sugden. 1987. *Transnational Monopoly Capitalism.* New York: St. Martin's.

Craven, Paul, and Tom Traves. 1979. "The Class Politics of the National Policy 1872–1933." *Journal of Canadian Studies* 14.

Cox, Robert. 1994. "Global Restructuring: Making Sense of the Changing International Political Economy." In Richard Stubbs and Geoffrey Underhill 1994.

Cross, Michael S., and Gregory S. Kealey (eds.). 1984. *Modern Canada, 1930s to 1980s.* Toronto: McClelland and Stewart.

Crotty, James, and Gerald Epstein. 1996. "In Defence of Capital Controls." In Panitch 1996.

Cutler, A. Claire, and Mark W. Zacher. 1992a. "Introduction." In Cutler and Zacher 1992b.

——— (eds.). 1992b. *Canadian Foreign Policy and International Economic Regimes.* Vancouver: UBC Press.

Dales, John. 1966. *The Protective Tariff in Canada's Development.* Toronto: University of Toronto Press.

Das, B.L. 1998. *An Introduction to the WTO Agreements.* Penang: Third World Network

David, Charles-Philippe, and Stephane Roussel. 1998. "'Middle Power Blues': Canadian Policy and International Security after the Cold War." *American Review of Canadian Studies* Spring and Summer.

Deakin, Nicholas. 1987. *The Politics of Welfare.* London: Methuen.

Dewitt, David, and John Kirton. 1983. *Canada as a Principal Power: A Study in Foreign Policy and International Relations.* Toronto: Wiley.

Di Matteo, Livio. 2000. "The Determinants of the Public-Private Mix in Canadian Health Care Expenditures, 1975–1996." *Health Policy* 52.

Dobbin, Murray. 1998. *The Myth of the Good Corporate Citizen: Democracy under the Rule of Big Business.* Toronto: Stoddart.

Dobuzinskis, Laurent. 2000. "Global Discord: The Confusing Discourse of Think Tanks." In Cohn, McBride and Wiseman 2000.

Doern, G. Bruce (ed.). 1981. *How Ottawa Spends Your Tax Dollars: Federal Priorities 1981.* Toronto: Lorimer.

——— (research coordinator). 1985. *The Politics of Economic Policy* Vol. 40 *Royal Commission on the Economic Union and Development Prospects for Canada.* Toronto: University of Toronto Press.

Doern, G. Bruce, and John Kirton. 1996. "Foreign Policy." In Doern, Pal and Tomlin 1996b.

Doern, G. Bruce, and Mark MacDonald. 1998. *Free Trade Federalism: Negotiating the Canadian Agreement on Internal Trade.* Toronto: University of Toronto Press.

Doern, G. Bruce, Allan M. Maslove and Michael J. Prince. 1988. *Public Budgeting in Canada: Politics, Economics and Management.* Ottawa: Carleton University Press.

Doern G. Bruce, Leslie A. Pal and Brian W. Tomlin. 1996a. "The Internationalization of Canadian Public Policy." In Doern, Pal and Tomlin 1996b.

_____. 1996b. *Border Crossings: The Internationalization of Canadian Public Policy.* Toronto: Oxford University Press.

Doern, G. Bruce, and Bryne B. Purchase (eds.). 1991. *Canada at Risk? Canadian Public Policy in the 1990s.* Toronto: C.D. Howe Institute.

Doern, G. Bruce, and Brian W. Tomlin. 1992. *Faith and Fear: The Free Trade Story.* Toronto: Stoddart.

Drache, Daniel. 1986. "The Macdonald Commission: The Politics of Neo-Conservatism." *Atkinson Review of Canadian Studies* 3, 1 (Spring).

_____. 1991. "Harold Innis and Canadian Capitalist Development." In Laxer 1991.

Drache, Daniel, and Meric S. Gertler (eds.). 1991. *The New Era of Global Competition: State Policy and Market Power.* Montreal and Kingston: McGill-Queen's University Press.

Dubuc, Alfred. 1966. "The Decline of Confederation and the New Nationalism." In Russell 1966.

Dunk, Thomas, Stephen McBride and Randle W. Nelsen (eds.). 1996. *The Training Trap: Ideology, Training and the Labour Market.* Halifax: Fernwood.

Dyck, Rand. 1993. *Canadian Politics.* Toronto: Nelson.

Eayrs, James. 1975. "Defining a New Place for Canada in the Hierarchy of World Powers." *International Perspectives* (May/June).

Economic Council of Canada. 1984. *Western Transition.* Ottawa: Minister of Supply and Services.

Eden, Lorraine, and Maureen A. Molot. 1993. "Canada's National Policies: Reflections on 125 Years." *Canadian Public Policy* (September).

Epstein, Gerald. 1996. "International Capital Mobility and the Scope for National Economic Management." In Boyer and Drache 1996.

Esping-Andersen, Gosta. 1983. "After the Welfare State." *Public Welfare* (Winter).

Evans, B. Mitchell, Stephen McBride and John Shields. 2000. "Globalization and the Challenge to Canadian Democracy: National Governance under Threat." In Burke, Mooers and Shields 2000.

Evans, Peter. 1997. "The Eclipse of the State? Reflections on Stateness." *World Politics* 50, 1.

Evans, Peter B., Dietrich Rueschemeyer and Theda Skocpol (eds.). 1985. *Bringing the State Back In.* Cambridge: Cambridge University Press

Evans, Robert G., Morris L. Baber, Steven Lewis, Michael Rachlis and Greg L. Stoddart. 2000. *Private Highway, One-way Street: The Deklein and Fall of Canadian Medicare.* Vancouver: UBC Centre for Health Services and Policy Research.

Fillmore, Nick. 1989. "The Big Oink: How Business Won the Free Trade Battle."

This Magazine (April).

Finance Canada. 1995. *Budget 1995.* Fact Sheets 9. Ottawa.

Finlayson, Jack A. 1985. "Canadian Business and Free Trade." *International Perspectives* (March/April).

Finlayson, Jack A., and Stefano Bertasi. 1992. "Evolution of Canadian Post-War International Trade Policy." In Cutler and Zacher 1992b.

Forbes, Ernest R. 1986. "Consolidating Disparity: The Maritimes and the Industrialization of Canada during the Second World War." *Acadiensis* 15.

Fossum, John Erik. 1997. *Oil, the State, and Federalism: The Rise and Demise of Petro-Canada as a Statist Impulse.* Toronto: University of Toronto Press.

Fowke, Vernon. 1967. "The National Policy—Old and New." *Canadian Journal of Economics and Political Science* 18.

Franks, C.E.S. 1987. *The Parliament of Canada.* Toronto: University of Toronto Press.

Fuller, Colleen. 1996. "Doctoring to NAFTA." *Canadian Forum* (June).

Gagnon Alain-G., and James P. Bickerton (eds.). 1990. *Canadian Politics: An Introduction to the Discipline.* Peterborough, Ont.: Broadview.

Gall, Gerald L. 1990. *The Canadian Legal System.* Calgary: Carswell.

Gamble, Andrew. 1988. *The Free Economy and the Strong State.* London: Macmillan.

Garrett, Geoffrey. 1998. *Partisan Politics in the Global Economy.* Cambridge: Cambridge University Press.

Germain, Randall D. (ed.). 2000. *Globalization and Its Critics.* London: Macmillan.

Gill, Stephen. 1995. "Globalisation, Market Civilisation and Disciplinary Neoliberalism." *Millennium* 5, 24 (Winter).

Glazebrook, G.P. de T. 1966. *A History of Canadian External Relations.* 2 vols. Toronto: McClelland and Stewart.

Gobeyn, Mark. 1995. "The Decline of Macro-Corporatism: A Rejoinder." *Governance* 8, 3 (July).

Gollner, Andrew B., and Daniel Salée (eds.). 1988. *Canada under Mulroney: An End-of-Term Report.* Montréal: Véhicule Press.

Gonick, Cy. 1987. *The Great Economic Debate.* Toronto: Lorimer.

Gonick, Cy, Paul Phillips and Jesse Vorst (eds.). 1995. *Labour Gains, Labour Pains: 50 Years of PC 1003.* Socialist Studies, vol 10. Winnipeg/Halifax: Society for Socialist Studies/Fernwood.

Goodman, James. 2000. "Transnational Contestation: Social Movements Beyond the State." In Cohn, McBride and Wiseman 2000.

Goodwin, Craufurd D.W. 1961. *Canadian Economic Thought: The Political Economy of a Developing Nation, 1814–1914.* Durham, N.C.: Duke University Commonwealth-Studies Center and Duke University Press.

Gotlieb, Allan. 1987. "Canada: A Nation Comes of Age." *Globe and Mail* 29 October: A7.

Grabb, Edward G. 1990. "Who Owns Canada? Concentration of Ownership and the Distribution of Economic Assets, 1975–1985." *Journal of Canadian Studies* 25 (Summer).

Grady, Patrick, and Kathleen Macmillan. 1999. *Seattle and Beyond: The WTO Millennium Round.* Ottawa: Global Economics Ltd. and International Trade

Policy Consultants Ltd.

Graham, Katherine A. (ed.). 1990. *How Ottawa Spends.* Ottawa: Carleton University Press.

Granatstein, J.L., and Norman Hillmer. 1991. *For Better or for Worse: Canada and the United States to the 1990s.* Toronto: Copp Clark Pitman.

Grant, George. 1965. *Lament for a Nation.* Toronto: McClelland & Stewart.

Gray, Herb et al. 1971. *Foreign Direct Investment in Canada (Gray Report).* Ottawa: Supply and Services Canada.

Graz, Jean-Christophe. 2000. "The Future of Seattle and Back." *Studies in Political Economy* (Summer).

Greider, William. 1997. *One World, Ready or Not.* New York: Simon and Schuster.

Grinspun, Ricardo, and Robert Kreklewich. 1994. "Consolidating Neoliberal Reforms: 'Free Trade' as a Conditioning Framework." *Studies in Political Economy* 43.

Guest, Dennis. 1987. "World War II and the Welfare State in Canada." In Moscovitch and Albert 1987.

Hall, Peter. 1990. "Policy Paradigms, Experts and the State: The Case of Macro-Economic Policy Making in Britain." In Brooks and Gagnon 1990.

Hampson, Fen Osler, and Christopher J. Maule (eds.). 1992. *Canada among Nations, 1992–93: A New World Order?* Ottawa: Carleton University Press.

Hardin, H. 1974. *A Nation Unaware: The Canadian Economic Culture.* Vancouver: J.J. Douglas.

_____. 1989. *The Privatization Putsch.* Halifax: Institute for Research on Public Policy.

Hart, Michael M. 1985. *Canadian Economic Development and the International Trading System: Constraints and Opportunities.* Toronto: University of Toronto Press.

Hart, Michael, with Bill Dymond and Colin Robertson. 1994. *Decision at Midnight: Inside the Canada–US Free-Trade Negotiations.* Vancouver: UBC Press.

Hartz, Louis. 1964. *The Founding of New Societies.* New York: Harcourt Brace.

Harvey, David. 1989. *The Condition of Postmodernity.* Oxford: Blackwell.

Hawes, Michael K. 1984. *Principal Power, Middle Power, or Satellite?* Toronto: York University Research Programme in Strategic Studies.

Heap, Shaun Hargreaves. 1980/81. "World Profitability Crisis in the 1970s: Some Empirical Evidence." *Capital and Class* 12.

Heard, Andrew. 1991. *Canadian Constitutional Conventions.* Toronto: Oxford University Press.

Helleiner, Eric. 1994. *States and the Reemergence of Global Finance: From Bretton Woods to the 1990s.* Ithaca, N.Y.: Cornell University Press.

_____. 1996. "Post-Globalization: Is the Financial Liberalization Trend Likely To Be Reversed?" In Boyer and Drache 1996.

Herman, Lawrence L. 1998. "Settlement of International Trade Disputes— Challenges to Sovereignty—A Canadian Perspective." *Canada-United States Law Journal* 24.

Hiebert, Janet. 1989–90. "Fair Elections and Freedom of Expression under the Charter." *Journal of Canadian Studies* 24 (Winter).

Hillmer, Norman, and Garth Stevenson (eds.). 1977. *Foremost Nation:*

CanadianForeign Policy and a Changing World. Toronto: McClelland and Stewart.

Hirst, Paul, and Grahame Thompson. 1996. *Globalization in Question: The International Economy and the Possibilities of Governance*. Cambridge, Mass.: Blackwell.

Hirst, Paul, and Grahame Thompson. 1999. *Globalization in Question: The International Economy and the Possibilities of Governance*. 2nd ed. Oxford: Polity.

Hobsbawm, Eric. 1995. *Age of Extremes: The Short Twentieth Century 1914–1991*. London: Abacus.

_____. 2000. *The New Century*. London: Abacus.

Hocking, Brian. 1993. "Introduction." In *Foreign Relations and Federal States*. New York: Leicester University Press.

Hogg, Peter W. 1992. *Constitutional Law of Canada*. Scarborough, Ont.: Carswell.

Holmes, John. 1976. "Canada's Role in International Organizations." *The Canadian Banker* 74.

Hoover, Kenneth, and Raymond Plant. 1989. *Conservative Capitalism in Britain and the United States*. London: Routledge.

Horowitz, Gad. 1968. *Canadian Labour in Politics*. Toronto: University of Toronto Press.

Houle, François. 1990. "Economic Renewal and Social Policy." In Gagnon and Bickerton 1990.

Howlett, Michael, Alex Netherton and M. Ramesh. 1999. *The Political Economy of Canada: An Introduction*. 2nd ed. Toronto: Oxford University Press.

Howse, Robert. 1996. *Securing the Canadian Economic Union—Legal and Constitutional Options for the Federal Government*. Toronto: C.D. Howe Institute.

Human Resources Development Canada (HRDC). 1995. *News Release*. Ottawa, 1 December.

_____. 1996a. *News Release: Government of Canada Offers Provinces and Territories Responsibility for Active Employment Measures*. Ottawa (30 May).

_____. 1996b. *Getting Canadians Back to Work*. Ottawa (30 May).

_____. 1996c. *Employment Insurance: A Guide to Employment Insurance*. Ottawa.

_____. 1997. "Delivery of Non-Decisional Activities; Agreements with Third Parties." Draft document, mineo. Ottawa.

_____. 1998. *1997 Employment Insurance: Monitoring and Assessment Report*. Ottawa.

Hurtig, Mel. 1991. *The Betrayal of Canada*. Toronto: Stoddart.

Hutton, Will. 1997. *The State to Come*. London: Vintage.

Innis, H.A. 1975. *The Fur Trade in Canada: An Introduction to Canadian Economic History*. Rev. ed. Toronto: University of Toronto Press.

Ismael, Jacqueline S. (ed.). 1987. *The Canadian Welfare State: Evolution and Transition*. Edmonton: University of Alberta Press.

Jackson, Andrew. 1995. *The Liberals' Labour Strategy (and its consequences for workers)*. Ottawa: Canadian Centre for Policy Alternatives.

Jackson, Andrew, and Matthew Sanger (eds.). 1998. *Dismantling Democracy: The Multilateral Agreement on Investment and Its Impact*. Toronto: Canadian Centre for Policy Alternatives and Lorimer.

Jackson, Robert J., and Doreen Jackson. 1998. *Politics in Canada*. Scarborough, Ont.: Prentice-Hall.

James, R. Warren. 1949. *Wartime Economic Co-operation: A Study of Relations Between Canada and the United States*. Toronto: Ryerson.

Jessop, Bob, Kevin Bonnett, Simon Bromley and Tom Ling. 1988. *Thatcherism: A Tale of Two Nations*. Oxford: Polity.

Johnson, Andrew F., and Andrew Stritch (eds.). 1997. *Canadian Public Policy: Globalization and Political Parties*. Toronto: Copp Clark.

Keating, Tom. 1993. *Canada and the World Order: The Multilateralist Tradition in Canadian Foreign Policy*. Toronto: McClelland and Stewart.

Keenes, Ernie. 1992. "Rearranging the Deck Chairs: A Political Economy Approach to Foreign Policy Management in Canada." *Canadian Public Administration*.

_____. 1995. "The Myth of Multilateralism: Exception and Bilateralism in Canadian International Economic Relations." *International Journal* (Autumn).

Keenleyside, Hugh. 1929. *Canada and the United States: Some Aspects of the History of the Republic and the Dominion*. New York: A.A. Knopf.

Keohane, Robert, and Helen Milner (eds.). 1994. *Internationalization and Domestic Politics*. New York: Cambridge University Press.

Kirton, John. 1999. "Canada as a Principal Power: G-7 and IMF Diplomacy in the Crisis of 1997–9." *International Journal* 56, 4 (Autumn).

Klein, Seth. 1996. "Good Sense Versus Common Sense: Canada's Debt Debate and Competing Hegemonic Projects." M.A. thesis, Department of Political Science, Simon Fraser University, Vancouver.

Knopff, Rainer, and F.L. Morton. 1992. *Charter Politics*. Toronto: Nelson.

Krasner, Stephen D. (ed.). 1983. *International Regimes*. Ithaca, N.Y.: Cornell University Press.

_____. 1999. *Sovereignty: Organized Hypocrisy*. Princeton, N.J.: Princeton University Press.

Krehm, William. 1993. *A Power unto Itself: The Bank of Canada*. Toronto: Stoddart.

Kroeger, Arthur. 1996. "Changing Course: The Federal Government's Program Review of 1994–95." In Armit and Bourgeault 1996.

Laird, Sam. 1999. "The WTO's Trade Policy Review Mechanism—From Through the Looking Glass." *The World Economy* 22, 6 (August).

Lalonde, Mark. 1982. *Statement on the Economic Outlook and the Financial Position of the Government of Canada: House of Commons, October 27, 1982*. Ottawa: Minister of Supply and Services Canada.

Lalumiere, Catherine, Jean-Pierre Landau and Emmanuel Glimet. 1998. "France's Official Position on Withdrawing From the MAI Negotiations." English translation at: <http://www.canadians.org/campaigns/campaigns-maipub03.html>. (The French original of this document is published by France's Ministry of the Economy, Finance, and Industry and is available on the Ministry's Internet site at: <http://www.finances.gouv.fr/pole_ecofin/international/ami0998/ami0998.htm>.)

Lang, Tim, and Colin Hines. 1993. *The New Protectionism: Protecting the Future against Free Trade.* London: Earthscan.

Langille, David. 1987. "The Business Council on National Issues and the Canadian State." *Studies in Political Economy* 24 (Autumn).

Langmore, John. 1995. "Restructuring Economic and Financial Power." *Futures* 27, 2.

Laux, Jeanne Kirk. 1991. "Shaping or Serving Markets? Public Ownership after Privatization." In Drache and Gertler 1991.

Laxer, Gordon. 1989. *Open for Business: The Roots of Foreign Ownership in Canada.* Toronto: Oxford University Press.

_____ (ed.). 1991. *Perspectives on Canadian Economic Development.* Toronto: Oxford University Press.

_____. 1992. "Constitutional Crisis and Continentalism: Twin Threats to Canada's Continued Existence." *Canadian Journal of Sociology* 17 (June).

Laxer, James. 1983. *Oil and Gas: Ottawa, the Provinces and the Petroleum Industry.* Toronto: Lorimer.

Layton, Jack. 1976. "Nationalism and the Canadian Bourgeoisie: Contradictions of Dependence." *Canadian Review of Studies in Nationalism* 3, 2 (Spring).

Lee, Marc. 2000. *In Search of a Problem: The Future of the Agreement on Internal Trade and Canadian Federalism.* Vancouver: Canadian Centre for Policy Alternatives.

_____. 2001. *Inside the Fortress: What's Going on at the FTAA Negotiations.* Ottawa: Canadian Centre for Policy Alternatives.

Lemieux, Denis, and Ana Stuhec. 1999. *Review of Administrative Action under NAFTA.* Scarborough, Ont.: Carswell.

Leslie, Peter. 1987. *Federal State, National Economy.* Toronto: University of Toronto Press.

Leys, Colin. 1980. "Neo-Conservatism and the Organic Crisis in Britain." *Studies in Political Economy: A Socialist Review* 4 (Autumn).

Liberal Party. 1993. *Creating Opportunity: The Liberal Plan for Canada.* Ottawa.

Lipset, Seymour Martin. 1990. *Continental Divide: The Values and Institutions of the United States and Canada.* New York: Routledge.

Lipsig-Mummé, Carla. 2000. "The Dilemma of Organizing: Trade Union Strategy in International Perspective." In Cohn, McBride and Wiseman 2000.

Lumsden, Ian (ed.). 1970. *Close the 49th Parallel, Etc: The Americanization of Canada.* Toronto: University of Toronto Press.

Lyon, Peyton, and Brian Tomlin. 1979. *Canada as an International Actor.* Toronto: Macmillan of Canada.

Macdonald, Donald S. 1998. "Chapter 11 of NAFTA: What Are the Implications for Sovereignty?" *Canada-United States Law Journal* 24.

MacDonald, L.R. 1975. "Merchants Against Industry: An Idea and Its Origins." *Canadian Historical Review* 56.

MacDonald, Martha. 1999. "Restructuring, Gender and Social Security reform in Canada." *Journal of Canadian Studies* (Summer).

Macdonald Report. See Canada 1985.

Macmillan, David S. (ed.). 1972. *Canadian Business History: Selected Studies, 1497–1971.* Toronto: McClelland and Stewart.

Magnusson, Warren (ed.). 1984. *The New Reality: The Politics of Restraint in British Columbia.* Vancouver: New Star.

Mahon, Rianne. 1990. "Adjusting to Win? The New Tory Training Initiative." In Graham 1990.

Mallory, J.R. 1954. *Social Credit and the Federal Power in Canada.* Toronto: University of Toronto Press.

Mandel, Michael. 1994. *The Charter of Rights and the Legalization of Politics in Canada.* Rev. ed. Toronto: Wall & Thompson.

Marchak, M. Patricia. 1991. *The Integrated Circus: The New Right and the Restructuring of Global Markets.* Montreal & Kingston: McGill-Queen's University Press.

Marr, William L., and Donald G. Paterson. 1980. *Canada: An Economic History.* Toronto: Gage Publishing.

Martin, Lawrence. 1993. *Pledge of Allegiance: The Americanization of Canada in the Mulroney Years.* Toronto: McClelland and Stewart.

Marx, Karl. 1971. *Capital.* 3 vols. Moscow: Progress Publishers.

Maslove, Allan M. 1981. "Tax Expenditures, Tax Credits and Equity." In Doern 1981.

Maxwell, Judith. 2001. *Towards a Common Citizenship: Canada's Social and Economic Choices.* Ottawa: Canadian Policy Research Networks.

May, Elizabeth. 1998. "Fighting the MAI." In Jackson and Sanger 1998.

McBride, Stephen. 1974. "Setting Naylor Straight." *Canadian Dimension* 10, 2.

_____. 1992. *Not Working: State, Unemployment, and Neo-Conservatism in Canada.* Toronto: University of Toronto Press.

_____. 1995. "Coercion and Consent: The Recurring Corporatist Temptation in Canadian Labour Relations." In Gonick, Phillips and Vorst 1995.

_____. 1996. "The Continuing Crisis of Social Democracy: Ontario's Social Contract in Perspective." *Studies in Political Economy* 50 (Summer).

McBride, Stephen, and John Shields. 1993. *Dismantling a Nation: Canada and the New World Order.* Halifax: Fernwood.

_____. 1997. Dismantling a Nation. 2nd ed. Halifax: Fernwood.

McBride, Stephen, and John Wiseman (eds.). 2000. *Globalization and Its Discontents.* London: Macmillan

McCullough, H.B. (ed.). 1989. *Political Ideologies and Political Philosophies.* Toronto: Thompson Educational Pub.

McEwan, Arthur. 1999. *Neo-liberalism or Democracy? Economic Strategy, Markets, and Alternatives for the 21st Century.* London: Zed.

McFettridge, D.G. 1997. *The Economics of Privatization.* Montreal: C.D. Howe Institute.

McIlveen, Murray, and Hideo Mimoto. 1990. "The Federal Government Deficit, 1975–76 to 1988–89." Mimeo. Ottawa: Statistics Canada.

McQuaig, Linda. 1987. *Behind Closed Doors: How the Rich Won Control of Canada's Tax System.* Markham, Ont.: Viking.

_____. 1992. *The Quick and the Dead: Brian Mulroney, Big Business and the Seduction of Canada.* Toronto: Penguin.

_____. 1995. *Shooting the Hippo: Death by Deficit and Other Canadian Myths.*

Toronto:Viking.

_____. 1998. *The Cult of Impotence: Selling the Myth of Powerlessness in the Global Economy.* Toronto:Viking.

McRoberts, Kenneth. 1997. *Misconceiving Canada:The Struggle for National Unity.* Toronto: Oxford University Press.

Meiksins Wood, Ellen. 1998. "Class Compacts, the Welfare State, and Epochal Shifts." *Monthly Review* 49, 8.

Merrett, Christopher D. 1996. *Free Trade: Neither Free Nor about Trade.* Montreal: Black Rose.

Michalos, Alex C. 1997. *Good Taxes:The Case for Taxing Foreign Currency Exchange and Other Financial Transactions.* Toronto: Dundurn

Miliband, Ralph. 1968. *The State in Capitalist Society.* London: Weidenfeld and Nicholson.

Milner, Helen. 1988. *Resisting Protectionism: Global Industries and the Politics of International Trade.* Princeton, N.J.: Princeton University Press.

Minifie, James. 1960. *Peacemaker or Powdermonkey: Canada's Role in a Revolutionary World.* Toronto: McClelland and Stewart.

Mishra, Ramesh. 1990. *The Welfare State in Capitalist Society: Policies of Retrenchment and Maintenance in Europe, North America and Australia.* Toronto: University of Toronto Press.

_____. 1999. "After Globalization: Social Policy in an Open Economy." *Canadian Review of Social Policy* 43.

Mitchie, Joanathan, and John Grieve Smith (eds.). 1995. *Managing the Global Economy.* Oxford: Oxford University Press.

Molot, Maureen Appel. 1990. "Where Do We, Should We, or Can We Sit? A Review of Canadian Foreign Policy Literature." *International Journal of Canadian Studies* 1–2.

_____. 1994. "The Canadian State in the International Economy." In Stubbs and Underhill 1994.

Moran, Jonathan. 1998. "The Dynamics of Class Politics & National Economies in Globalization." *Capital and Class* 66 (November).

Moscovitch, Allan, and Jim Albert (eds.). 1987. *The "Benevolent" State:The Growth of Welfare in Canada.* Toronto: Garamond.

Muirhead, B.W. 1999. *Against the Odds:The Public Life and Times of Louis Rasminsky.* Toronto: University of Toronto Press.

Myers, Gustavus. 1972. *A History of Canadian Wealth.* Toronto: James, Lewis & Samuel.

Naylor, Tom. 1972. "The Rise and Fall of the Third Commercial Empire of the St. Lawrence." In Teeple 1972.

_____. 1975. *The History of Canadian Business, 1867–1914.* Vol. 1. *The Banks and Finance Capital.* Toronto: Lorimer.

Neill, Robin. 1991. *A History of Canadian Economic Thought.* London and New York: Routledge.

Neufeld, Mark. 1995. "Hegemony and Foreign Policy Analysis: The Case of Canada as Middle Power." *Studies in Political Economy* 48 (Autumn).

Newman, Peter C. 1975. *The Canadian Establishment.* Toronto: McClelland and

Stewart.

Niosi, Jorge.1985a. "Continental Nationalism: The Strategy of the Canadian Bourgeoisie." In Brym 1985.

_____. 1985b. *Canadian Multinationals.* Toronto: Garamond.

Norman, Wayne. 1991. "Network Seminar on Economics." In Network Seminar on the Constitution. *Taking Stock.* Ottawa.

Nossal, Kim Richard. 1983–84. "Analyzing the Domestic Sources of Canadian Foreign Policy." *International Journal* 39 (Winter).

_____. 1993. "The Impact of Provincial Governments on Canadian Foreign Policy." In Brown, Fry and Groen 1993.

_____. 1997. *The Politics of Canadian Foreign Policy.* Scarborough, On: Prentice-Hall.

O'Brien, Robert, Ann Marie Goetz, Jan Aart Scholte and Marc Williams. 2000. *Contesting Global Governance: Multilateral Economic Institutions and Global Social Movements.* Cambridge: Cambridge University Press.

Ohmae, Ken'ichi. 1990. *The Borderless World: Power and Strategy in the Interlinked World Economy.* New York: Harper Business.

Organization for Economic Cooperation and Development (OECD). 1997. *MAI: Consolidated Text and Commentary.* Draft (May).

Ornstein, Michael. 1985. "Canadian Capital and the Canadian State: Ideology in an Era of Crisis." In Brym 1985.

Osborne, Andrew. 2000. "EU 'Power in U.S. firms' on GM foods." *Guardian Weekly* 20–26 July.

Otero, Gerardo (ed.). 1996. *Neoliberalism Revisited: Economic Restructuring and Mexico's Political Future.* Boulder, Col: Westview.

Pal, Leslie A. (ed.). 1999. *How Ottawa Spends 1999–2000.* Toronto: Oxford University Press.

Palan, Ronen, and Jason Abbott with Phil Deans. 1999. *State Strategies in the Global Political Economy.* London: Pinter.

Palast, Gregory. 2000. "Keep Taking Our Tablets (no-one else's): The WTO's Response to the African AIDS Crisis Is a Chilling Reminder of Where Power Lies." *Guardian Weekly* 27 July–2 August.

Panitch, Leo (ed.). 1977. *The Canadian State: Political Economy and Political Power.* Toronto: University of Toronto Press.

_____. 1996. *Socialist Register: Are There Alternatives?* London: Merlin.

_____. 2000. "The New Imperial State." *New Left Review* (March–April).

Panitch, Leo, and Colin Leys. 1997. *The End of Parliamentary Socialism: From New Left to New Labour.* London: Verso

Park, Libbie, and Frank Park. 1962. *Anatomy of Big Business.* Toronto: Progress.

Pauly, Louis, and Simon Reich. 1997. "National Structures and Multinational Corporate Behaviour: Enduring Differences." *International Organization* 51, 1.

Pearson, Frederic S., and Simon Payaslian. 1999. *International Political Economy.* Boston: McGraw Hill.

Pentland, H.C. 1950. "The Role of Capital in Canadian Economic Development Before 1875." *Canadian Journal of Economic and Political Science* 16.

Peters, B. Guy, and Donald J. Savoie (eds.). 1995. *Governance in a Changing Environment*. Montreal: McGill-Queen's University Press.

Phillips, Paul. 1999. "Why Were We Bombing Yugoslavia?" *Studies in Political Economy* (Autumn).

Phillips, Stephen. 1999. "The Demise of Universality: The Politics of Federal Income Security in Canada, 1978–1993." Ph.D. dissertation, University of British Columbia, Vancouver.

_____. 2000. "The Demise of Universality: The Politics of Federal Income Security in Canada, 1978–1993." Paper presented at the annual meeting of the British Columbia Political Studies Association, Victoria (May).

Pierre, Jon. 1995. "The Marketization of the State." In Peters and Savoie 1995.

Pomfret, Richard. 1981. *The Economic Development of Canada*. Toronto: Methuen.

Porter, John. 1965. *The Vertical Mosaic: An Analysis of Social Class and Power in Canada*. Toronto: University of Toronto Press.

Potter, Evan. 1997. "Niche Diplomacy as Canadian Foreign Policy." *International Journal* 52 (Winter).

Pratt, Cranford. 1983–84. "Dominant Class Theory and Canadian Foreign Policy: The Case of the Counter-Consensus." *International Journal* (Winter).

_____. 1990. "Middle Power Internationalism and Global Poverty." In *Middle Power Internationalism: The North-South Dimension*. Montreal: McGill-Queen's University Press.

Pratt, Larry. 1982. "Energy: The Roots of National Policy." *Studies in Political Economy: A Socialist Review* 7 (Winter).

Prince, Michael J. 1999. "From Health and Welfare to Stealth and Farewell: Federal Social Policy, 1980–2000." In Pal 1999.

Public Citizen, Global Trade Watch. 1998. "MAI Provisions and Proposals: An Analysis of the April 1998 Text." <http://www.citizen.org/pctrade/otherissues/MAI/what%20is/ANALYSIS.htm>.

Pulkingham, Jane, and Gordon Ternowetsky (eds.). 1996. *Remaking Canadian Social Policy: Social Security in the Late 1990s*. Halifax: Fernwood.

Putnam, Robert D., and Nicholas Bayne. 1987. *Hanging Together: Co-operation and Conflict in the Seven-Power Summits*. London: Sage.

Rehnby, Nadene, and Stephen McBride. 1997. *Help Wanted: Economic Security for Youth*. Ottawa: Canadian Centre for Policy Alternatives.

Resnick, Phillip. 1970. "Canadian Defence Policy and the American Empire." In Lumsden 1970.

_____. 1989. "The Ideology of Neo-Conservatism." In McCullough 1989.

_____. 1990. *The Mask of Proteus: Canadian Reflections on the State*. Montreal: McGill-Queen's University Press.

_____. 1991. *Toward a Canada-Quebec Union*. Montreal: McGill-Queen's University Press.

Rice, James J., and Michael J. Prince. 2000. *Changing Politics of Canadian Social Policy*. Toronto: University of Toronto Press.

Richards, Robert G. 1991 "The Canadian Constitution and International Economic relations." In Brown and Smith 1991.

Richardson, Jack. 1991. "Economic Concentration and Social Power in Contemporary Canada." In J. Curtis and L. Tepperman (eds.), *Images of Canada.* Scarborough, Ont.: Prentice-Hall.

_____. 1992. "Free Trade: Why Did it Happen?" *Canadian Review of Sociology and Anthropology* (August).

Richardson, J.J. (ed.). 1990. *Privatisation and Deregulation in Canada and Britain.* Aldershot, Eng.: Dartmouth.

Richardson, R.J. 1982. "'Merchants Against Industry': An Empirical Study of the Canadian Debate." *Canadian Journal of Sociology* 7.

Robertson, R. 1992. *Globalization.* London: Sage.

Robinson, Ian. 1993. *North American Trade as if Democracy Mattered: What's Wrong with NAFTA and What Are the Alternatives?* Ottawa: Canadian Centre for Policy Alternatives.

_____. 1995. "Trade Policy, Globalization and the Future of Canadian Federalism." In Rocher and Smith 1995.

Rocher, Francois. 1991. "Canadian Business, Free Trade and the Rhetoric of Economic Continentalization." *Studies in Political Economy* 35 (Summer).

Rocher, Francois, and Miriam Smith (eds.). 1995. *New Trends in Canadian Federalism.* Peterborough, Ont.: Broadview Press.

Rosenbaum, N. 1969. "An Effective Foreign Policy for Canada." *Behind the Headlines* 27, 5–6 (June).

Ruggeri, G.C. 1987. *The Canadian Economy: Problems and Policies.* 3rd ed. Toronto: Gage Publishing Company.

Ruggie, John G. 1983. "International Regimes, Transactions, and Change: Embedded Liberalism in the Postwar Economic Order." In Krasner 1983.

Russell, Bob. 1991. "The Welfare State and the Politics of Constraint." In Bolaria 1991.

_____. 2000. "From the Workhouse to Workfare: The Welfare State and Shifting Policy Terrains." In Burke, Mooers and Shields 2000.

Russell, Peter (ed.). 1966. *Nationalism in Canada.* Toronto: McGraw-Hill.

Russell, Peter H., Rainer Knopff and Ted Morton. 1989. *Federalism and the Charter: Leading Constitutional Decisions.* Ottawa: Carleton University Press.

Ryerson, Stanley B. 1973. *Unequal Union: Roots of Crisis in the Canadas 1815– 1873.* Toronto: Progress Books.

Safarian, A.E. 1974. *Canadian Federalism and Economic Integration.* Ottawa: Privy Council Office.

Sanger, Matthew. 1993. "Public Services." In Cameron and Watkins 1993.

Savoie, Donald J. 1995. "Globalization, Nation States and the Civil Service." In Peters and Savoie 1995.

_____. 1999. *Governing from the Centre: The Concentration of Power in Canadian Politics.* Toronto: University of Toronto Press.

Scharpf, Fritz W. 1987. *Crisis and Choice in European Social Democracy.* Ithaca, N.Y.: Cornell University Press.

Scheinberg, Stephen. 1973. "Invitation to Empire: Tariffs and American Economic Expansion in Canada." *Business History Review* 47.

Schneiderman, David. 2000. "Investment Rules and the New Constitutionalism." *Law and Social Inquiry* 25 (Summer).

Scholte, Jan Aart. 1997. "Global Capitalism and the State." *International Affairs* 73, 3.

Schwanen, Daniel. 2000. "Happy Birthday, AIT!" *Policy Options* (July–August).

Schwartz, Herman M. 1994. *States versus Markets*. New York: St. Martin's Press.

Sears, Alan. 1999. "The 'Lean' State and Restructuring: Towards a Theoretical Account." *Studies in Political Economy* 59 (Summer).

Seccareccia, Mario. 1995. "Keynesianism and Public Investment: A Left-Keynesian Perspective on the Role of Government Expenditures and Debt." *Studies in Political Economy* 46 (Spring).

Sharp, Mitchell. 1972. "Canada–U.S. Relations: Options for the Future." *International Perspectives* (Special Edition) 17 Oct.

Shields, John. 1990. "Democracy Versus Leviathan: The State, Democracy and Neoconservatism." *Journal of History and Politics* 9.

Shields, John, and B. Mitchell Evans. 1998. *Shrinking the State*. Halifax: Fernwood.

Shrybman, Steven. 1999. *Citizen's Guide to the World Trade Organization*. Toronto: Lorimer.

Silver, Susan. 1996. "The Struggle for National Standards: Lessons From the Federal Role in Health Care." In Pulkingham and Ternowetsky 1996.

Simeon, Richard. 1987. "Inside the Macdonald Commission." *Studies in Political Economy* 22 (Spring).

_____. 1991. "Globalization and the Canadian Nation-State." In Doern and Purchase 1991.

Simeon, Richard, George Hoberg and Keith Banting. 1997. "Globalization, Fragmentation, and the Social Contract." In Banting, Hoberg and Simeon 1997a.

Simeon, Richard, and Mary Janigan (eds.). 1991. *Toolkits and Building Blocks: Constructing a New Canada*. Toronto: C.D. Howe Institute.

Sinclair, Scott. 2000. "After Seattle: How the New WTO Services 2000: Negotiations Threaten Democratic Governance." Ottawa: Canadian Centre for Policy Alternatives (electronic version).

Sinclair, Timothy J. 2000. "Deficit Discourse: The Social Construction of Fiscal Rectitude." In Germain 2000.

Skilling, H.G. 1945. *Canadian Representation Abroad: From Agency to Embassy*. Toronto: Ryerson.

Smiley, Donald. 1967. *The Canadian Political Nationality*. Toronto: Methuen.

_____. 1975. "Canada and the Quest for a National Policy." *Canadian Journal of Political Science* 8, 1 (March).

Smith, David E. 1995. *The Invisible Crown*. Toronto: University of Toronto Press.

Smith, Janet. 1990. "Canada's Privatisation Programme." In Richardson 1990.

Smith, Miriam. 1992. "The Canadian Labour Congress: From Continentalism to Economic Nationalism." *Studies in Political Economy* 38.

Stairs, Dennis. 1994–95. "Will and Circumstance and the Postwar Study of Canada's Foreign Policy." *International Journal* 50 (Winter).

Stanbury, William T. 1988. "Privatization and the Mulroney Government, 1984–1988." In Gollner and Salée 1988.

Stanford, Jim. 1993 "Investment." In Cameron and Watkins 1993.

_____. 2000. "The Facts Ma'am. Just the Facts: Assessing the Liberals' Allocation of the Fiscal Dividend." *Behind the Numbers* 3, 2 (November).

Stevenson, Garth. 1982. *Unfulfilled Union: Canadian Federalism and National Unity.* Toronto: Gage.

Stone, Frank. 1992. *Canada, the GATT, and the International Trade System.* 2nd ed. Montreal: Institute for Research on Public Policy.

Stubbs, Richard, and Geoffrey R.D. Underhill (eds.). 1994. *Political Economy and the Changing Global Order.* Oxford: Oxford University Press.

_____. 2000. Political Economy and the Changing Global Order. 2nd ed. Oxford: Oxford University Press.

Swenarchuk, Michelle. 2000. "The International Confederation of Free Trade Unions Labour Clause Proposal: A Legal and Political Critique." In McBride and Wiseman 2000.

Taylor, D. Wayne. 1991. *Business and Government Relations: Partners in the 1990s.* Toronto: Gage.

Taylor, Malcolm. 1987. "The Canadian Health Care System After Medicare." In Coburn et al. 1987.

Teeple, Gary (ed.). 1972. *Capitalism and the National Question in Canada.* Toronto: University of Toronto Press.

_____. 1995. *Globalization and the Decline of Social Reform.* Toronto: Garamond.

_____. 2000. *Globalization and the Decline of Social Reform Into the Twenty-First Century.* Toronto: Garamond.

Ternowetsky, Gordon W. 1987. "Controlling the Deficit and a Private Sector Led Recovery: Contemporary Themes of the Welfare State." In Ismael 1987.

Thomas, Christopher. 1992. "Reflexions on the Canada–US Free Trade Agreement in the Context of the Multilateral trading System." In Cutler and Zacher 1992b.

Valihora, Michael S. 1998. "Chapter 19 or the WTO's Dispute Settlement Body: A Hobson's Choice for Canada?" *Case Western Reserve Journal of International Law* (Spring/Summer).

Vanier Institute of the Family. 2001. *The Current State of Canadian Family Finances—2000 Report.* Ottawa.

Veltmeyer, Henry. 1986. *The Canadian Class Structure.* Toronto: Garamond.

_____. 1987. *Canadian Corporate Power.* Toronto: Garamond.

Wade, E.C.S., and G. Godfrey Phillips. 1965. *Constitutional Law.* 7th ed. by E.C.S. Wade and A.W. Bradley. London: Longmans Green.

Wade, Robert. 1996. "Globalization and Its Limits: Reports of the Death of the National Economy Are Greatly Exaggerated." In Berger and Dore 1996.

Waters, Malcolm. 1995. *Globalization.* London: Routledge.

Watkins, Mel. 1989. "The Political Economy of Growth." In Clement and Williams 1989b.

Watkins Report. 1968. *Foreign Ownership and the Structure of Canadian Industry.* Ottawa: Supply and Services Canada

Webb, Michael. 1992. "Canada and the International Monetary Regime." In Cutler and Zacher 1992b.

Webber, Michael J., and David L. Rigby. 1996. *The Golden Age Illusion: Rethinking*

Postwar Capitalism. New York: Guilford.

Weiss, Linda. 1997. "Globalization and the Myth of the Powerless State." *New Left Review* 225.

_____. 1998. *The Myth of the Powerless State: Governing the Economy in a Global Era.* Cambridge: Polity.

Weiss, Thomas G., and Tatiana Carayannis. 2001. "Whither United Nations Economic and Social Ideas? A Research Agenda." *Global Social Policy* (April).

Weller, Geoffrey R. 1996. "Strengthening Society I: Health Care." In Johnson and Stritch 1997.

Whitaker, Reg. 1977. "Images of the State in Canada." In Panitch 1977.

White, Randall. 1989. *From Fur Trade to Free Trade: Putting the Canada–U.S. Trade Agreement in Historical Perspective.* 2nd ed. Toronto: Dundurn Press.

Williams, Glen. 1986. *Not for Export: Towards a Political Economy of Canada's Arrested Industrialization.* Toronto: McClelland and Stewart.

Wilson, Michael H. 1984. *Economic and Fiscal Statement.* Ottawa. Department of Finance.

_____. 1991. *The Budget.* Ottawa: Department of Finance.

Winham, Gilbert R. 1992. "Canada, GATT, and the Future of the World Trading System." In Hampson and Maule 1992.

_____. 1994. "NAFTA and the Trade Policy Revolution of the 1980s: A Canadian Perspective." *International Journal* (Summer).

Wiseman, John. 1998. *Global Nation? Australia and the Politics of Globalization.* London: Cambridge University Press.

_____. 2000a. "Alternatives to Oppressive Globalization." In McBride and Wiseman 2000.

_____. 2000b. "Here to Stay? The 1998 Australian Waterfront Dispute and its Implications." In Cohn, McBride and Wiseman 2000.

Wolfe, David A. 1984. "The Rise and Demise of the Keynesian Era in Canada: Economic Policy, 1930–1982." In Cross and Kealey 1984.

_____. 1985. "The Politics of the Deficit." In Doern 1985.

Wolfe, Robert. 1996. "Global Trade as a Single Undertaking: The Role of Ministers in the WTO." *International Journal* (Autumn).

Woodside, Kenneth B. 1993. "Trade and Industrial Policy: Hard Choices." In Michael M. Atkinson (ed.), *Governing Canada.* Toronto: Harcourt Brace Jovanovich.

Workman, Thom. 1996. *Banking on Deception: The Discourse of Fiscal Crisis.* Halifax: Fernwood.

World Trade Organization (WTO). 1999. "About the WTO." <http://.wto.org/wto/about/facts2.htm>.

World Trade Organization Secretariat. 1999a. An Introduction to the GATS. Geneva.

_____. 1999b. The GATS: Objectives, Coverage and Disciplines. Geneva.

Yalnizyan, Armine. 1998. *The Growing Gap: A Report on Growing Inequality between the Rich and the Poor in Canada.* Toronto: Centre for Social Justice.

Index

Kirton, John 51, 52, 53, 138, 146
Korean War 48
Kosovo 51
Krasner, Stephen 19, 134
Kreklewich, Robert 29, 103, 104

L

labour 24, 30, 31, 32, 35, 38, 41, 59, 60, 79,
 81, 82, 87, 96, 100, 119, 124, 140,
 142, 149, 152, 154, 158
Labour Conventions case 140
Labour Market Development 98
labour markets 27, 82, 97, 98, 99, 141
Laxer, Gordon 7, 35, 40, 56, 58, 61, 77, 146
Lee, Marc 107, 114, 142, 144
legitimacy 73, 80, 92, 147, 150, 151, 152,
 154
lend-lease 47
Liberal Party of Canada 43, 89, 95
Lumley, Ed 71

M

Macdonald Commission/Report 61, 62,
 63, 73, 74, 76, 77, 81
Macdonald, Donald 10, 63, 71, 72, 73, 75,
 78, 140
Macdonald, John A. 9, 38, 39, 58, 130, 131
MacDonald, Mark 143, 144, 145
Mackintosh, W.A. 40
magazines case 117, 120, 121, 136
Mahon, Rianne 60
Major Projects Task Force 60
Malaysia 158
Maritime provinces 47
markets 13–25, 27, 35, 36, 46, 57, 58, 65,
 67, 73, 81, 82, 94, 104, 109, 114, 115,
 121, 125, 139, 151, 158, 160, 161
Marsh Report 9, 42
May, Elizabeth 150
McCain Foods 76
McCall, Christina 48
McEwan, Arthur 156
McQuaig, Linda 30, 66, 68, 71, 72, 75, 76,
 77, 83, 84
Medical Care Act 10, 43, 94
Meech Lake 10
megaprojects 44, 60
Metalclad case 112
Methanex case 112
Mexico 32, 103, 112, 113
Michalos, Alex 158
middle power, Canada as 48, 49, 50, 51, 52
Miliband, Ralph 19, 20

Mimoto study 83
Mishra, Ramesh 81, 89
modernization 21
monetarism 83, 100
monetary policy 27, 41, 81, 82, 83, 84
Moran, Jonathan 30, 31
most-favoured nation 106, 108, 110, 113,
 114, 117, 119, 122, 143
Mulroney, Brian 10, 48, 53, 63, 72, 78, 149
Mulroney Conservatives 10, 48, 53, 61, 72,
 76, 82, 89, 95, 133
multilateral, multilateralism 23, 49, 50, 51,
 52, 53, 62, 74, 104, 105, , 122, 124,
 125, 134, 135, 148, 150
Multilateral Agreement on Investment 11,
 17, 32, 114, 116, 122, 123, 124, 150,
 153, 154
multinational corporations 15, 24, 25, 79,
 81, 109, 110, 117
multinational corporations, Canadian 65,
 67
Myers case 112

N

nation-building 9, 13, 38, 58, 59
nation-state 13, 14, 15, 16, 19, 20, 21, 22,
 23, 24, 26, 28, 36, 103, 122, 139, 156,
 158, 160, 161
National Energy Program 10, 44, 48, 60,
 61, 62, 65, 67, 111, 133
national policy/policies 9, 16, 24, 36, 38,
 39, 40, 44, 45, 46, 47, 53, 57, 58, 59,
 60, 76, 107, 133, 136, 145
national standards 43, 91, 95
national treatment 106, 108, 110, 113, 114,
 115, 119, 120, 122, 143, 145
nationalism/nationalists 19, 21, 23, 40, 43,
 48, 52, 53, 55, 57, 59, 60, 61, 63, 69,
 71, 73, 75, 76, 80, 133, 149, 150
natural resources 16, 35, 73, 109, 122
Naylor, Tom 38, 58
neo-classical economics 27, 38, 75, 80
neo-liberalism 13, 14, 21, 22, 27, 32, 62,
 79, 127, 134, 137, 138, 145, 147, 151,
 155, 157, 159
new constitutionalism 103, 104
New Public Management 137
Niosi, Jorge 60, 65
Nixon, Richard 53
Non-discrimination 114
non-governmental organizations 13, 117,
 151, 152
NORAD 48